EDWARD MCWHINNEY is Professor of Law at Simon Fraser University and author of *Quebec and the Constitution 1960–1978.*

In response to the general crisis in law and society in contemporary western and communist nations alike, and to the need for new relations between man and the state, Professor McWhinney presents a comparative study of constitutions and constitution-making.

This book begins with a discussion of constitutional government in western societies – the United States, France, Germany, and Great Britain – the challenges it faces, its philosophy, and its practice. It then draws comparisons to major non-western societies such as Japan and India and to the major powers of the communist world – the Soviet Union and China.

McWhinney discusses in detail the essential aspects of constitution-making – when, why, and by whom it is done, as well as the art of drafting a constitution. He presents the various options: presidential executive or government by assembly, centralization or decentralization, the rule of law and emergency powers, the open society and affirmative action, and direct and indirect elections. All are examined against an empirical record of the experience of major countries.

In conclusion, McWhinney enquires into the claimed socio-economic limits to contemporary constitutionalism, its alleged western ethnocentricity, and the effective political limits to constitutional government today. He offers canons of prudence for contemporary constitution-making.

EDWARD McWHINNEY

Constitution-making:
Principles, Process, Practice

UNIVERSITY OF TORONTO PRESS
Toronto Buffalo London

© University of Toronto Press 1981
Toronto Buffalo London
Printed in Canada
ISBN 0-8020-5553-2

Canadian Cataloguing in Publication Data

McWhinney, Edward, 1926–
Constitution-making
Bibliography: p.
Includes index.
ISBN 0-8020-5553-2
1. Constitutional history. 2. Comparative
government. I. Title.
JF51.M38   342'.029   C81-094155-4

TO THE MEMORY OF
HAROLD DWIGHT LASSWELL

Acknowledgments

Some parts of the present study draw upon papers prepared by the author at earlier periods for special sessions of the Institut universitaire of Luxembourg that were directed jointly by Judge Pierre Pescatore and the author and that were devoted to the themes, respectively, of legislative power in the modern state and of executive power in the modern state. The treatment of federalism and supra-national integration derives, in part, from earlier studies for international colloquia on federalism held, variously, at the Institut Gosudarstvo i Pravo in Moscow under the auspices of the Association Internationale des Sciences Juridiques and UNESCO, and at the Australian National University in Canberra under the auspices of the World Congress on Philosophy of Law and Social Philosophy.

The analysis of the most recent, 1978, Constitution of the People's Republic of China and the inevitable comparisons with the earlier, 1975, Constitution have benefited from seminar discussions with members of the Chinese Academy of Social Sciences (International Law and Constitutional Law section) in Peking, the Peking University Department of Law, and the East China Institute of Law and Political Science in Shanghai, in the spring of 1980.

Responsibility for interpretations advanced or opinions offered in the present manuscript remains, of course, that of the author alone.

Publication of this book is made possible by a grant from the Social Science Federation of Canada, using funds provided by the Social Sciences and Humanities Research Council of Canada, and a grant from the Publications Fund of the University of Toronto Press.

E.McW.

Contents

x Contents

Preface

We are facing a new wave of constitution-making today. 'New' countries in Asia and Africa that obtained constitutional charters to accompany the grant of self-determination and independence from imperial, European 'parent' countries are finding, after one or two decades of trial-and-error experience, that their original 'made-in-Europe,' or at least 'received European' constitutions hardly correspond to their urgent political, social, and economic needs today, and they are either replacing those original charters altogether or else ignoring them in significant measure. 'Older,' western European countries, already in the post-industrial phase of development and with presumably stable social systems, are finding themselves rent by centrifugal, separatist pressures for local autonomy and regional devolution, at the same time as centripetal pressures for supra-national political and economic integration and association on a continent-wide basis. Countries like Canada, after a century or more of seemingly orderly national development, are experiencing the cultural shock and the political perils of the contemporary movement for national self-determination for Quebec and French-Canadians. The United States has hardly recovered, as yet, from the traumatic experience of the Watergate crisis and the downfall of the so-called 'imperial' presidency; while within the rival, communist countries, the Soviet Union has just given itself a new constitutional charter in place of the Stalin Constitution of 1936, and the People's Republic of China has also come up with a new, essentially programmatic constitutional charter.

For some, a new constitution may be largely a rhetorical or public relations exercise, conceived and designed as such from the beginning. For others it may be a too often necessarily vain exercise in trying to resolve, by legal means and legal formulae, essentially non-constitutional problems of an ethnic-cultural, social, or economic character that are better disposed of by fundamental political compromises in other, non-legal arenas, using other, non-legal techniques. For some countries, however, a venture in constitutional novation, or at least fundamental constitutional change, may be a politically worthwhile and useful community exercise allowing for a balancing and resolution of competing community interests and the achievement of a genuinely new, or renewed social contract as the *Grundnorm* or authoritative starting point for a new constitutional system. Social control through law has its place in these cases, and the search for paradigms or models of basic constitutional institutions and their mutual and reciprocal relationships and of constitutional processes and procedures for the peaceful resolving of interests-conflicts becomes a necessary and inevitable task. While the best models are drawn from one's own society and its past successes and mistakes, there is by now a certain common core of comparative constitutional experience, going to institutions and processes and also, to some extent, fundamental philosophic principles which are subsumed today under the rubric of 'constitutionalism.' In the present study, the attempt is to identify and also to sketch out in some more or less precise way the lessons and experience of those societies where modern democratic constitutionalism may be said to find its principal historical legal sources or origins: Great Britain and the United States, certainly, as representing the two main streams of 'Anglo-Saxon,' common law constitutionalism today; France and Germany as representing the 'alternative,' continental European, civil law constitutional traditions, in their own separate and distinct ways; and a number of other countries – Japan and India, for example – that have 'received' a good deal of either Anglo-Saxon common law constitutionalism or continental European civil law constitutionalism, but have then had the crucial practical problem of digesting that foreign experience and creatively adapting it to their own distinctive, indigenous cultures and to their own special local social and economic conditions and problems. The emphasis, in the present study, is upon synthesis so far as possible of the frequently seemingly disparate practice of those countries that can be said to have had some continuing experience with constitutional government, over a reasonable period of time.

The quest is for general propositions as to constitutional law and constitutional government that can aid other countries venturing upon their own national exercises in constitution-making, or even aid those countries that are themselves chosen as the source of constitutional models if their own constitutional systems become, through passage of time, overcome by attrition or even seem in danger of breaking down altogether through having lost the inherent capacity of creative self-renewal. The questions asked and sought to be answered are of the nature of *when* and *why* one should venture on acts of constitution-making; to *whom* one should entrust the tasks of producing the fundamental political compromises that are a condition precedent to wise constitution-making; what balance one should make between general political talents and specialist legal expertise in the actual drafting of a constitutional charter; and, finally, what one should put in the charter when one is ready to draft it. This last question is, of course, the most difficult one; for the empirical record suggests that there are a number of different roads to Rome, and that the adoption, for example, of one particular pattern of institutional balancing rather than another requires careful study of basic political, social, and economic facts that underlie the positive law and that are a condition to its effective operation. The response, here, must be in terms of an identification of the range of alternative constitutional models available for choice at any particular time – what Radbruch would call the constitutional antinomies, for they are not, strictly, contradictions as in conventional Marxist-Leninist terminology – with some attempt at quantification of their relative social costs in the particular space-time situation. There are, of course, some clear general rules that can be induced from comparative constitutional legal science as to matters of technical drafting and 'style' in constitution-making, and these are set out wherever appropriate.

One very important caveat or warning should be offered at the outset. One should be at pains to avoid at all times that peculiarly barren and mechanical form of legal eclecticism – so popular, unfortunately, with constitution-makers today – of taking odd snippets from constitutional systems here and there and seeking to transplant them, unaltered, to other countries without at least enquiring beforehand whether the particular political, social, and economic conditions under which those constitutional institutions or processes developed in the host country and which help to make them politically viable and operational there are also present in the 'receiving' country. Constitutional institutions and processes need to be seen and understood against a background of what Ehrlich called the 'living law' of the communities in which they originated. The present study tries to render this extra, 'sociological' element in law – in this case, constitutional law – as a necessary accompaniment to the comprehension of the otherwise too abstract positive law of constitutional charters and related texts.

EDWARD McWHINNEY
Vancouver, Canada

CONSTITUTION-MAKING

4 Constitution-making

A second wave of constitution-making after the Second World War brought several quite different tendencies to the fore. In eastern Europe, in those countries that had been liberated by the advancing Red Army, there appeared a form of 'popular democracy' that was hailed in 1945 as marking a transition from 'bourgeois democracy' to 'Soviet democracy' – as uniting democratic principle to revolutionary dynamism in a popular (Jacobin) type of government. As a basic pattern, there was to be in each popular democracy a single chamber, the assembly, elected by universal suffrage, and this assembly was to control the executive. In the presence of a single dominant political party, questions of countervailing power and of constitutional checks and balances or separation of powers tended to become somewhat academic, with elections tending to reduce to plebiscites.

A further main tendency in post-Second World War constitution-making was that of 'post-colonial' constitutionalism. With the progressive liquidation of the European colonial empires – in Asia, Africa, and the Caribbean – in some cases voluntarily, and with perhaps a certain sense of relief of being able to shed a military or economic burden, and in other cases reluctantly and most tardily, the process of decolonization usually involved, in stages, the progressive devolution of qualified home rule, then self-government, and finally independence. The new post-colonial constitutions were invariably highly derivative, and tended to borrow very heavily from the constitutional institutions and developed practices of the 'parent' European colonial power involved: since the approach to self-government and independence on the part of the colonial territory concerned was usually conditioned upon the development, within that territory, of a democratic system of government as evidence of its capacity finally to govern itself, free from the benevolent paternalism of the erstwhile colonial power, it is perhaps not surprising that the emerging new, post-colonial, indigenous local political élite should find it good practical politics to copy the constitutional models of the colonial power, and that the influence of the old colonial office legal draftsmen should often be pervasive. Some of the later political and economic problems of this new group of 'succession' states, after the Second World War, undoubtedly stem from this constitutionalist eclecticism – the too-ready application to non-European societies of essentially European constitutional stereotypes, without prior examination of whether the different communities concerned were at the same essential stages of political and economic development, and whether, in consequence, the socio-economic infrastructures that inevitably condition the operation of positive law prescriptions were the same. A certain minimum equivalence or identity of underlying basic societal conditions is a pre-condition to the successful reception or transfer of legal models from one system to another.

1

Constitutions and constitutionalism

THE CONTEMPORARY SPATE OF CONSTITUTION-MAKING

The present era is one of unprecedented activity in constitution-makii
consequence in considerable part of the political culmination throughc
twentieth century of the dominant European historical trends of the
teenth century towards liberalism, nationalism, and independence
downfall of the continental European imperial dynastic states in Ger
Austria-Hungary, and Russia, with defeat or military disaster in the
1914-18, brought a flood of new, 'succession' states in a first, 'Eur
liberal,' wave of constitution-making that lasted throughout the dec
the 1920s. Power in the 'succession' states generally passed to a cult
intelligent, bourgeois élite whose principal preoccupation, after gener
of more or less authoritarian and often alien rule, was with the rationali
of power – the seeking to replace the extra-legal facts of power by rigi
extensive rules of written law. The constitutions that these groups pro
were essentially 'professorial constitutions,' with common key charac
tics: a notable heaviness of construction in conjunction with compl
rules that attempted to provide, in advance, for all foreseeable continge
The influence of the professors – especially of Preuss with the W
Constitution, and Kelsen with the Austrian constitution – was domina
constitution-making after the First World War, which was not, perhaps
prising considering that the revolutions that gave rise to the new con
tional systems occurred in countries without substantial, continuing,
democratic experience. In the end, the elaborate constitutional prescrip
directed against the exercise of executive power and the impressive con
tional catalogues of human freedoms that accompanied them proved
incapable of checking the onset of dictatorial regimes, military or Fasci
the countries for which they were devised.

A final main tendency in the post-Second World War wave of constitution-making was what we may call 'revived,' or 'modernized,' classical western constitutionalism. One great source of western constitutionalism – German civil law constitutionalism – was, after the short-lived adventure of Weimar democracy, suppressed during the Nazi regime of the 1930s and the war years. It succumbed altogether with the final military defeat in 1945 and the Four-Power military occupation, and the partition of Germany itself into the two political-geographical zones, East and West. French civil law constitu-tionalism, by the same token, suffered the traumatic military defeat of 1940 and the German military occupation from 1940 to 1944. In the political rebuilding of both countries – in West Germany in 1948-9, as the three west-ern powers, in default of a general, Four-Power peace treaty in Europe, pre-pared to return sovereignty to the three western military occupation zones; and in France in 1944-5 as General de Gaulle's provisional government dis-placed the Vichy regime – one of the felt imperatives was a fresh constitu-tional start and an abandonment of the pre-war constitutional system. In the case of West Germany, in the immediate historical context of Allied military occupation, it was necessary to demonstrate to the Allied authorities that they would, indeed, be handing over sovereignty to a genuinely democratic state that had been effectively purged of all dictatorial or Nazi elements and with appropriate legal safeguards against any revival of authoritarian tenden-cies in the future. In the case of France, by contrast, since the military defeat of 1940 was widely blamed upon the political weakness thought to be inhe-rent in the 'government-by-Assembly' of the Third French Republic, the first and strongest constitutional initiatives in 1944-5 were in the direction of building strong executive leadership to undertake the challenges of post-war social and economic reconstruction and of emphasizing, in particular, the role of the president of the republic. That these plans failed and that the constitutional system of the Fourth French Republic ended up not very different from that of the old Third French Republic was due more to the triumph of traditional forces in French political life and the 'unholy alliance' formed between Communists, Socialists, and the old right-of-centre Radi-cals against a Gaullist led return to an executive dominated government than to any confidence in the constitutional virtues of the old system. The failure, in turn, of the Fourth French Republic to solve the economic problems of the post-war period and its inability to implement firm policies of decoloniza-tion made inevitable its own breakdown, and paved the way to the Fifth French Republic and a strong presidential regime as a delayed recognition and implementation of the principal constitutional truth thought to be derived from the unhappy experiences of the Third French Republic's 'gov-ernment by Assembly.'

6 Constitution-making

The 1958 constitution of the Fifth French Republic and the Bonn Constitution of 1949 represent, together with the British constitutional system and the American constitution, the principal alternative models or stereotypes for democratic constitution-making at the present time. Is it altogether by accident that they have so emerged as the textbook examples for study and application in communities other than their own, often differing very widely in terms of basic social and economic conditions and political history and experience? One first question that suggests itself is whether the very notion of a constitutional system is inherently ethnocentric and western in character. If a constitution is thought of as no more than a recording of the basic institutions of decision-making in the contemporary state, and an identification of the alternative instruments for achievement and application (concretization) of those decisions, then the term is no doubt value-neutral and can be applied to any particular ideological system with equal impartiality. If, however, we think of a constitutional system as meaning something more than the mere formal source of decision-making competence in the state but as implying, in addition, certain notions about the manner and quality of the decision-making act and its exercise, and perhaps, beyond that, even the substantive content of the actual decisions, then we are rooting our conceptions of constitutional law in ideas of the nature and quality of government itself; and our very definition of law does begin to take on a quality of historical particularism or ethnic-cultural relativism. The original Anglo-Saxon common law conceptions of equality of government official and private citizen before the law, and of basic fairness and absence of surprise in legal process and procedure – worked out especially in the constitutional battles of the seventeenth century between the common law courts and parliament on the one hand and royal prerogative power on the other – are refined, elaborated, and extended by the late nineteenth century so as to be codified, in legal-literary form, as Dicey's celebrated 'Rule of Law' concept. Clearly, in substantive law terms, this is English constitutionalism quite as much as, or more than, the essentially institutions-based concept of the sovereignty of parliament.

At a slightly earlier period than Dicey's, Coke's seventeenth-century, common law, procedural due process, as further interpreted by Blackstone, had entered American constitutional law by the front door, through the new constitutional Bill of Rights, adopted virtually simultaneously with the Constitution of 1787 and intended to be part of it. The Bill of Rights, as interpreted by the United States Supreme Court in the post-Civil War era – in the so-called 'gilded age' of American capitalism right up to the time of the 'Court Revolution' of 1937 – began to take on a new and different note. Relying perhaps more on Blackstone than on Coke, the court gave procedural due process a new, *substantive* connotation, involving the reading into it of a notion of fundamental 'liberty of contract' that is constitutionally infringed by the state when it begins to venture upon social and economic planning legislation – the fixation of maximum hours of labour in industry, or minimum wages. Read in this special way, *substantive* due process equated with liberty-of-contract in the abstract ceased to be concerned with the manner and mode of exercise of governmental decision-making power vis-à-vis the private citizen, but looked instead to the content of the actual decisions and the values inherent in them. The constitution, as law-in-action, became – under the liberty-of-contract notion as developed and applied by the judges – equated with economic laissez-faire and its preservation long after it has ceased to be politically viable in electoral terms. Those who could no longer control the legislatures looked to the courts as guardian of their economic special interests, and did so right up to the time of the 'Court Revolution' of 1937 and the new wave of Roosevelt 'New Deal' judges on the court.

Most constitutional authorities today would say that the United States Supreme Court's development and application of substantive due process norms represented a very substantial and historically unwarranted and, in the end, politically dangerous extension of the notion of constitutionalism and of inherent constitutional values that the courts, qua institution of government, are obligated to defend. Other Anglo-Saxon common law, or common law-influenced, federal supreme courts reveal a tendency to find similar economic laissez-faire values – designed to protect private enterprise or private property against government regulation or control – inherent in their constitutional system, relying sometimes on language similar to the American due process clause and even sometimes on language that was deliberately designed to be different from the American model. The economic laissez-faire extension is politically dangerous because of its becoming very quickly politically dated: it was rooted in a specific, and very limited, period in American historical development. But the more general notion of constitutional fairness which procedural due process in its common law historical origins implies remains, as does the concomitant notion of keeping the political processes open and unobstructed, and free from unnecessary clogs in their operation – leading on to the concept of freedom of speech and discussion as the constitutional 'preferred freedom,' and to fair and honest election laws as the basis of any constitutional government. These latter 'open society' values are certainly rooted historically in nineteenth-century political liberalism, but they have a quality of permanence and immutability, nevertheless, that quite transcends issues of temporary economic advantage. In so far as the notion of constitutionalism has a meaning going beyond the positivism of a constitutional charter or constitutional texts, as written, it is this; and it seems common to all western European and western European derived constitutionalism, whether under the rubric of constitutional due process, 'preferred freedoms,' the rule of law, *le principe de la légalité*, or the *Rechtsstaat*, or some similar synonym.

THE LAW-IN-BOOKS AND THE LAW-IN-ACTION: OF THE NECESSARY DISTINCTION BETWEEN NOMINAL AND NORMATIVE CONSTITUTIONS

The pre-First World War legal philosopher of the Austro-Hungarian Empire Ehrlich developed the concept of the 'living law' to explain the sociological phenomenon that the positive law rules and prescriptions developed by the imperial bureaucracy in Vienna for application on a uniform basis throughout the empire were applied, nevertheless, in rather different ways in the different imperial regions, in accordance with local ethnic-cultural community attitudes and expectations. Ehrlich's general propositions were derived from his detailed case study of the Austrian civil code provisions on family law, and their operation in the remote province of Bukovina on the then imperial border with Roumania.

The phenomenon is not limited to the private law and, indeed, exists even more strongly in the domain of public and constitutional law. Leaders of the sociological approach to law in the United States – the School of Sociological Jurisprudence, as it was called – distinguished between the law-in-books and the law-in-action: the positive law as originally enacted by the legislature and the de facto community attitudes and expectations, and hence practice, in regard to that law. The textbook example usually cited by American jurists was the 18th (Prohibition) Amendment to the United States Constitution, launched after the American entry into the First World War and ratified after the conclusion of that war in 1919, formally prohibiting the manufacture, sale, or consumption of alcoholic liquors in the United States. The 18th Amendment was a dead letter, almost from the date of its coming into legal effect, ignored alike by private citizens and the law enforcement officials sworn to apply it. The fate of the 18th Amendment raises interesting questions about the long-range utility and merits of trying to concretise transient community social or moral attitudes by putting them, in permanent form, into the constitutional charter itself. But, more important, in the immediate context, it underlines the importance of underlying community attitudes in regard to law, and the importance of having a certain minimum societal support for the positive law. Some degree of non-correspondence between the positive law, as written, and de facto community attitudes and practices, is no doubt inevitable and even desirable in order to permit and encourage administrative flexibility in the application of the law. But how big a gap is permissible for the positive law rules concerned still to deserve the accolade of law, and for us to be able to speak of the existence of a viable, operational legal system?

Certainly, in the case of the United States, with the adoption of the 13th, 14th, and 15th amendments to the constitution in the immediate aftermath of the American Civil War, the principle of racial equality, to which those amendments were specifically directed, remained largely a dead letter in many parts of the United States, in regard to basic social and economic rights, and even voting rights for almost three quarters of a century. It was not until a series of courageous, imaginative Supreme Court decisions in the 1940s and the 1950s that the gap between the constitutional law-in-books and the constitutional law-in-action could be narrowed to the point of more substantial correspondence with the historical intentions of the original drafters of the 13th, 14th, and 15th amendments, and the principle of racial equality accepted as a constitutional 'living law' imperative.

This dichotomy between abstract constitutional principle, as drafted, and concrete governmental application of that principle exists, as we can see, even in regard to the classical constitutional systems where the constitution really is a going concern and has endured over a certain period of years. It is the more marked, however, in the case of some more recent ventures in constitution-making where the constitutional charter takes on a politically hortatory, programmatic character, and reads more in the nature of a statement of ideological principles than a practical blue-print for government. The constitution, in this case, has a symbolic rather than a functional quality and seems designed more for public relations at home or abroad than as a genuinely operational legal charter. The more rhetorical the formulations in the charter, the more it may appear that the constitution is intended to be nominal and not normative, and not in any case controlling as to the modalities of governmental decision-making, its procedural application in concrete cases, and its substantive content and compliance or otherwise with the postulated fundamental principles.

CONSTITUTIONS AND CONSTITUTIONALISM: OF THE SPIRIT OF THE LAWS, AND THE CONSTITUTIONAL 'RULES OF THE GAME'

A further necessary distinction is that between constitutions and constitutionalism. A particular governmental action – whether legislative act, or executive decree, or administrative application of a law – may happen to conflict with no express stipulation in the constitutional charter; and it may even, in certain cases, positively accord with the constitution-as-written. And yet it may be successfully impugned as being 'unconstitutional.'

Constitutional charters are normally, and necessarily, framed in fairly broad terms, and cannot cover every specific problem situation in terms before it has arisen in fact. There is a lapidarian quality of generality in the more successful constitutional charters that facilitates their continuing application and adaptation to rapidly changing societal conditions and expectations. Rather than try to cover the field exhaustively, these charters content themselves when they go beyond the outlining of the institutional machinery of government, to establishing high-level general principles – what might be called the primary or imperative principles of government – whose further elaboration, in terms of more concrete and low-level, secondary principles can then be left to empirical development on a case by case basis in the future. This is the essence, for example, of the English constitutional principle of the Rule of Law, first adumbrated by Dicey and embodying basic concepts like the absence of arbitrary power and equality before the law, as recognized in executive-legislative practice and applied and enforced by the regular courts. The Rule of Law is, in essence, a distillation of English common law legal history from the great constitutional battles of the seventeenth century onwards. We may call it the 'spirit of the laws'; but it is, in the sense used by Montesquieu, a historically received notion and not an a priori natural law postulate. The notion of the *Volksgeist*, at least in its nineteenth-century juridical formulation by von Savigny as the accumulated weight of the national legal tradition, is a German civil law analogue. The idea of constitutionalism seems to introduce, in any case, a further, supra-positivist element of evaluation to the constitutional law processes by insisting that even though a governmental act be 'legal' in the strict sense of conformity to the letter of the pre-existing positive law, it may still be 'unconstitutional' and so invalid and inoperative because in conflict with historically received, imperative constitutional norms.

By the same token, the correlative proposition is sometimes advanced that a governmental action may be 'constitutional' in the sense of being in the full spirit of the constitution, even though not 'legal' in the sense of strictly complying with pre-existing positive law stipulations or settled practice. Thus President de Gaulle defended his decision, in 1962, to use the special 'presidential powers' section of the 1958 Constitution of the Fifth Republic (Article 11), rather than the regular constitutional amending machinery (Article 89), to reform the constitutional charter, on the argument, reported by Raymond Tournoix: 'I don't want to let France die by respect for legalisms. When one wants to escape from legalisms, one does, even if the texts haven't foreseen it. Legalisms, yes, certainly one must pay attention to them; but they are secondary and even tertiary.'

2

Constituent power: the *when* and *why* of constitution-making

The starting point for any constitutional system is, necessarily, a political fact – a political decision. In this – what Kelsen called the *Grundnorm* and what we may call, ourselves, the *prior* constitutional question – the answer is necessarily pre-legal or meta-legal, in the realm of political science or sociology and not of law in the strict sense. The decision whether particular geographical areas with their own distinct ethnic-cultural groups may be grouped together into one larger political-territorial unit; or whether, by comparison, an existing, larger political-territorial unit may be split up into several smaller regions, or else lose some of its original territory and populations to other states, is, in the end, a high political one whether or not it may subsequently be rationalised in legal terms by a militarily-imposed peace treaty or else given some more genuine, democratic legitimation through ratification by popular plebiscite or referendum. And so it is that within an existing nation-state, a fundamental change in the existing social and economic base, effected by popular revolution or similar cataclysmic political event, usually means a corresponding change in the basic constitutional system and the postulation of a new legal starting point, or *Grundnorm*, as the basic premise of the new constitutional system. Presumably, if no *Grundnorm* is to be found, the political society concerned may be in process of disintegration or else in a condition of anarchy with no clear coalition or combination of political forces as yet prevailing. This was perhaps the case with revolutionary France during the Reign of Terror; or Russia between the deposition of the Czar and the 'October Revolution' of 1917; or Iran in the interregnum after the enforced departure of the Shah when no balance had been struck between the army, the bourgeois intellectual and business groups, the fundamentalist religious forces, and the local Communist party leaders and thus no unchallenged political power in the state had yet emerged. A parallel situation might be that of pre-1973 Vietnam, with one set of rulers during the day and another at night.

Within existing nation-states, and especially those blessed with some stable and continuing experience in constitutional government, restatement or redefinition of the main political and social premises may also occur on a fully consensual, voluntaristic basis without the *force majeure* of revolution or internal political upheaval. One may cite the case of Belgium where, in the spring of 1977, the so-called Pact of the Egmont Palace seemed to signal a far-reaching, binding compromise between the two great contending ethnic-linguistic communities within the Belgian state, the Flemish and the Walloon, on a basis of two separate and distinct, territorially-based, unilingual regions, Flanders and Wallonie, together with a common, bilingual capital region, Brussels. Unfortunately, supervening political conflicts between the two communities soon put in jeopardy the special status of Brussels, already agreed upon, and thus the substance of the inter-community compromise that had been established as the *Grundnorm* for the future continuance of a Belgian state based on constitutional coexistence and co-operation of the two races.

A further example of attempt at consensual redefinition of the fundamental political premise or *Grundnorm* of a state that is already a going concern may be seen in Canada, with the recommendation of a federal government constitutional commission of enquiry, the Pépin-Robarts Commission, early in 1979, for a massive restructuring of the Canadian federal system for the future, inter alia, on a constitutionally dualist ('Two Nations' – French and English) basis.

It may, indeed, be argued in relation to Canada that while it has had the one constitutional charter since 1867, it has had more than one *Grundnorm* during that time, operating at successive time periods and responding to changing societal conditions within Canada: from the initial, post-confederation centralized federalism, through the more consciously pluralistic, 'Provincial Rights' era from the 1890s to the 1930s, on finally to the neo-Keynesian, renewed centralization from the 1930s onwards.

Once the *prior* constitutional question has been answered and the new *Grundnorm* identified, the primary and secondary principles of the resulting new legal order can be developed by a process of logical deduction and application as the basic norm, in Kelsen's terms, progressively unfolds or concretizes itself. The choice of the *Grundnorm* itself, qua legal exercise, remains value-neutral. The courts have, with rare exceptions only (*The State* v *Dosso*

[1958] S. Ct 533 (Pakistan); reversed in *Asma Jilani* v *Government of Punjab* [1972] S. Ct 139 (Pakistan)), avoided giving direct rulings on the constitutionality of achievement of a new *Grundnorm*, where the political transition has not been made compatibly with the legal processes established in the pre-existing *Grundnorm*. But the courts have also invariably acquiesced in or assisted the lower level and essentially internal municipal law consequences flowing logically from the new *Grundnorm*, especially after the political events concerned when the courts' recognition is, in effect, retrospective only. (*Madzimbamuto* v *Lardner-Burke N.O and others* (Rhodesia) [1969] 1 A.C. 645 (P.C.).) Kelsen himself, in his later years, tried to reconcile his theories with his own personal political commitment by arguing that their application was always predicated upon the maintenance of a democratic constitutional system – thereby seeking to refute the argument that, in their very ideological neutrality or relativism, his theories paved the way to the fascist state. Obviously, too, the *Grundnorm*, as the starting point for a social science exercise, must bear some minimum correspondence to political reality; otherwise we would still be engaged in building legal systems for the Stuart kings, long after the 'Glorious Revolution' of 1688, or for the *ancien régime* after the fall of the Bastille. For those actually engaged in the exercise of constituent power, however, the decision to proceed to the adoption of a new constitution remains a political *donnée*, which they must accept under pains of having to turn in their mandate.

THE TIME ELEMENT IN CONSTITUTION-MAKING

Are there certain periods in the political development of a society when it is ripe to venture upon acts of constitution-making, and other periods when it is not? In the great debate of the early nineteenth century among German jurists over the issue of codification of the German civil law – codification, in the sense of enactment into one single, concise and comprehensive legal instrument, being not too dissimilar in intrinsic philosophy and purpose to the adoption of a constitutional charter – the legal historians were ranged in battle against the natural law school. The latter, led by Thibaut, impressed by the clarity and rationality and apparent claims to universality of the Code Napoléon, as carried throughout Europe and introduced into the German Rhineland in particular by Napoleon's military victories, argued for just such an act of codification of the German civil law as an aid to good government and good legal administration. They were answered by the historicists, led by von Savigny, who contended that the Code Napoléon was an alien, French civil law creation that could not be successfully imposed upon the German people. To the argument that both the French civil law and the German civil law had a 'received' Roman law base, von Savigny pointed to some centuries of different historical development since the reception and revival of Roman law in Germany from the fourteenth century onwards. The argument was that the fusion of Roman law and Germanic customary law by German jurists and German courts, over that period, had given the German civil law its own distinctively German character in spite of the Roman law heritage, and that this should be built upon in any attempt at German codification. Von Savigny developed the concept of the *Volksgeist*, or the distinctive legal genius of a people, the better to present his arguments, and suggested that the only time to codify successfully was when a nation had reached its full political and legal maturity. To do so before this would be to venture upon a premature codification that would prevent or limit national development; to do so afterwards would be to engage in an act of futility, since incapable of stemming national decline and decay.

There are strong elements of historical fatalism present in von Savigny's analysis, successful as it was in its immediate, early nineteenth-century German political context in delaying the approach to codification of the German civil law until after the establishment of the German Empire in 1871, and delaying the final codification act itself until the close of the century. But the emphasis upon the *Volksgeist* and upon the element of national popular support as a necessary pre-condition for codification does draw attention to the fact that the successful acts of legal codification – whether of the private (civil) law or the public (constitutional) law – almost invariably occur in or immediately after a period of great public excitement and resultant public euphoria when it is relatively easy to build, and to retain for a sufficiency of time to enable codification, a certain climate of popular political consensus. These periods normally occur during and after great political crises – victory in a great war, when the wartime consensus will extend to imaginative projects of post-war reconstruction; even a major military defeat, when there is a rallying of popular support to overcome any lasting effects of that past disaster; and certainly after a great political or social revolution when the original enthusiasm that spearheaded it usually insists upon some more concrete, secondary, follow-up measures. To this catalogue we might add, in a contemporary context, successful assertions of national self-determination and independence, whether occurring compatibly with, and in orderly legal succession from, the pre-existing constitutional regime, or else asserted only through *force majeure* and successful wars of national liberation. In such circumstances, if the new political élite is resolute and also categorical in its instructions to its constitutional advisers, we can expect to see the major political event fairly quickly succeeded by a major new constitutional act.

The art of constitution-making is to profit from such periods, using a constituent assembly if at all possible in order to enlist popular enthusiasm or public support to the full, and thus to proceed boldly to the elaboration of a new constitutional charter during the time – often, unfortunately, very brief – that a sufficient popular consensus still subsists. Thus 1848, 1871, 1919, and 1949 were peculiarly favourable periods for constitutional novation in Germany, even though the immediate background political events – the Frankfurt Liberal Assembly; the victory in the Franco-Prussian War; the military disaster of the First World War; and, after the Second World War, the three western military occupation powers' ill-concealed desires to return sovereignty to a new West German state as a potential western ally in the 'cold war' – were somewhat different in each case and the long-term results certainly not the same. The period 1944-5, immediately after the Gaullist liberation, was ripe for constitution-making and fundamental constitutional novation in France, but the political challenge was not fully met and so the opportunity was largely missed. The politicians, for the most part, were simply not intellectually or morally equal to the task at that time; though when the occasion came round again in 1958, with all the then current popular disillusionment with the Fourth French Republic's politicians and their proven inability to resolve either the nation's economic problems or the continuing crisis of the Algerian War, a new French political élite was able to marshal public opinion successfully in support of a fresh constitutional start. In a certain way, it is not surprising that Chairman Hua should profit from the public furore surrounding the overthrow of the 'Gang of Four' in 1976 successfully to initiate and to have adopted by the Fifth National People's Congress the new, 1978 Constitution of the People's Republic.

THE NECESSARY RELATION BETWEEN
CONSTITUTIONAL AND SOCIETAL CONSENSUS

The oldest and most durable of the written constitutional charters is the American one which was adopted in 1787, immediately after the conclusion of the Revolutionary War of Independence, when the points of weakness and improvisation in the original Articles of Confederation that had been adopted in 1777 for purposes of the colonial war against Great Britain, and that had finally been ratified and come into force in 1781, had become apparent, and when natural law ideas of the rights of man – the progenitor of the constitutional Bill of Rights – were at the flood-tide in the full flush of the victory over the imperial forces. A second, major innovation in the American constitution, sufficiently dramatic and sweeping in its political and social implications to amount, almost, to a new constitutional order – namely, the 13th, 14th, and 15th amendments to the constitution, with their mandate of racial equality – was effectuated in the immediate aftermath of the American Civil War, the amendments being rushed through Congress and the state legislatures with the requisite majorities by Radical Republican coalitions.

In the case of France, each major epoch in political development since the French Revolution is accompanied by its own appropriate constitutional instrument, representing the successful coalition of political and social forces that has brought about the change of political power in the first place. There is a dialectical character to the development of French constitutionalism over the years since the first constitutional settlement of 1791, with an ebb and flow of representative, government-by-Assembly principles, and caesarean, plebiscitarian approaches to government. The Constitution of 1791, conservative and still monarchical in character, was highlighted mainly by its inclusion, as its starting chapter, of the celebrated Declaration of the Rights of Man and of the Citizen of 26 August 1789. It gave way, very soon, to the constitution of the revolutionary Convention of 1793, which consciously created only a very weak executive authority, intended at all times to be subordinate to the all-powerful, populist Assembly. Reaction to the revolutionary excesses of this Assembly produced increasingly oligarchic, executive-weighted, governmental systems, through the Directory (1795), the Consulate (1799) and Consulate-for-Life (1802), and finally the Empire (1804), where the regime was frankly authoritarian in tone, legitimated in constitutional terms by overwhelming popular plebiscite support. We need not linger too long on the Restoration era from 1814 onwards, or the Second Empire interlude. Suffice it to say that, with the French military defeat in the Franco-Prussian war of 1870-1, and the reaction both to the revived caesarean constitution created under Napoleon III and to the 'democratic' excesses of the Paris Revolutionary Commune during the wartime German siege, the National Assembly that had been elected in February 1871 after the conclusion of the military armistice, specifically in order to conclude a formal treaty of peace with Germany, resolved to proceed also to the establishment of its own new constitutional system. The Assembly's task was complicated by the undoubted preferences, initially, of a majority of members of the Assembly for a restoration of the monarchy in some form or other; but by an inability of the monarchical majority to agree among itself as to the choice between the rival monarchical factions, and then, when the issue seemed finally resolved in favour of the Comte de Chambord's claims, by the latter's intransigent insistence upon a return to the old Bourbon fleur de lys flag in place of the revolutionary and Napoleonic tricolour. The Assembly resolved this particular problem – as it turned out finally – by adopting a law in November 1873 providing for the election of the president of the republic for a term of seven years. The republic, thus provisionally proclaimed in September 1870 with the defeat at Sedan and the downfall of Napoleon III, and already effectively functioning for more than three years, was thus confirmed. It remained only to record the event and to delineate its institutions and modalities in constitutional form, and this was achieved in a series of basic constitutional laws in early and mid-1875, the main features of which were a revival of the power of the legislature, composed of a popularly elected lower chamber and an indirectly elected senate. It was this body that, meeting together in assembly, elected the president of the republic and also had the capacity to amend the Constitution. The return to government-by-Assembly, at the expense of strong executive power, was completed by the disappearance, for practical purposes and as a matter of customary constitutional law, of the president's right to dissolve the lower house of the legislature on his own initiative, as a result of President MacMahon's maladroit use of that power in 1877.

After the French capitulation in 1940, the government-by-Assembly of the Third French Republic, with its emphasis on parliamentary fractionalism and weak and fleeting governments, was widely, if not entirely accurately, blamed for the military disaster. After the French liberation in 1944, General de Gaulle, as head of the provisional government, attempted to influence the adoption of a new, 'presidential' constitutional regime in France, to be marked by a preponderance of executive power on a general, American constitutional model. Faced from the start with the opposition of the Socialist and Communist parties, de Gaulle was eventually forced to give way. The Constituent Assembly elected in October 1945 soon lapsed into traditional habits of constitutional thinking and traditional fears of strong executive authority. In the end, and after General de Gaulle's resignation as head of the provisional government in January 1946, members of the Assembly voted to replace the Third French Republic by a Fourth French Republic on the same, government-by-Assembly model, but, if anything, with even more diminished powers on the part of the president of the republic than before. After two public referenda the constitution was finally adopted in October 1946 by a very weak popular plurality and with an extraordinary number of abstentions. The constitution, in the end, had the approval of only 36 per cent of the voters. Such a feeble popular mandate, succeeded by a recrudescence of the parliamentary fractionalism of the pre-war period and by the evident inability of the parliamentary leaders to resolve the economic and also the political (post-colonial) problems of the late 1940s and the 1950s, demonstrated the loss of popular legitimation for the constitutional system of 1946, and made inevitable its collapse and replacement by a new, executive weighted constitutional regime. This is the Fifth French Republic's Constitution of 1958, approved by overwhelming popular vote in public referendum; and the switch back from government by Assembly to strong executive power was accentuated by the adoption, in 1962, of a constitutional amendment substituting for the purely indirect system of presidential election provided under the Constitution of 1958 an election, henceforward, by direct, universal suffrage.

In the case of Germany, every major exercise in constitution-making, from the abortive, liberal democratic constitutional draft of 1849 to the present day, has succeeded upon some cataclysmic political or military upheaval. The constitutional draft of 1849 was the work of the so-called Frankfurt Assembly, a bourgeois liberal gathering stemming directly from the intellectual ferment and debate of the revolutionary year 1848. German unification, in the form of the new German Empire of 1871, was consummated by victory of the German states' alliance against France, on the battlefield in Bismarck's war launched for that purpose. In contrast to the bourgeois liberal draft of 1849, which commanded the enthusiasm of intellectual and professional groups but failed to rally significant support among the high civil service functionaries or the military or the industrial leaders, the constitutional system of 1871, with its frank deference to Prussian hegemony within the new federation of states, correctly reflected the dominant political facts of life of that era. The detailed federal constitutional arrangements follow directly from that *Grundnorm*: the relation between constitutional and societal consensus as represented by the prevailing political élite is thus proximate and direct.

The Bismarckian constitutional system of 1871 collapsed with the German military surrender in 1918. While liberal intellectual and professional groups now pressed strongly for an institutionalization of the *Rechtsstaat* as a counter to the overarching executive power of the old Imperial era and for an elaborate scheme of constitutional checks and balances, (including a constitutional bill of rights and the legal innovation, for Europe, of judicial review and control of constitutionality), the new republican regime suffered, from the outset, from a two-fold 'legitimacy gap.' First, the conservative groups who dominated industry, commerce, the army, and the upper strata of the civil service and the judiciary, were hostile in mind and outlook to a *republi-*

can state. Again, worker and syndicalist organizations preferred to build a Communist mass party in opposition to the idea of a *democratic* state.

The differences in intellectual sympathies and ideological expectations among the disparate political, social, and economic groupings that were the heirs to the old Bismarckian, imperial regime and thus effectively charged with finding a replacement for it, are reflected in the constitutional arrangements that they ended up by drafting. The new republican system has, certainly, an impressive catalogue of constitutional checks and balances, reflecting the enlightened legal eclecticism of the cultivated, civilized lawyers and professors who played such a very large part in the actual constitutional drafting. But these checks and balances, with the legal restraints on arbitrary executive or legislative power that they imply, are balanced by a sweeping concept of special or exceptional powers of State authority to meet claimed constitutional emergencies. This antinomy in terms of basic constitutional principle is reflected, if not indeed concretised, in another antinomy, in terms of basic constitutional institutions, between a parliamentary and a presidential system of government, involving the executive dualism of a legislature based chancellor and a popularly elected president. The Weimar constitutional charter maintained, in Karl Loewenstein's terms, a conspiracy of silence as to the existence of political parties and, in consequence, as to their regulation and integration, on a representative, interest-group basis, in associations or clusters having some minimum degree of political cohesiveness and viability. In the result, and in the actual historical unfolding of the Weimar constitutional era, there was not so much a 'democracy without democrats' as a democracy without a solid majority of democrats. The proliferation of splinter political parties ensured that chancellors could only rarely – in periods of economic and general international stability – build a successful multiparty coalition of rational and reasonable republicans. The weakness (and, eventually, in crisis times, the vacuum) as to effective executive decision-making power at the chancellor level, reciprocally compelled a filling of the constitutional gap by burgeoning presidential power, armed by the plebiscitarian legitimation conferred by direct popular election of the president in contradistinction to the chancellor. The point is that, in its ambiguity or ambivalence as to basic constitutional provisions, the Weimar system more or less faithfully reflected the imperfect or mixed character of the post-November 1918 German societal consensus immediately preceding the actual exercise in constituent power. Facing often seemingly contradictory trends and preferences in the legal 'special community' to whom they were ultimately responsible, the Weimar constitution-makers sought to express this fact, fairly and accurately, in their charter, by putting everything in together and leaving it up to history eventually to resolve any contradictions. The constitutional lessons from the Weimar experience are thus, themselves, complex and mixed, corresponding to the underlying frequent ambivalence in the Weimar constitutional charter's own stipulations: the dangers of an overly weak, parliamentary based executive power on the one hand, and the perils of an overly strong, caesarean, presidential executive power on the other.

The Weimar system was effectively ended with the Nazi takeover of power in 1933, Hitler's actual appointment to the chancellorship being effected, ironically enough, in accordance with the pre-existing constitutional 'rules of the game.' The formal ending came with the German military collapse and unconditional surrender in May 1945. The post-Second World War German reaction against all the legal abuses of the Nazi era ensured that when the time came to set up a new West German basic law or constitutional system in 1949, the West German societal consensus encompassed the elimination of all those elements of the preceding Weimar system that were thought to have destroyed it by facilitating the eventual Nazi takeover: the caesarean presidential executive established by direct popular election; the provision for direct popular plebiscite, having a law making character, on key political and social issues; and the decisive role of the president in the actual choice of the chancellor. Instead, under the 1949 (Bonn) system, the office of president of the republic is dramatically weakened, reduced to largely honorific functions, while the post of chancellor is given the extra constitutional legitimacy and prestige of being filled by election by the lower house (Bundestag) of the federal legislature. The constitution-makers of 1949, drawn from the three western powers' zones of military occupation in Germany, and committed to the principle of a democratic constitution as a condition of restoration of political sovereignty in West Germany, opted for a vibrant federalism, a judicially based control of constitutionality, and a parliament based executive, all within the framework of a republican presidential regime. The Bonn Constitution of 1949 correctly reflects the felt experience – the lessons from the recent past and also the hopes for the future – of the West German leaders to whom political power and sovereignty was handed over in 1949 by the Western allies.

THE POLITICAL-SOCIAL UTILITY OF CONSTITUTION-MAKING

If constitution-making requires, as a condition of its successful operation and application, a certain fortuitous timing ideally involving an already existing societal consensus in favour both of the principle of fundamental constitutional change, as such, and also of the grand lines and directions of the substantive changes involved, why do we sometimes see ventures in constitution-making when these prior conditions of popular approval hardly exist? First, in the case of non-democratic societies, the decision whether or not to have a new constitution will normally be imposed from above, by executive fiat, as it were. The exercise in constitution-making involved may, for example, become something in the nature of a public relations exercise, designed in considerable measure to impress governments and public opinion in foreign countries. Or, it may be designed deliberately, for purposes of domestic audiences to herald, in high-level, symbolic character, a change in basic policy imperatives or a new five or ten-year economic plan, much in the way that the Soviet Constitution of 1936 signalled the new, accentuated centralization of decision-making following upon Stalin's complete takeover of the governmental apparatus and the elimination of his party opponents. In the same way, the Brezhnev constitution of the late 1970s seems intended to lead to a newer, more inclusive and pluralistic, participatory governmental system.

Again, in the case of 'new' countries that have suddenly emerged to statehood as a result of decolonization or separation from some larger pre-existing unit, there may be little or no choice as to either the timing or the political-geographical *données* or limits, of constitution-making. The old imperial countries of Europe were, in the end, often in a hurry to decolonize, having left it until politically very late in the day in the first place. The Indian subcontinent would no doubt have benefited by more time and opportunity for working out fundamental compromises in the devolution of self-government and independence from British power. But Prime Minister Attlee, who had unexpectedly succeeded Mr Churchill in the elections of 1945, was resolute as to the decision to decolonize, and had set an absolute deadline of 1949 for its legal consummation. It was just not possible, in that brief time span, even with all the goodwill in the world, to work out sophisticated plural-constitutional forms and institutions, from available British Empire and Commonwealth constitutional stereotypes and models, to accommodate predominantly Hindu and Muslim drives for self-determination. Fission, and the creation of two separate, often mutually opposing states, was, *faute de mieux*, the solution.

Towards the end of the process of decolonization, by the late 1950s certainly, the colonial power often seemed to lose interest or to become impatient with detail in balancing, on the one hand, the political-economic advantages and disadvantages of colonialism, and on the other hand the undoubted political unpopularity, in world community terms of that era, in retaining colonies. Instead of an orderly process, decolonization seemed to become a rush, with too little thought given, in passing, to the rationality in ethnic-cultural and other terms of the original colonial boundaries, and to the propriety of handing over power in post-colonial terms to one claimed representative local, indigenous political élite rather than to another. Local, indigenous political élites, however, faced with the alternative of accepting an offer of transfer of power *tout court* or else letting the opportunity pass by and not return, can be pardoned, I think, for taking it, even if the terms and conditions were not to their liking. These could always be corrected later, of course. This perhaps accounts for the rapidly supervening dissatisfaction, in so many post-colonial, succession states, for the public order system that they 'received' or inherited on independence, and for the frequency with which those same systems were radically recast or overthrown in the post-decolonization period.

Finally, in the case of countries whose constitutional system is already a going concern, in continuing operation over a period of years without any marked evidence either of public dissatisfaction with it or else of its inability to respond to changing societal needs, the decision to novate or not to novate the constitutional system may indicate either a very stable society in which the task of updating the constitutional text can be undertaken soberly and deliberately as an ordinary housekeeping measure, or else a society that is unable to solve other, more substantial, *non-constitutional* problems (economic recession, high unemployment and inflation, and demands for national self-determination and political breakaway on the part of a regionally based, national ethnic-cultural minority) by other, *non-constitutional* means, and that turns to constitution-making as a last resort to divert public attention from those other, more pressing non-constitutional problems and its own inability to develop viable solutions for them.

3

The constitution-makers: *who* does *what*?

CONSTITUTION-MAKING: AN ÉLITIST OR A POPULAR VENTURE?

The decision for any state whether to embrace direct democracy, and to seek active popular participation in the actual processes of constitutional drafting and constitutional enactment, may in some cases be foreclosed in advance. In instances of decolonization, where a parent, imperial government finally resolves to devolve political-legal authority to an indigenous, local, colonial community, the imperial government – normally in control of the constitutional rules of the game from the beginning – may prefer an orderly, 'arranged' state succession from its own government to a new, local government created, ad hoc, for the purpose. The transfer of constitutional power thus becomes an élitist, oligarchic exercise, with the constitutional charter of the newly created state often being one prepared in advance by the imperial government's own colonial office functionaries. When there has been adequate time, the British Empire practice was, as far as possible, to try to co-ordinate the imperial initiative in favour of constitutional devolution with some form of local constituent activity in the colonial territory concerned and on the part of the local people on some more or less genuinely representative basis. This was easy enough to effectuate in the case of that older and narrower European segment of the empire – Canada, Australia, and even the Union of South Africa – and it was also possible successfully to apply this example in the late 1940s, in the case of decolonization and devolution of constitutional self-government and independence on the Indian subcontinent, where a local, representative constituent assembly functioned from the beginning – once the British decision to go had been made in London – in order to work out the general principles as well as the detailed institutions of the new constitutional system or systems. But decolonization by apparent voluntary act of the imperial power was sufficiently novel and imaginative and inducive of goodwill, immediately after the Second World War, for it to be able to proceed at a leisurely pace in regard to post-independence fundamental constitutional imperatives. By the late 1950s, decolonization had become a 'new' international law imperative which the United Nations and the emerging Third World sought to impose on often unwilling or uncooperative parent imperial states or governments. Sometimes these latter moved too late, when political events had already passed them by, so that the actual transfer of power became often ungracious and hurried, with the consequence that the post-independence constitutional systems, in their turn, were often improvised or makeshift arrangements, with a predominantly European 'colonial office' personality reflected in constitutional institutions that had originally been developed for European societies but never empirically tested in terms of their capacity for being usefully received and applied in non-European societies at rather different levels of social and economic development than the parent powers. This might not perhaps have mattered too much if the post-decolonization 'succession states' of the late 1950s and thereafter had had the time to develop, in comparative leisure and on their own proper constitutional initiative, their own genuinely local source of sovereignty in place of the 'received,' imperial *Grundnorm* at the time of independence. This would have implied locally developed constitutional institutions and practices more nearly reflecting the local, indigenous society and its aspirations. Unfortunately, most of the 'new countries' of the late 1950s and the 1960s were soon overwhelmed by post-independence economic and political problems – the latter stemming from the fact that the territorial frontiers inherited from the colonial era often involved the compulsory political union of quite distinct and different ethnic-cultural communities that could not coexist easily in the post-colonial phase. *Faute de mieux*, the post-decolonization, 'made in Europe' constitutional systems of that period survived uneasily while the other, non-constitutional problems of the post-colonial phase were battled; and when they were replaced it was too often by the extra-constitutional route of a military coup d'état, civil war, or military repression of local autonomy and minority self-determination claims.

CONSTITUTION-MAKERS IN PROFILE:
THE TECHNICIANS AND THE POLICY-MAKERS

These 'decolonization' era exercises may perhaps be considered as a special historical example or exception to the operation of constituent power in democratic constitutionalism, even if, numerically, they no doubt amount to much the largest category of cases. But even within the older 'classical' constitutional systems, concrete practice indicates that the choice between direct democracy on the one hand, involving active popular participation in constitutional drafting through a representative, elected constituent assembly and later ratification by a referendum and, on the other hand, élitist or at least oligarchic approaches to constituent power, is not a clear-cut one. A great deal will turn on the particular state and its particular national legal tradition.

In the case of France, it would be unthinkable, with the perceived constitutional traditions from the revolution onwards, not to utilize direct democracy in the major steps of the constituent process. It was noted in criticism of the Constitution of 1799 (the *Consulate*), that it was the first of the four revolutionary era constitutional charters to be adopted by a small committee and not by an elected assembly; but the new first consul, General Bonaparte, had asked that the constitution include a provision for its submission to a plebiscite and this was in fact done, creating a sort of ex post facto popular involvement in the constituent process. In fact, the Constitution of 1799 reflects, in its origins, the intellectual dominance of two key personalities operating through the committee or commission system: the Abbé Sieyès, politician and politicologue of the revolution and noted for his constitutional aphorisms, and, with increasing ascendancy, the man-on-horseback and man-of-action of the hour, General Bonaparte. By the end of this particular exercise in constituent power, Bonaparte had become first consul and therefore the dominant executive personality in the new constitutional system, while Sieyès had been effectively shunted aside or 'kicked upstairs' as president of the Senate.

This illustrates, of course, one of the principal practical dilemmas of constitution-making. If it is intended to be a meaningful public exercise, producing a constitutional charter that really will be operational as constitutional law-in-action and not simply political window-dressing, then the charter must go beyond the postulation of abstract general principles (always fairly easy to draft) and get down to the details of institutions and processes and of their mutual interaction. This is an inherently technical domain, demanding some degree of specialist constitutional expertise going beyond actual governmental, policy-making experience. How much is constitution-making a technical function, and how much a more general, community policy-making exercise? If the answer is that it is both, then how is one to strike the balance between the two? Ideally, the politicians (policy-makers) would assume the law-making, enacting role, assisted by the technicians (constitutional specialists) as their professional or civil service advisers. But, at a certain point, the professionals – the legal *honoratiores*, in Weber's term – seem bound to dominate the amateurs, by virtue, simply, of their innate professionalism just as the Prussian law professor and civil servant, Preuss, dominated the Weimar constitution-making in 1919, and the law professor, Kelsen, dominated the post-1918 Austrian constitution-making. It would take a very gifted amateur, with the added ability of mastering technical detail, to reverse this condition as did General Bonaparte with the Constitution of 1799, and General de Gaulle with the Fifth French Republic Constitution of 1958. The better approach, and one in accord with all the trends in democratic constitutionalism today, would seem to be to open up the constituent process as much as possible by rendering it public: open charters openly arrived at – through popularly elected constituent assemblies and through open plebiscitarian ratification of the final constitutional text.

CONSTITUTION-MAKERS AND THEIR ARENAS

Study of the different modalities of exercise of constituent power in different countries indicates a wide variety of options as to the arenas for constitutional drafting and enactment. The choice among these different options may be made casually or inadvertently, but it will never be value-neutral in its consequences. What looks like a simple, technical, machinery choice may in fact predetermine or influence the final substantive recommendations as to the content and direction of a new, or 'renewed,' constitutional system. The evidence would suggest that governments are very often aware of this truth, and shape their choice of the instruments of constitution-making accordingly.

The expert commission
Theoretically, an expert commission will be availed of by any government genuinely concerned with improving or modernizing its constitutional system. But the constitutional and the political domains are very close, and a government, through naming the members of an expert commission, is in a position to determine, or at least to decisively influence the commission's thinking in advance of its commencing its work. The distinguished French jurist, Georges Scelle has identified a certain professional bias or at least in-built intellectual disposition – a *dédoublement fonctionnel* – on the part of certain jurists, law professors, and even judges who, if they are not 'government' jurists in the crude sense of the word, are at least eminently predictable, on the basis of their past performance, as favouring their own government in adversary situations that cry out for an independent, objec-

tive professional scientific judgment. An expert commission, therefore, tends to become politically suspect, unless its members are selected on some genuinely independent, non-partisan basis, or unless its terms of reference are so precisely and narrowly defined in advance that it will be compelled to limit itself, in its work, to a purely technical, non-partisan, non-political function.

In the case of the countries that in recent years have used the expert committee or commission as an aid to constitution-making, the actual exercise of constituent power – to be made only after the expert commission report has been completed – has tended to remain under the firm control of the political decision-makers, and so the possibility of their being overwhelmed by the experts' opinions has never been substantial, even assuming the experts had wanted to play such a role.

The expert commission was used by the Supreme Soviet in its approach to enactment of the 1977 ('Brezhnev') Constitution of the USSR, the titular head of the constitution committee being, not inappropriately, L.I. Brezhnev himself. This was also the route taken by the Swiss Ministry of Justice in 1974 in naming an expert commission, composed of forty-six members, to take up the project for total revision of the Swiss federal constitution launched as early as 1965 by two federal deputies and continuing at measured pace – some might say, at deliberately leisurely pace – thereafter.

The British Commonwealth practice of using a royal commission of inquiry, or a public (as distinct from expert) commission or task force, raises much the same questions as already posed in regard to the expert commissions, and seems to offer some additional problems. The government of the day, in naming the royal commissioner or commissioners, or the members of the public commission or task force, is in a position to shape the final outcome, so that some parliamentary role to ensure independence in choice of the commission's members would seem desirable if public confidence is to be maintained.

In April 1969, the British government appointed a multi-member royal commission of inquiry to 'examine the present functions of the central legislature and government in relation to the several countries, nations and regions of the United Kingdom ... [and] whether any changes are desirable in those functions or otherwise in present constitutional and economic relationships.' The task of the royal commission, in essence, was to examine regional alienation and disaffection in Great Britain and to recommend for or against some form of constitutional devolution for Scotland and Wales. The royal commission membership covered a wide range of public and professional experience, and it does not seem to have been viewed as partisan in character, either at the time of appointment or at the time of final submission of its report in October 1973.

In 1977, the Canadian government appointed the Task Force on National Unity, a multi-member public commission of inquiry to look into problems of regional alienation within Canada and particularly in the province of Quebec. The task force, to give it a non-partisan image, had two designated co-chairmen, one a former Liberal federal cabinet minister, Jean-Luc Pépin, and the other a former Conservative premier of the province of Ontario, John Robarts, although the remaining members of the commission seemed to be members of the ruling federal Liberal party. The task force's terms of reference were rather more loosely drawn than those of the British royal commission, with the result that in its final report made early in 1979, it tended to run the gamut of constitutional change, thereby acting rather more as a constituent assembly than as an expert commission of inquiry. Since the task force members tended to be lay rather than professional in their training and experience, this, rather than any complaint of political partisanship, was perhaps what militated against the political persuasiveness of the report upon the government that had appointed it in the first place. The Trudeau government had not acted on the report in any way by the time of the government's defeat in the general elections of May 1979.

Parliamentary enactment
A constitutional system committed to the principle of flexibility will normally choose the national legislature as the principal or sole arena for constitutional change, whether particular or general. The commitment to constitutional flexibility stems from the French revolutionary experience that to erect too many or too difficult barriers to constitutional change in the charter itself is an exercise in futility and an encouragement to the resort to force if all else fails. More ambitiously, however, the commitment to constitutional flexibility and the making of the legislature as the main repository of the processes of change, bespeaks a certain confidence in representative government and in the capacity of duly elected legislators to provide wisely for their country's future. This is why – building on their own national experience – the constitution-makers in France, in the case of the constitution of the Third Republic in particular, but also the Fourth and the Fifth Republic, give such a large role to the legislature in the processes of constitutional revision. The situation in France, which might otherwise be viewed as a simple reflex of that occasional French constitutional emphasis on government-by-Assembly, is complicated by the existence of that other, and somewhat countervailing French constitutional principle of plebiscitarian

democracy: the practical reconciliation of the two principles, built into the constitutional charters of the Fourth and the Fifth Republic, is to utilize both approaches – the legislative processes, albeit with extraordinary majorities and involving the two houses of parliament; and the referendum/plebiscite, as co-ordinate or alternative instruments of constitutional change.

The Bonn Constitution of 1949, after Germany's own direct experience of plebiscitarian democracy in the Weimar and Hitler periods, entrusts constitutional revision to the federal legislature, but specifying extraordinary (two-thirds) majority votes in each house (Article 79). The Weimar Constitution of 1919 had had a similar provision for constitutional revision through two-thirds majority votes in the two houses, but accompanied by provision for a binding popular referendum vote in the case of disagreement between the lower and upper house or in the case of a popular initiative coming from ten per cent of the registered voters.

In 1973, the lower house (Bundestag) of the West German federal legislature voted unanimously on an all-party proposal to set up a commission of inquiry on constitutional reform. The membership of the commission was novel in that, while one-third of the commission's twenty-one members were to be members of the Bundestag, another third were to be named by the governments of the member-states (*Länder*), while the remaining third were to be experts named by the different political parties in the Bundestag. Among the seven members thus selected from the ranks of the Bundestag, three came from the principal government party, the Social Democrats (SPD); three from the combined opposition forces, the Christian Democrats (CDU/CSU); and one from the tiny centre, Liberal party (FDP), which was currently a part of the government coalition. To a quite remarkable extent, the members of the commission, including those chosen from the Bundestag party ranks, were professors or doctors of law. The commission of inquiry, though initiating through the parliamentary processes, was thus, in its basic character, a 'mixed' commission – parliamentary, federal-state, and expert – with its claims to political detachment and scientific objectivity reinforced by the multiparty elements in its composition and the deference to professional training and expertise accorded by the various political parties, government and opposition, in their actual selection of members of the commission. The commission produced, in a four year period, two separate reports, one on institutional interactions within the federal government itself and the other on *Bund-Länder* (federal-state) relationships. Perhaps in part because of the technical character of the commission's membership – though in principal part, no doubt, because the Bonn constitutional system of 1949 is an evident operational success as it now stands – the commission's conclusions and recommendations for future change have tended to be rather modest and technical in themselves.

It may, indeed, be suggested that when the constitutional system is already a going concern, so that what is wanted is considered to be incremental changes that build on existing constitutional values and constitutional institutions, without any perceived need for radical restructuring, then other modes of constitutional change, involving large-scale, direct popular participation like the constituent assembly, may become not merely expensive and time consuming but functionally unnecessary or irrelevant. The strictly technical, scientific, expert committee or commission as an aid to legislative drafting then comes into its own as, for example, in the case of the Brezhnev Constitution of 1977. But, it may be suggested, it is in this type of situation, that the parliamentary committee finds its special role: either a wholly *intra*-legislature group, or else a cabinet sub-committee, utilizing expert advice of necessity but on a largely non-public basis. In a general sense, and making appropriate allowances for certain basic structural differences applying in the case of a Socialist, eastern European state, we could say this has been the case with the successive, post-Stalin constitutional systems of the Socialist Federal Republic of Yugoslavia – of 1963 and 1974 especially.

The British constitutional system, in embracing the constitutional principle of the sovereignty of parliament, renders the constitution totally flexible, and makes the legislature the instrument of such flexibility. The Anglo-Saxon federal systems, among which the United States and the main commonwealth countries may be numbered, make use of the national (federal) legislature, too, but as part of the larger constitutional machinery of federalism; and they are perhaps better dealt with separately and in that special context.

Executive diplomacy
Executive action as the prime solvent for constitutional change occurs most naturally and spontaneously in a federal system or else in some other form of plural-constitutional system resting upon the association, in constitutional or, less than that, contractual (treaty) form of two or more states or governmental units. It may then be found politically prudent, even if not legally obligatory, to negotiate a new political-social consensus between the political leaders of those different units before entering upon any fundamental changes – in effect, a re-definition of the original political-social *Grundnorm*. We are, of course, speaking at the level of constitutional law-in-action: the actual machinery for formal constitutional amendment may be quite other than inter-governmental agreement or contractual accord and might involve,

as in Canada under the constitutional system of 1867, for example, formal application to the British government for a British, imperial statute applicable to Canada; or, as in Australia, federal legislation followed by a popular referendum with special constitutional stipulations as to the quality (range) of the popular majorities at the referendum. Executive diplomacy, in this case, is simply a political prerequisite or catalyst for fundamental constitutional change or novation. Where it has tended to be employed over a period of years, as it has in Canada, it offers the disadvantage of becoming viewed, in time, as a form of constitutional custom or convention conferring a *right* on the constituent units of the federal or plural-constitutional system to exercise a veto over any proposals for constitutional change. What emerged, then, as a measure of political expediency on the part of the federal or central government, involving the conferring of a mere *privilege* of prior consultation upon the political leaders of the constituent units, may become an element of constitutional rigidity, tying up the process of constitutional change into cumbersome consultative procedures, with the implicit claim of a liberum veto (eighteenth-century, Polish-style) on the part of anyone consulted. It may also lock a federal system into an original, historically quite static conception of the nature of the constitutional union that was created in the first place – the notion that the federal system remains no more than a loose contractual association of German princes – a *Staatenbund* or Holy Roman Empire, rather than a genuine *Bundesstaat* with its own autonomous legal personality. A plural-constitutional system may sensibly decide to maintain, or even retroactively to recognize, a form of special 'contractual' status for one or more of its constituent units in response to pressing internal political factors: this may be the case, for example, in Canada, where the emergence of French-Canadian claims for national self-determination might seem to call for acceptance of a *deux nations* conception of Canadian confederation, with some form of special constitutional status for Quebec within it. The *Grundnorm* or political basic premise for the federal state, in this case, would have changed to take on a genuinely dualist (French-English) character, with the subsidiary constitutional norms being modified or adjusted accordingly. It would be quite another matter, however – neither historically true nor valid in contemporary societal terms – to argue that French-Canadian drives for national self-determination compelled transformation of the existing Canadian federal system into a league of ten provinces in which all the political leaders (of the nine English-speaking provinces, plus Quebec) were seen as having a postulated natural law *right* to put in question the original federal union by demanding re-negotiation of its fundamental terms. Legal fictions can be carried too far!

Executive diplomacy may also be seen in operation in non-federal and non-plural, purely unitary states; but then it is part of the ordinary constitutional machinery of separation of powers and constitutional checks and balances. The constitutional head of state, particularly where he is an elected president, may sensibly claim to have a direct, national political mandate, whereas the mandates of members of the legislature and the cabinet may be more local and particularist, or, at least, represent coalitions of regional or sectional forces. The merits of balancing the general interest against the particular, and so counteracting parochialism, not less than the desire to ensure efficacy in the operation of the constitutional amending processes, may suggest conferring a constitutional role on executive (presidential) initiatives in the amendment formulae, with or without subsequent ratification by popular referendum. The French constitutional traditions since the revolution – at least, those aspects of it stressing direct, popular democracy and the plebiscitarian approach – reflect this method most strongly: not merely the two Napoleons, but also President de Gaulle in a contemporary context, have demonstrated the capacities and opportunities for a strong executive personality to introduce fundamental changes in this way.

Constituent assembly
It is, however, the constituent assembly – albeit a constituent assembly elected by direct, popular vote and therefore having its own direct political mandate and claims to political, as well as constitutional legitimation – that represents the culmination of the constitutional thinking of the Age of Enlightenment. It is not surprising, therefore, that it is one of the principal constitutional heritages of the French Revolution and of the liberal constitutionalist tradition that, historically, followed it from throughout the nineteenth and a good part of the twentieth century. Its apogee, post-Second World War, is to be found in the Gaullist constitutionalism of the Fifth French Republic, though Chairman Hua's 1978 Constitution of the People's Republic, as adopted by the Fifth National People's Congress, has an avowedly popular and populist root or source of state sovereignty that would have delighted French revolutionary era constitution-makers.

For its most effective operation, a constituent assembly would seem to require to be elected against a background of an already existing, and continuing, societal consensus as to the nature and desired direction of fundamental political, social and economic – and hence constitutional – change. Either that, or the constituent assembly must itself be conceded enough time, within the definition of its mandate, to wait for such a societal consensus to develop or to get out itself and try to build it. Normally, of course, one does not have time: the 1946 temporal tribulations of the combined, All-India Constituent Assembly over the issue of a united or fissured subcontinent for the post-decolonization era, or (if unity was to be the final solution) of a unitary versus a plural constitutional form, were foreseeable, and could not be overcome even by the substantial prior consensus on many of the machinery, processual aspects of the post-independence government still to be established. In most instances, however, the motive power of constituent assemblies will come from acting quickly, in periods of great public euphoria where natural law ideas are dominant – normally, as noted, following on some great political or social revolution or similar upheaval, when there is little difficulty for the constitution-makers in perceiving the nature of the public mood and in translating it into technical legal form.

The constituent assembly is almost *de rigueur* with constitution-making ventures in France: the constitution of 1799 was the first of the revolutionary era to be adopted by a small committee and not by a constituent assembly, and it is not an example that has commended itself to subsequent history, in spite of its having received a form of ex post facto legitimation by being submitted to a popular plebiscite vote. Where the constituent assembly can make an ally of time and thereby itself adjust to new problems and needs as they arise, it can be surprisingly successful from the viewpoint of constitutional durability. The constitutional system of the Third French Republic of 1875 is an example of this. Prevented by the obstinacy and intransigence of mutually conflicting Royalist claimants from adopting a monarchical constitutional system quickly – which a majority of the members clearly wanted, at the time of their election, as a national assembly to conclude peace with the German states at the beginning of 1871 – the constituent assembly that succeeded upon the Second Empire continued on a pragmatic basis. It confirmed particular institutions – for example, the president of the republic, to be indirectly elected for a seven-year term – when the occasion arose, as it did in November 1873, in the case of the presidency; it went on, in 1875, to a series of three organic laws setting out the main governmental institutions of the new republic and their relations inter se. The republic had in fact functioned successfully for four years, and it remained simply to confirm it in positive law terms, which the National Assembly, renewed by partial elections since it was first elected in 1871, finally did.

Reflections on the role of pragmatism, or 'operationalism,' in the act of constitution-making for the Third French Republic tend to suggest that constitutions made with a large degree of commonsense and without too much practical deference to a priori conceptions of eternal truth, tend to have a way of lasting, where more perfect, abstract blueprints may fail because of their own intellectual absolutism. The 'temporary' character of the origins of the Third French Republic – a monarchical republic, with the possibilities of future revision to a genuine monarchical regime – reminds us that the present-day Bonn Constitution of 1949 was also officially designed as a transitional regime for the three western zones of Germany to which sovereignty had been restored by the three Western military occupation powers, pending an eventual reunification of East and West Germany. In 1974, the then federal president, Gustav Heinemann, rightly reminded people on the twenty-fifth anniversary of the Bonn *Grundgesetz* – or basic law, as distinct from constitution, so called to emphasize its provisional character – that the Federal Republic of West Germany was not built in a day. It was only with the passage of time that it had become a state in the full sense of the word. 1955, the date of return of sovereignty to West Germany by the three western occupation powers, must be considered, together with 1949 the date of coming into force of the *Grundgesetz*, as one among a number of separate dates marking the establishment, on a step-by-step basis, of the Bonn constitution.

The references in the preamble and elsewhere in the constitution (Article 23, on territorial jurisdiction, for example), to a possible eventual extension of the Bonn constitution to all of Germany, should not gainsay the fact that the political-territorial division of Germany in 1945 into two conflicting spheres of influence has taken on, by now, a quasi-permanent character, legal perhaps as well as political; but that has not prevented the Bonn constitution, temporary or transitional though it may have been intended to be in its origins, from becoming a model of contemporary democratic constitutionalism, at the level of law-in-action as well as in abstract charter form.

Both the Bonn Constitution of 1949 and the earlier Weimar Constitution of 1919 can be considered as the products of constituent assemblies – the Bonn constitution being the work of the sixty-five member parliamentary council formed from leading political figures drawn from the three western military zones of occupation of Germany, and confirmed by the legislative councils of more than two-thirds of the participating units (*Länder*) within those western zones. The parliamentary council, in particular, seems to have acted as a genuine debating chamber, with key personalities from the subsequent Bonn republic dominating the discussions and effectively determining the final shape of the constitutional system, all this notwithstanding the continuing political reality of Allied military occupation of Germany. By contrast, the Weimar Constitution of 1919, which had also followed on a military defeat, was adopted by a national assembly democratically elected in January 1919, after the overthrow of the old monarchical regime. The national assembly was immensely aided by the expert drafting role already undertaken by Professor Preuss at the request of the transitional government; but the final constitutional draft, adopted at the end of July 1919, and coming into force the following month, still represents the give-and-take and political compromise inherent in any genuinely functioning, multiparty assembly. It is not without justification that the preamble of the Weimar constitution, in marked contrast to that of the empire of 1871, proclaims an unimpeachable popular source or *Grundnorm* for the new constitutional system.

Though the Constitution of the United States of 1787, in contrast to the earlier, wartime Articles of Confederation that had been adopted in 1777, ratified and come into force in 1781, is the product of a constituent assembly, this has not been the universal way for Anglo-Saxon constitutional systems. The British-style constitutional systems, when they were limited to the 'older' (essentially European, Anglo-Saxon) countries, had their formal juridical origins in statutes of the (imperial) British parliament; though one sees them preceded – in the case of Canada and Australia, for example – by what might be characterized as local constituent assembly-style activity, grouping together local political leaders. The second-wave, British Empire constitutional systems, being designed for non-European colonies in process of rapid decolonization, were (with the notable exception of the Indian subcontinent already referred to) normally devolved from above from the parent authority. They thus tend to have an élitist or expert, and certainly non-popular, root of political and legal sovereignty. British and British-received constitutional systems on the whole favour putting one's trust in parliamentary majorities, and there is not the continental European tradition or experience in direct, plebiscitarian democracy; so that it is not surprising, perhaps, that discussions in Canada for a species of constitutional novation in response to French-Canadian drives for national self-determination show no enthusiasm for the principle of popular constitutional involvement, by way either of an elected constituent assembly charged with the task of constitutional drafting, or of a popular referendum on any new constitutional proposals.

Popular initiative
Direct popular initiative, as a source of constitutional change, is usually associated with Swiss constitutionalism. The present Swiss constitution, adopted in 1874, was amended in 1891 so as to allow, for the first time, the popular initiative as a mode of introducing proposals for constitutional amendment. Prior to that time it was the federal legislature alone that could initiate such proposed amendments: after 1891, proposed amendments could also be

introduced by a petition of 50,000 voters, whether the projects simply covered partial revision of the constitution or a total revision involving a wholly new constitutional charter (Articles 120, 121). In either case, the proposed constitutional amendment is not legally adopted until ratified by popular referendum majority, requiring both a majority overall vote and also a majority of the votes cast within a majority of the cantons (member-states of the federation). The popular initiative approach to the introduction of proposals for constitutional amendment has been widely and frequently availed of since the time of its insertion into the federal constitution. No doubt the frequency of its utilization has been facilitated by the simple and straightforward conditions for its application: 50,000 voters by way of petition is not a difficult constitutional hurdle to surmount, and in addition there is provision for the federal legislature itself rendering an initiative proposal into appropriate constitutional-legal form if it should not be presented in precise statutory form in the first place. It is noticeable that the success record, at the referendum, ratification stage, of popular initiative-originating proposals for constitutional amendment, as opposed to federal legislature-originating proposals, is not very great; but this may be a commentary much more upon the relatively greater freedom and disposition to break new social or economic ground of the popular initiative proposals than upon the intrinsic institutional merits of the popular, as opposed to the federal, legislative initiative.

Outside Switzerland, however, the popular initiative has found little application. The short-lived Weimar Constitution of 1919 allowed for a popular initiative approach to the introduction of proposals for constitutional amendment, though it had not been present under the earlier federal constitution of 1871. Though the more normal method – initiation by federal legislation – remained, as it had under the Constitution of 1871, proposals for constitutional amendment could, in terms of Article 73 of the Weimar constitution, be introduced by petition of one-tenth of the qualified voters. The proposal for constitutional amendment had then to be submitted to popular referendum vote for purposes of legal adoption, unless it had been accepted, in the meantime, without alteration by vote of the Reichstag (lower house of the federal legislature). At any popular referendum held upon a popular initiative-originating proposal for constitutional amendment, the consent of a majority of those entitled to vote was required (Article 76).

The popular initiative approach to constitutional change has, however, enjoyed notable public enthusiasm in recent years in some of the member-states of the American federal system, particularly in the state of California where it was the focus of the 'taxpayers' revolt' and the successful insertion into the state constitution of the so-called Proposition 13, establishing ceiling limits to state governmental expenditures for the future.

The popular initiative is not part of the constitution of the United States itself. It tends, qua constitutional institution, to remain somewhat avant-garde in character, cherished by people like the Swiss and the citizens of some of the American states who see in it an ultimate expression of popular democracy and of faith in the commonsense and goodwill of the individual voter. It is, as such, the other side of the coin to the use of the popular referendum as part of the constituent processes.

THE LEGITIMATION OF THE CONSTITUENT ACT: POPULAR REFERENDUM

A trend that is unmistakable in the history of democratic constitutionalism in modern times is towards the legitimation of exercises in constituent power – particularly those of a fundamental or far-reaching character – by plebiscite vote, so that the constitutional charter may be said to have acquired, even if only ex post facto in the ratification stage, an unimpeachable popular root or source of sovereignty. The historical dichotomy between the direct, 'popu- list' approach to fundamental constitutional change (through popularly elected constituent assembly; popular initiative; popular referendum) and the indirect, parliamentary approach (through a sovereign legislature, albeit one that is sometimes required to operate with extraordinary majorities) may be disappearing, even in countries as wedded to the constitutional principle of the sovereignty of parliament as Great Britain: on the issue of constitu- tional devolution to Wales and Scotland, and even more on the issue of the British joining of the European communities, which seems to imply, at least long-range, a change in the British constitutional *Grundnorm*, the govern- ment applied the rule of direct popular consultation in referendum form. The 'yes' vote on the European communities issue was followed by immediate governmental action to effect Britain's legal adhesion to the communities: the 'no' vote on the issue of devolution for Wales and for Scotland brought a shelving of both proposals.

In France, the plebiscitarian constitutional tradition has alternated with the concept of government-by-Assembly as the key emphasis in French con- stitutionalism at any particular time period. Muted in the case of the Third French Republic in reaction to the supposed excesses of the Second Empire, the plebiscite as part of the constituent processes makes a qualified reappear- ance in the 1946 Constitution of the Fourth French Republic, and then emerges in full flower in the case of the 1958 Constitution of the Fifth French Republic as part not merely of the processes for formal adoption of the new charter but also of the procedures for amendment of the constitution; in the latter context, it was used very actively by President de Gaulle – in the case of the constitutional amendment of 1962 on the election of the president of the republic by universal suffrage, to augment still further the caesarean qualities of the new constitutional system.

The distinction sometimes made between a referendum and a plebiscite – between a popular vote that is immediately legally normative and binding, and a popular vote that carries merely moral authority – is one that seems limited to the English-speaking, common law, world. For the record, a popular referendum (with an overall majority vote, and majority vote also in a majority of the member-states of the federal system – a provision borrowed directly from the Swiss constitution of 1874), is legally binding for purposes of ratification of proposals for amendment of the Australian constitution. Facultative, non-legal binding plebiscites have been held in Canada on the issue of compulsory military service overseas, during the Second World War, with what have been considered politically unfortunate and divisive consequences, though Prime Minister Trudeau flirted with the idea of direct, mandatory, popular referendum vote in the matter of changes to the Canadian federal system in response to Quebec self-determination, in case he should fail to secure the prior accord of the premiers of the member-states or provinces to changes that he considered necessary and within the federal government's constitutional competence.

The Weimar Constitution of 1919 recognized direct democracy in its constitutional processes in several distinct elements, including popular referendum provision on the motion of the president of the republic in certain instances of disagreement between' different state organs – between the president and the lower house of the federal legislature, or between the two houses of the federal legislature, for example (Articles 73, 76). There was also, as noted, provision for popular referendum following a popular initiative by ten per cent of the legally qualified voters. These constitutional gestures to the principle of popular democracy foundered, perhaps because the overall political climate was too difficult and obsessed with larger issues of political and economic survival: popular initiatives on questions like the expropriation of the assets of the former ruling houses in 1926, or the building of highway overpasses (1928), or the acceptance of the latest United States government plan over Germany's First World War financial reparations obligations (the Young Plan) in 1929, all failed either to obtain the ten per cent of the electorate in petition form necessary to constitute a popular initiative, or to obtain a popular majority in the ensuing referendum. In the general reaction of West German constitution-makers, after the Second World War, to the 'populist' elements in the Weimar constitutional system which were supposed to have favoured the rise of strong presidential executive authority at the expense of the legislature and thus to have facilitated the political onset of the Nazi regime, these constitutional concessions to direct democracy were largely discarded in the Bonn Constitution of 1949, though there remain some complicated procedures for such popular initiative and consultation in the matter of reorganization of the member-states (*Länder*) of the new (Bonn) federal system and their territorial boundaries (Articles 29, 118); and perhaps also popular consultation would be requisite in the event of any new, all-German constitution for a reunited Germany of the future (Article 146).

Where the legally binding, popular referendum does not exist as part of the general constitutional machinery, a government may still try to achieve the same essential result by maximizing the psychological or 'moral' weight of a majority vote in a legally purely facultative plebiscite. This has been the tactic of the separatist-leaning government of Quebec, within federal Canada. Though a popular vote, within Quebec, on national self-determination for French Canada, would have no automatically constitutionally binding consequences for the federal government of Canada, Prime Minister Trudeau had indicated that he would not apply military force to counter such a popular majority in favour of separation from Canada. The factual – in this case, any clear and unequivocal Quebec majority favouring separation in the future – may thus acquire its own normative legal quality: *die normative Kraft des Faktischen*, in Jellinek's terms.

Within the Soviet Union, the principle of 'participatory democracy,' involving nationwide public discussion and debate, as well as referendum vote in regard to 'the most important questions of state life,' was formally recognized in the first draft of the Brezhnev constitutional charter of 1977 that was officially published on 4 June 1977 (Articles 5 and 114). The obligation of public discussion was applied immediately to the draft constitutional charter itself. Allowing for differences in structure and practice from standard western constitutional-governmental models, the public discussion that emerged on the draft constitutional charter seems to have been both intensive and significant, and to have come both from party and general community interest groups and associations as well as technical, scientific-legal groups and academicians. A number of changes were in fact made in the text of the constitutional charter, between its first publication on 4 June 1977 and its formal enactment in Autumn of the same year, as a result of the public and professional comments and contributions, including some amelioration of the procedural due process guarantees included in the charter under the rubric of the 'principle of Socialist legality.' Ironically enough, the popular referendum provision – though not the all-important public discussion stipulation – was deleted from Article 114 where the machinery for concretely implementing it existed in supplement to the general principle in Article 5.

4

The art of constitution-making:
the *how* and *what* of drafting

The decision to proceed to a single act of constitution-making – a constitutional charter adopted all in the one exercise and in timely fashion – is normally the consequence of the understanding, by those who actually exercise constituent power, that it is best to profit from an existing societal consensus or public euphoria, following on a revolution, a military victory or similar great public event. To delay too long, as General de Gaulle and the political leaders of the French resistance movement did in 1945-6, is to risk losing both the impetus to constitutional change, as such, and also the popoular will to accept something imaginative and far-reaching that really does amount to a break with the past. The practical dilemma remains, however, that with a society that is in any way complex or plural – in ethnic-cultural or even political-ideological terms – the rendition of the revolutionary or wartime consensus into permanent, written, institutionalized form may involve substantial political compromises or sacrifices on the part of different groups, something that normally requires either making an ally of time and so delaying the final act of constitution-making accordingly, or else glossing over the substantive differences through purely verbal formulae – the language of calculated ambiguities and diplomatic vagueness.

If the achievement of a new constitutional charter is perceived of as necessary for the political legitimation of a new governmental regime succeeding on social-economic revolution or military victory or defeat, then the skills of essentially verbal compromises must come to the fore. Something of this process can be seen, perhaps, in the drafting of the Weimar constitution for the post-1918 Germany: faced with irreconcilable differences between the forces of the right and the left within the constituent assembly, the key figures in the constitution-making concluded that the only possible solution – short of either reporting failure or else postponing their conclusion indefinitely, neither of which would have been politically acceptable in the crisis events of the era – was to put everything together in the constitutional instrument, and to leave it to history and the subsequent unfolding of political events to resolve the contradictions.

On the other hand, if one has more reason for confidence in the long-range political stability of one's society, and also some more continuing constitutional tradition to build upon, then it may be best to play for time, by adopting a step-by-step approach and doing what one can, and no more than that, as opportunity presents itself, to effectuate ad hoc compromises on particular problems. Thus the National Assembly, elected in 1871 and acting also as constituent assembly for the drafting of the constitution of the Third French Republic after the military defeat of the Second Empire, had a clear majority, at the outset, in favour of a monarchical restoration. Unable satisfactorily to resolve the conflicts between the rival monarchical factions or to overcome their obduracy over the symbols, as distinct from the substance of government – in sum, the choice of the national flag – the assembly temporized in masterly fashion with its interim president, Thiers, inclining more and more towards a conservative republic. Although Thiers was compelled to resign by the monarchical forces early in 1873, his successor MacMahon was promptly confirmed and the monarchical issue effectively eliminated, once and for all, by the adoption by the National Assembly in November 1873 of a law providing for the election of the president of the republic for a seven year term. It remained only to inscribe in statutory form the republican system that had already been functioning in practical, institutional form for now more than three years. There was no need to draft a constitutional charter, as such. In fact, the Third French Republic – the most long-lived of all the French constitutional systems since the Revolution of 1789 – rests on a series of organic acts, adopted seriatim and concretizing, in pragmatic fashion, already existing constitutional practice. Three such laws – of February and July 1875 – on the organization of public powers (the presidency, the two houses of parliament, and the cabinet), on the senate, and on the relations inter se of the different institutions of government, complete the process of adoption of organic laws for a republican constitutional system.

In a more contemporary context, the new state of Israel, beset by the threat of military attack both external and internal from the moment of its creation, had neither the time among so many other pressing problems, nor perhaps the felt need (many of its early leaders being familiar with British constitutional experience), to establish constitution-making as a priority obligation. The way to achievement of an Israeli constitutional system became the essentially pragmatic, empirical, problem oriented, step-by-step approach that characterized the development of British constitutionalism over the centuries. In place of one grand, over-arching charter, adopted in one blow, the Israeli constitutional system was, of necessity, a series of organic measures adopted ad hoc as the need for constitutional rationalization developed and the opportunity presented itself. The problem was not, apparently, at any time any lack of societal consensus on substantive measures; though perhaps if the task of constitution-making had been engaged upon a systematic, continuing basis, the divisions between traditionalist or conservative, orthodox religious forces and more radical, reformist groups in the new Israeli society would have become apparent with resulting dangers for the continued political viability of the new state.

In the special context of post-Second World War Germany, the same essentially pragmatic impulse on the part of local, West German political leaders, facing the unpleasant political reality of long-term foreign military occupation after Germany's unconditional surrender in 1945, led to acceptance of a step-by-step tactical approach both to the recovery of political and legal sovereignty and also the exercise of constituent power. A temporary constitutional document, styled deliberately as a basic law (*Grundgesetz*) and not a constitution (*Verfassung*), and stipulated, in its final article (Article 146), as ceasing to be in force upon the achievement of a reunified, all-German state in the future, was adopted for the new West German political entity created by the administrative fusion of the three western Allies' zones of military occupation. May 1949, the date of the official coming into force of the *Grundgesetz*, is thus simply one point in a continuum of political-legal events that include, certainly, May 1955 – the date of formal restoration of sovereignty to West Germany by the three western occupation powers – and that mark the founding and achievement of the West German federal constitutional system after the Second World War. It is not without historical irony that the conceivedly 'temporary' Basic Law of 1949 survives to this day as a particularly vigorous and well regarded species of constitutional law-in-action, where so many other new constitutional systems, launched about the same time and under far more favourable political auspices (including the French military occupation power's own Fourth Republic constitutional system of 1946), have sundered.

The western European constitution-makers after 1945, looking to the building of a new European political community in the face of the cold war threats to western Europe's political survival, deliberately eschewed all the temptations to begin the easy way with a single, abstract act of constitution-

-making – in effect, a western European constitutional charter. This, in their view, would have been to pursue an illusion, like those earlier professorial pan-Europeanists, between the two world wars, who were excessively concerned with constitutional drafting at the expense of study of the basic facts of political power. Instead, the post-1945 western European leaders applied an essentially pragmatic, empirical, step-by-step approach, beginning with major problem areas and trying to resolve these situations functionally. In this way, building on the earlier Schuman Plan of 1950 which had provided for the pooling of the entire French and German production of coal and steel under a joint high authority in an organization which would be open to other European countries, the European Coal and Steel Community was achieved between the six key western European countries – France, West Germany, Italy, and the Benelux countries – the treaty being signed in 1951 and the community itself coming into effect in 1952. The European Atomic Energy Community (Euratom) treaty was signed in 1957 and entered into force in 1958. Finally, the European Economic Community treaty, the so-called Treaty of Rome, was also signed in 1957 and entered into force in 1958. It was this latter community, in particular, that came to be regarded as both the core of the movement for western European political integration in the post-Second World War era and also the focal point for the endeavours to expand and develop the association of the Six Countries into some even more comprehensive and ambitious undertaking, going beyond the Six Countries' then existing institutional links with each other.

The early project for a European defence community, the treaty for which was signed in Paris in 1952 and which was intended to set up a common defence structure for the Six Countries against the cold war dangers, involving, inter alia, the merger of their armed forces, had come to naught because of the failure in 1954 to obtain ratification of the treaty in the French legislature – due in part to residual national suspicions and hostilities dating from before the Second World War. The parallel project for a European political community, a draft treaty for which was prepared by a special ad hoc assembly of the Six Countries meeting in Strasbourg in the winter of 1952-3, had hoped to merge the already established and operational European Coal and Steel Community and the European Defense Community then awaiting ratification into something greater – a European community which would have the powers of both communities, plus additional powers relating to foreign affairs and economic policy.

While the project for a European political community fell, in 1954, with the failure of the project for a European defence community, mutual exchanges of views between the foreign ministers of the Six Countries convinced them that the resulting political setback to the pan-European movement in 1954 had not been through any flaw in the grand design of western European integration but simply in the techniques for achieving it; and that the failure had been due to proceeding too quickly, or, more strictly, to establishing the wrong priorities for political action. The new slogan was to become the pragmatist one of 'hasten slowly,' with the European community movement itself being seen clearly, thereafter, as far less a technical exercise in rationalizing trade and commercial relations between the Six Countries than a new venture in supra-national political association which had happened, for historical reasons peculiarly related to the post-Second World War European scene, to have focused on economic methods as the best techniques available for achieving that objective. It was thus a revolutionary experiment in federalism, viewing federalism here as a dynamic *process* of functional association and co-operation on an institutional basis and as something to be realized progressively through pragmatic, empirical, problem oriented, step-by-step methods, rather than by attempting to begin with enactment of a single, abstract constitutional charter.

The European parliament that emerged in Strasbourg in 1958 as a form of parliamentary assembly for the then existing three European communities was a historically logical and predictable outcome of this process, just as was the later admission of three new member-states (Great Britain, Denmark, and Ireland) to join the original Six Countries, and the establishment, in 1979, of a system of direct popular elections to the European parliament itself.

TECHNICAL BLUEPRINT, *OR* IDEOLOGICAL PROGRAMME?

A second crucial decision, in the approach to constitution-making, is whether to confine the constitutional charter to a matter-of-fact detailing of the main institutions and arenas of community decision-making, the processes and procedures through which decision-making operates and is applied, and the reciprocal relations and interactions of those institutions; or whether, instead, to try for something more and add some oratorical flourishes. The decision as between a prosaic and a rhetorical draft is partly a matter of national, legal tradition, whether inherited (intrinsic) or received ('export variety'); and partly a consequence of the time factor in constitutional drafting, charters conceived in a period of political euphoria tending to be rich in fundamental, natural law-style affirmations. British constitutional acts, and particularly the exported, British colonial charters intended for the far-flung dominions and crown colonies overseas, tend to be somewhat dull and intellectually low-level and light in philosophical affirmations: these imperial export constitutions may be didactic in purpose in so far as intended to instruct in the elements and first principles of constitutional government, British-style, but they are rarely moralizing in tone. They are the archetype of the prosaic, 'bread and butter' constitutional charters. By contrast, the champagne touch is most recognizable in French constitutional drafts, particularly those conceived in the more optimistic eras in French history: no more magnificent example of inspired natural law in constitutional form exists than the Declaration of the Rights of Man and the Citizen of 26 August 1789, placed at the head of the first revolutionary era constitution of 1791. The American Declaration of Independence of 1776 – an earlier project, influenced in some part by the same French philosophical rationalism that produced the French Declaration of 1789 – represents the same felicitous combination of high ideals of government and lucid literary formulation. The American articles of confederation that followed shortly thereafter are, by comparison, somewhat more functional and consequently pedestrian, though the final Constitution of the United States of 1787, and the accompanying American Bill of Rights, do succeed in recapturing some of the nobility and lyricism of the Declaration of 1776. These are the main archetypes or models of what may be called, without any disrespect, the rhetorical constitutions. They have had some less than skilful imitations in more recent years; but these have too often been examples of nominal, and not normative, constitutional charters, or else have been intended as harbingers of new trends or directions in ideological programmes within the state rather than as genuinely operational blueprints for constitutional government.

The constitution of the People's Republic of China, adopted by the Fifth National People's Congress in 1978, in reaction to the immediately preceding constitutional charter – associated with the anti-Party 'gang of four' – that had been adopted by the Fourth National People's Congress in 1975, is designed, evidently, to fulfil the two objectives. First, in Yeh Chien-Ying's words, uttered before the first session of the Fifth National People's Congress on 1 March 1978, the constitution establishes a 'set of general rules for managing the affairs of the state in the new period'; and these, essentially machinery (institutions and processes of community decision-making) provisions are quite extensive and detailed, and, particularly in the sections on self-government of national autonomous areas (Articles 38 to 40), the people's courts and people's procuracies (Articles 41 to 43), and fundamental rights and duties of citizens (Articles 44 to 59), go well beyond the preceding constitution in seeking to offer concrete, institutionally based procedures for guaranteeing the implementation of the constitutional text. The constitutional charter also offers, however, a catalogue of general principles providing political, social, and economic guidelines for the development of state policy in what is characterized by Yeh Chien-Ying as the 'new period of development in China's socialist revolution and socialist construction,' following on the downfall of the 'gang of four': the five principles of peaceful coexistence and also the theory of the three worlds (classical, Western-style imperialism; Soviet-style, social imperialism; and the Third World, of which China considers herself part) as a guide to foreign policy; the concepts of the three great revolutionary movements (class struggle, the struggle for production, and scientific experiment) and of the four modernizations (of agriculture, industry, national defence, and science and technology) as operational indices for the development of Chinese domestic policy for the balance of the century. The programmatic character of these essentially preambular stipulations is clear, while the actual formulation, if often unnecessarily redundant and prolix according to normal western canons of constitutional drafting, is, in compensation, frequently elegant, even poetic, in a literary sense. Where else but in the constitution of the People's Republic could one expect to find direct citation, in the constitutional text itself, of the late Chairman Mao's celebrated parable of the 'fragrant flowers and the poisonous weeds'? In the formulation of the criteria for the guidance of the development of government policies in the arts and sciences, it is expressly stipulated (Article 14) that the state is to apply Mao's 'policy of "letting a hundred flowers blossom and a hundred schools of thought contend."'

Chinese jurists admit, frankly, that the 1978 constitution was not, and could not have been in the time available, as comprehensively researched or as thorough in its preparation as the first post-liberation constitution of 1954 which had been the product of five years of intensive study and discussion. But they view the 1978 constitution, nevertheless, as a necessary attempt at speedy correction of the governmental and administrative errors and abuses inherent in the earlier constitutional system of 1975 which had involved such gross violations of the principle of socialist legality (rule of law) as the extortion of confessions through torture, and the arbitrary arrest and imprisonment of citizens on the order of security police officials without prior decision of the courts or sanction of the procurator's office. The Constitution of 1978, in particular, attempts systematic institutional extension of the principle of socialist legality through the strengthening of the procuracy – often called the 'watchdog of socialist legality'; and it also ventures very far towards the goal of socialist democracy through the postulation of more comprehensive and more detailed fundamental rights and duties of citizens.

Evidence that the constitutional charter of 1978 is not viewed as a collection of timeless absolutes graven on tablets of stone, but as open to empirically-based adjustment and change in the light of concrete operation and experience, is to be seen in the pragmatic approach to the issue of constitutional amendment present at the first and second sessions of the Fifth National People's Congress in 1978 and 1979, and thereafter. Concrete new constitutional measures involve the idea of direct elections to the organs of local self-government, with machinery provisions for enforcement, if need be, against local party officials, and further strengthening of the grass roots, neighbourhood committees. What, on first sight, might be seen as a retrograde step – namely, the suspension for the time being, in February 1980, of the right, under article 45 of the 1978 constitutional charter, to 'write big-character posters' – is considered as a necessary response to the experience of abusive exercise of that right in libellous attacks on public officials. Amendment of the criminal code, as proposed in June 1979 at the second session of the Fifth National People's Congress, so as to provide for criminal law (as distinct from constitutional law) follow-up, in appropriate cases, of libel through public posters, might render the suspension of the Article 45 right constitutionally otiose and thus permit its revival at some future stage. It is worth noting in this regard, however, that classical western constitutionalism, for its part, has never viewed constitutional free speech claims as constitutional absolutes in themselves, but rather as needing to be weighed pragmatically against other, competing social interests in concrete cases.

Chinese jurists also offer supplement to the otherwise too abstract constitutional text, as to governmental decision-making institutions and processes. The National People's Congress, established under Article 20 of the constitution as the 'highest organ of state power,' is obviously far too large, with 3,497 members, to be able ever to become functional and operational in itself as a legislative body. In fact, the National People's Congress functions at the level of constitutional law-in-action, through its 197-member Standing Committee; and its elaborate committee structure is the key to its working success, including a special legal committee for purposes of proposing and considering constitutional revision.

On the more general question of the balance or relation between the hortatory or didactic, programmatic elements of the 1978 constitutional charter, and the governmental-institutional machinery and processes sections, Chinese jurists view the 1978 charter as having established the main societal goals with a specific time dimension – the end of the present century, according to the preamble of the charter – for achievement or completion of those goals. Presumably, in the new spirit of social empiricism and pragmatism that seems to be guiding the Chinese approach to law, not less than to economics and international relations, at the beginning of the 1980s, this would mean that the programmatic sections of the constitutional charter should themselves be open to amendment or revision or recall, as specific societal goals should be progressively attained or demonstrated as unnecessary or irrelevant.

The 1977 Constitution of the Soviet Union is somewhat more prosaic in language and styling than the constitution of the People's Republic, even though, as a charter that must also respond to Marxist-Leninist ideals and that is drafted at almost the same time, it does give programmatic expression to contemporary scientific-Marxist teachings on law and society and chooses an essentially rhetorical preamble as a principal vehicle to that end. The basic antinomy between constitutional charter as description of the main power relationships and decision-making institutions and processes within the state, and constitutional charter as affirmation of the goal values of society, shaping and controlling concrete community decision-making for the future, is reflected in the text of the Brezhnev constitution. The latter-day emphasis on 'participatory democracy' in the Soviet political processes envisaged, in relation to the final adoption of the new constitutional charter, a process of public discussion and debate and criticism similar in kind though much more concentrated in time to that applied, years before, to the German civil code in the period between publication of its official draft in 1896 and its formal enactment in 1900. (This participatory-democratic element is in fact entrenched in the so-called public discussion sections [Articles 5 and 114] of the new constitutional charter.) The expert constitutional commission, composed of seventy-five members, that prepared the official draft of the new charter published on 4 June 1977 was mixed political and technical-legal in the background and experience of its members. In between publication of the official draft and its formal ratification in the autumn of 1977, party organizations and also general community interest groups and associations, in addition to the strictly specialist scientific-legal groups and individuals, were expected to offer their comments and suggestions on the draft, with the expectation that their input would be taken into account in the making of the final revisions. Within the scientific-legal community, the intellectual debate between the partisans of the more traditional Marxist thinking on state and law and the more innovative group of jurists continued. The former argued, after the manner of the Stalin Constitution of 1936, that the constitutional charter should be no more than a description or codification of the structure of state power prevailing at the time of drafting. The latter more innovative group of jurists contended for a separate and distinct science of constitutional law that would necessarily include its own inherent, autonomous constitutional values with obvious normative quality and potential for future community policy-making. The conflict between the two groups is clearly reflected both in the intra-commission adjustments and compromises present in the draft published at the beginning of June 1977, and also in the public contributions and discussions that succeeded that publication. In fact, the Brezhnev constitutional charter reflects the influences of both schools of thought, for it is at once a cataloguing or recording of state institutions and procedures and processes, and an authoritative definition of party goals and policies for the future – in the substantive articles as well as in the constitutional preamble. In President Brezhnev's own words to the May 1977 *Plenum* of the Communist Party Central Committee: 'V.I. Lenin and the Bolshevik Party maintained that a constitution is not only a legal document but a political one of the utmost importance. The Party regarded the Constitution as an affirmation of the gains of the revolution and, at the same time, as a proclamation of the basic tasks and goals of the building of socialism.'

In the result, high-level, 'motherhood' style principles like scientific, technical, and artistic creation and the development of scientific research, invention, and rationalization (Article 47), and the protection of nature and the safeguarding of its riches (Article 67), accompany the very substantial list of articles on the administration of justice and the role of the courts (Articles 151 to 163), and on the rights, liberties, and duties of citizens (Articles 39 to 69). Precisely because these latter represented the official openings to the so-called principle of socialist legality, they seem to have attracted the professionally and scientifically most informed public discussion and criticism, including contributions from the best known Soviet academicians concerned with reform of criminal procedure and procedural due process generally.

VAGARIES OF LITERARY STYLE IN CONSTITUTIONAL DRAFTING

There is a casual, fortuitous element in constitutional drafting to which ideological issues are often quite irrelevant. One can often 'date' a constitutional charter, simply by these vagaries in the verbal formulations.

Formal constitutional bills of rights containing the catalogue of liberal, political and civil rights of man, though never the new social democratic and economic rights, were an inevitable part of the 'rationalized constitutionalism' of the central and eastern European constitutional charters of the era between the two world wars. They reflected the intellectual style of the enlightened bourgeois-liberal professional and professorial groups that were so heavily represented in the drafting committees or constituent assemblies set up to draft those charters; though, in the end, since unaccompanied by appropriate institutional machinery for their constitutional enforcement and application, they proved quite incapable of stemming the rise of the very authoritarian political groups that they had been intended to restrain and to confine.

After the Second World War, by comparison, a prime lesson drawn from the disappointment of all the liberal constitutional hopes of the 1920s and the early 1930s was the need to set up strong institutional checks and balances for the control of legality, without, however, so completely denying executive power as to institute yet another round of government-by-Assembly. The partial solution, in West Germany, in Italy, and later in Yugoslavia, was the institution of a special constitutional court – a final judicial tribunal with juris-diction over constitutional questions, involving conflicts between different institutions of government, or between different levels of government (national and regional), or complaints by private citizens and interest groups as to alleged violations of the fundamental principles of the constitution. The influence of the Supreme Court of the United States, as a model for such a special constitutional tribunal, was considerable, though it would be an error to underestimate the influence, also, of local, indigenous German experi-ence under the Weimar constitution, in the case of the Western German federal constitutional court which has become the archetype of continental European civil law-inspired constitutional court.

Another area where transient elements of taste in literary draughtsman-ship have played a role, irrespective of particularistic, national historical legal traditions, is in the so-called directive principles of state policy. These gen-eral propositions, formulated at a high level of generality and abstraction and couched in larger, philosophical terms, make their appearance for the first time in the short-lived Spanish Republic's Constitution of 1931. They are apparently intended, then, as canons of good governmental policy-making addressed to executive and legislative authority, and not (in the Spanish legal context, anyway) designed or intended to allow for court review or control of their application or non-application. From Spain they make their way to the Republic of Ireland, by way of the refugee German civil law jurist, Leo Kohn, who became constitutional adviser to the Irish government (and still later, after the Second World War, constitutional adviser to the new Israeli government) and who was most influential in the drafting of the Irish Constitution of 1937, in which a catalogue of such principles is enshrined. Under the rubric 'Directive Principles of *Social* Policy' (constitution, Article

45), these principles are stated to be 'intended for the general guidance of the *Oireachtas* [legislature]. The application of these principles in the making of laws shall be the care of the *Oireachtas* exclusively, and shall not be cognisable by any Court ...'

In substantive content, the directive principles, being posited upon 'a social order in which justice and charity shall inform all the institutions of the national life,' and reflecting, no doubt in measure, their general continental European and specifically Spanish Republic derivations, add an important social democratic element to a constitutional enumeration of fundamental rights (Articles 40 to 44) that is liberal and laissez-faire in basic philosophical orientation, albeit with a strongly Roman Catholic, Christian Democratic tinge (Article 41 [the family]; Article 42 [education]; Article 44 [religion]). For the directive principles of social policy guarantee the 'right to an adequate means of livelihood,' and impose limitations upon ownership and control of material resources and upon the operation of free competition in the interest of 'the common good' (Article 45). Unlike the fundamental rights, which have had a continuing record of (somewhat traditional and conservative) judicial application, the directive principles, being non-justiciable, are of an essentially hortatory character and do not seem to have had any practical application in Irish political and constitutional life.

From Ireland, however, the directive principles, this time renamed 'Directive Principles of *State* Policy,' pass to the notice of the members of the Indian constituent assembly drafting the post-independence republican Constitution of 1949. The Indian constitution-makers were richly eclectic in their intellectual outlook and very well informed as to British and Commonwealth constitutional experience, including that of Ireland. From Spain, by way of Ireland, the directive principles turn up as a catalogue of general propositions in the new Indian constitution. Sir B.N. Rau, the constitutional adviser to the Constituent Assembly, who was the main sponsor of the idea of such non-justiciable principles (Constitution, part IV, Articles 36 to 51), in supplement to the fully justiciable fundamental rights (constitution, part III, Articles 12 to 35), seems to have envisaged the directive principles as something equivalent to the constitutional doctrine of the state police power under the United States constitution. The directive principles would, however, in India not less than in Ireland, probably have remained no more than a stylistic curiosity in constitutional drafting except for the controversy that later developed over their constitutional compatibility with the fundamental rights sections and the issue of which should legally prevail in case of conflict.

Being much more contemporary in their legal antecedents and borrowings, the directive principles were also much more contemporary in their philosophic and ideological orientation than the fundamental rights. These latter, with their more obvious debts to nineteenth-century western liberal constitutionalism, had a strong laissez-faire quality to their stipulations as to the right to property, or at least were so perceived by the courts. Further, the fundamental rights stipulations as to the right to equality tended to be interpreted by the judges according to essentially abstract, western, nineteenth-century liberal social and economic thinking, thus effectively excluding any constitutionally based, 'affirmative action' programmes by the federal or the state governments designed to correct marked imbalances in terms of social and economic opportunity for particular individuals or minority groups, and thereby to render equality in the concrete. A constitutional antinomy was thus created between the fundamental rights and the directive principles: in the view of Chief Justice Gajendragadkar (expressed after his retirement from the Supreme Court of India), the fundamental rights, important though they were, were in a very real sense static, whereas the directive principles had a dynamic quality and were designed to promote a transition to welfare state principles – distribution of the ownership and control of the material resources of the community, avoidance of the concentration of wealth and means of production, equal pay for equal work for both men and women (Article 39); the right to work, to education, and to public assistance in cases of unemployment, old age, sickness, and disablement (Article 41); free and compulsory education for all children until they complete the age of fourteen years (Article 45); promotion of the educational and economic interests of the weaker sections of the people, and, in particular, of the Scheduled Castes and the Scheduled Tribes (Article 46).

In its earlier jurisprudence, the Supreme Court of India, responding to the express stipulation, in the opening directive principle (Article 37), that the principles themselves should 'not be enforceable by any court,' and lacking any Indian or indeed any inherited British Empire and Commonwealth judicial precedents supporting any contrary interpretation, ruled that the directive principles had to conform to the fundamental rights sections of the constitution, and were subsidiary to them in cases of conflict. These essentially conservative judicial interpretations, restricting the social democratic openings provided by the directive principles and thus the practical implementation of governmental 'affirmative action' programmes advancing the backward classes of citizens and redistributing wealth in the interests of social justice, led directly, in the federal executive-legislative arena, to the adoption of the first and the fourth amendments to the constitution, in 1951 and 1955 respectively, redefining and amplifying existing fundamental rights articles touching on these major problem-areas, so as to immunize corrective governmental programmes from frustration by hostile supreme court rulings. These executive-legislative attempts to counter a judicially based social and economic laissez-faire had themselves to run the gauntlet of further judicial harassment, culminating in the 1967 landmark supreme court decision, rendered by a 6 to 5 vote, in the *Golak Nath* case [A.I.R. (1967) s.c. 1643], and holding, inter alia, that the constitutional amending power (Article 368) was itself subject to the fundamental rights sections and that constitutional amendments could therefore be struck down by the courts on the basis that they conflicted with them. While the *Golak Nath* decision was subsequently over-ruled by the supreme court on that point [in the *Keshavananda Bharati* case, A.I.R. (1973) s.c. 1461], the 7 to 6 split within the court on that occasion meant no single, clear ground of decision (*ratio decidendi*) to guide future executive-legislative policy, and thus led on, more or less inevitably, to the prospect of fresh political conflicts between government and judiciary, a fresh 'correcting' constitutional amendment, and a fresh judicial ruling thereon. In the meantime, however, the potential conflict between conceivedly static fundamental rights and more dynamic directive principles of state policy had been partially resolved, as a matter of constitutional interpretation, by the judicially developed canon of 'harmonious construction' under which the attempt would be made to give effect to both fundamental rights and directive principles as much as possible, though not in such a way as to make the fundamental rights a 'mere rope of sand' [see the *Quareshi* case, A.I.R. (1958) s.c. 731; the *Kerala Education Bill, 1957* Advisory Opinion, A.I.R. (1958) s.c. 956].

If the directive principles are viewed, in the words of one Indian constitutional specialist, M.P. Jain, as 'more akin to moral, rather than to legal, precepts,' then the similarities to the programmatic, policy declarations to be found in recent Marxist-Leninist influenced constitutional charters, particularly in their preambular declarations, as in the 1977 Soviet Constitution and the 1978 People's Republic Constitution, become marked. Constitutional preambles, indeed, in their changing tastes and also their changing utility and relevance in the interpretation and application of the constitutional charters that follow them, are further fascinating examples of literary vagaries of style in the art of constitution-making. Constitutions framed in eras when natural law sentiments are still dominant tend to be endowed with highly poetic preambular statements, rich in solemn proclamations of the asserted popular (or popular and divine) origins of the charter. This is especially true of the early French revolutionary era constitutions – those of 1791, 1793 (the Convention), and even 1795 (the Directory) – though not of the later ones which are much more prosaic and down-to-earth in their stipulations. It is true of the American Constitution of 1787; and also, for that matter, of the United Nations Charter. By contrast, British-derived constitutional charters seem consciously to eschew any such verbal flights of fancy – in the preamble as much as in the substantive parts of the constitution – though even reasonably simple, descriptive touches in a British-derived charter – like the reference in the preamble to the Canadian constitution (the British North America Act of 1867) to a 'Constitution similar in Principle to that of the United Kingdom' – may be used by courts as points of departure for natural law-style glosses on the constitutional charter, as happened when judges of the Supreme Court of Canada, in the *Alberta Press* case in 1937 [*Re Alberta Statutes* 1938, 2 D.L.R. 81], read a sort of common law bill of rights into the constitution in reliance on that general phrase in the preamble.

Sometimes, a country already endowed with a dully formal, opening gambit for its constitutional charter may decide to upgrade its literary and philosophical style with a more elegant re-formulation. This happened with the Union of South Africa, whose British-made constitutional charter opened, very simply, with the bald statement that the charter might be styled as the South Africa Act, 1909 – a fairly standard opening touch for a British-trained parliamentary draughtsman. In 1925, a somewhat more nationalistic and fundamentalist regime in South Africa amended the charter by eliminating this provision and substituting the assertion: 'The people of the Union acknowledge the sovereignty and guidance of Almighty God.' In such a case, as a constitutional scholar, Richard Latham, remarked at the time, sovereignty becomes less a scientific term of art than a complimentary expression. Those who search in constitutional preambles for true and accurate identifications of the constitutional law-in-action of the ultimate source of constituent power in the state – that ever-elusive constitutional *Grundnorm* – are likely to be disappointed.

The extended, programmatic, essentially philosophical recitals to be found in the preambles of Marxist-Leninist constitutional charters – the new Soviet and Chinese constitutions already referred to – and which are often derided by Western critics as largely rhetorical exercises, can be justified, in strictly technical constitutional terms at least, having regard to the rather different institutional structure and organization of government in those countries. With the dominant role given to executive decision-making authority in comparison to western and particularly Anglo-Saxon models where the constitutional functions of the courts tend to be of major importance, the preambular statements in the Marxist-Leninist constitutional charters can serve as policy guidelines and directives for governmental and party leaders for the future, as educational norms for governmental administrators and for the public at large, and finally, not least as counsels of prudence, in appropriate cases, for those specialist bureaucrats of the procurator's office who are given prime responsibility for administering the 'Principle of Socialist Legality' as a constitutional protection against administrative arbitrariness.

LAPIDARIAN TEXT OR EXHAUSTIVE BLUEPRINT?

Those who look for general rules or axioms as to constitutional drafting will find none. Instead, there are alternative conventions or models, depending on the particular national legal style and on the predominance of particular schools of legal and constitutional philosophy at the particular time of drafting. The Abbé Sieyès, a veteran of many constitutional draftings, ventured the proposition that a constitution should be both short and obscure. The first quality, brevity, is to emphasize its uniqueness or distinctiveness in relation to ordinary forms of law-making: a constitution is, after all, rather different from a municipal ordinance on sewers and drains. A shorter text can also, by its very simplicity, be more readily comprehended by the general public, and this facilitates that national consensus-building that is one of the prime objectives of democratic constitutionalism. The obscurity referred to by the Abbé is, rather, a lapidarian quality of generality that enables new meaning and content to be built into the constitution, according to changing societal conditions and demands. Without that element of generality and the inherent quality of continuing change as constitutional law-in-action coming from it, an impossible tension would otherwise grow up between the constitutional text as originally written and the society for which it was designed: the text would either have to be recast, by way of formal constitutional amendment – not an easy condition to achieve with most constitutional charters – or else the constitutional system would fly apart because of those inner tensions.

The Abbé Sieyès was not altogether successful in selling his ideas on the merits of succinctness in constitutional drafting to his colleagues and contemporaries of the post-French Revolution era, though the actual, machinery parts of the constitutions of that time period tend to be brief: it is the declarations on the right of man that tend, in compensation, to be prolix. Perhaps the American constitution can be accepted as the model of a short and generally lapidarian text; though, even here, the overly specific responses to transitory public irritation of the moment of drafting – for example, the provision in Article III of the Bill of Rights that 'No Soldier shall, in time of peace be quartered in any house, without the consent of the Owner' – coexist oddly with the constitutionally sublime and eternal. Constitutions are better kept free from such casual, ad hoc responses to the exigent here-and-how: the 18th (Prohibition) Amendment to the Constitution of the United States, adopted in 1919 and prohibiting the manufacture, sale, or transportation of intoxicating liquors within the United States or their importation, surely did not belong in a constitutional charter, and it should not have required its repeal by the 21st Amendment fourteen years later to demonstrate the point. But, leaving these limited and often short-lived aberrations to one side, the constitution of the United States, in its clarity and universality, and also its basic comprehensibility – its 'educational' component – does seem to meet the criteria of what a constitutional charter should look like. The ultimate test, perhaps, is that it has stood the test of time, as the oldest of the still operational constitutions today.

The British constitutions, export variety, are by contrast much longer and more diffuse. The British Colonial Office and the later Commonwealth Office seemed to think that these constitutional charters, being devised for overseas, colonial subjects – even those of wholly British origin as in Australia and New Zealand or those where the British element in the population tended to be politically dominant, at least at the outset, as in Canada and South Africa – had a didactic role to fulfil in instructing those colonial peoples in the principles and practice of British constitutionalism, including a very great deal that, in Great Britain itself, was sensibly left to unwritten, purely customary law as the 'conventions of the constitution.' In this category fall, for example, the prerogative powers of the crown and the colonial governor designated by the crown.

In the case even of newly decolonized independent countries that had once been part of the empire and commonealth, the lessons from British constitutionalism, export variety, remain pervasive even after independence. The 1949 Constitution of the Indian Republic not merely reveals these qualities, but beyond that, ranks as the longest of the contemporary constitutional charters – the didactic constitutional charter par excellence – 395 articles, plus nine schedules, and running to 254 pages in the official version published by the Government of India Press. The justification for this, apart from the residual British constitutional-legal heritage, has to be that it must operate in a vast country with a vast population, a very great percentage of which was either illiterate or else not schooled in the refinements of constitutional government. The constitution thus performs a public educational function in itself.

But even with these lengthy, discursive, and exhaustive constitutional charters we can note a pronounced tendency, at the level of constitutional law-in-action, for the constitutional charter to operate selectively. A few key sections, sometimes seemingly chosen quite casually, will do all the work, while the remaining sections of the constitution, though not repealed, are largely forgotten, even on the part of the legal establishment. Thus it is that in the case even of the quite succinct United States constitution, a few choice provisions, such as the First Amendment free speech guarantee, and the Fifth and Fourteenth amendments' due process clauses, will carry most of the case load; where other, equally promising provisions that in some cases seem more constitutionally apt, in strictly verbal, drafting terms, will be passed by. In Canada, in the post-Second World War period, two sections establishing, in effect, a dichotomy of legislative powers – sections 91 and 92 of the constitution – were consistently applied in court jurisprudence, to the exclusion of other sections, even to the point of serving, in their interplay, as the basis for a sort of judicially created, interstitial bill of rights.

THE TRANSITORY AND THE PERMANENT:
EVOLUTION AND CHANGE IN CONSTITUTIONAL SYSTEMS

Constitutional charters, as we have said, should not generally be used as receptacles for changing public conceptions of morality or approved social behaviour. A constitution should not be confused with a general code of private morality: private morality is the domain, normally, of the criminal law which, being either judicially developed customary law or statute law, is not subject to the same legal and psychological impediments as to reform and updating as a constitutional charter. The sole exception perhaps is where a particular religious or moral ethic is the raison d'être of a new state. The Republic of Ireland Constitution of 1937, following on the earlier constitution of the Irish Free State (Saorstat Eireann) of 1922, and in keeping with the sharp, almost revolutionary character of the severance of legal ties with Great Britain and the British Empire as a whole, emphasizes the profoundly religious, Roman Catholic, scholastic tone of the new constitutional system and the new political society for whom it is being created; though the actual application of those particularist religious norms, over the years, by courts and administration, has proved to be relatively modest as a matter of constitutional law-in-action and with a high degree of deference to the claims of religious minorities or similar out-groups.

By the same token, the state of Pakistan found its political origin in the decision by the Muslim delegates to the Constituent Assembly, convened in December 1946 to adopt a new constitutional system for the Indian subcontinent with the pending withdrawal of British imperial power, to break with the majority Hindu forces who were pressing for the establishment of a modern, secularized state. It is possible that, given more time and more goodwill – and also a considerably greater degree of technical sophistication in the then available, British-derived federal constitutional forms and precedents, as to the possibilities of political pluralism and the accommodation of radically different conceptions of man and the state within the one constitutional-governmental system – a viable, plural federal system could have been worked out to embrace the whole Indian subcontinent. Such political pluralism, translated and institutionalized into constitutional pluralism, would no doubt have meant the quest for separate political electorates and electoral systems within the one state, the notion of 'reserved' blocs of seats within the legislature, and other, 'complex' constitutional-legal arrangements of this nature. The special Indian experience in this regard under the British Raj, though limited largely to the era following the 1919 Government of India Act, and the somewhat more liberalized 1935 Government of India Act, was hardly suspicious: the 'blight of communalism' was regarded, rightly perhaps, as among the worst direct legacies of British rule. Nor was that obvious constitutional alternative – a massive decentralization or devolution of power on a regional, provincial basis within a necessarily weak federal state – appealing to a majority of the emerging new 'succession' political élite, having regard to the range and difficulty of the social and economic problems that would have to be solved in the immediate aftermath of independence. A strong central executive authority was clearly essential for decision-making in these key areas, whatever the consequences it might have for hopes for still maintaining, after independence, a plural political society embracing Hindu and Muslim communities together.

In the face of the apparent intransigence of the majority, Hindu leaders on these points, and in the seeming absence of any politically viable, plural constitutional options, the Muslim delegates to the All-India Constituent Assembly walked out and proceeded to form their own separate constituent assembly, and then went on from there to form an independent, sovereign, Muslim state of Pakistan. This is not the place to record the tribulations of the Pakistan Constituent Assembly which soon manifested its own internal contradictions – in political-geographical terms, between West Pakistan and East Pakistan (which latter, many years later, itself broke away and, after a war of secession, formed its own independent state of Bangladesh); and in philosophical terms, between those who wanted an essentially Islamic, theocratic organization for the government of the new state and those who still inclined to the elements of a liberal democratic constitution along western secular lines. Taken to its logical conclusion, the incorporation of the basic moral principles of Islam into the constitution would involve, according to some Muslim fundamentalist members of the Constituent Assembly, the proscribing of legislation repugnant to the Holy Koran and the Sunnah (traditions of the Prophet Muhammad); and there would then be the issue of whether the Supreme Court, or, rather, a committee learned in Islamic law should decide such repugnancy. The interminable conflicts within the ranks of the Constituent Assembly between the progressive and the conservative forces seemed resolved with the decision to adopt directive principles of state policy establishing the supremacy, over legislation, of the Koran and the Sunnah, and with the award of the power to impose and control such supremacy to the full bench of the Supreme Court. But the worsening crisis between divergent West Pakistan and East Pakistan political and economic interests and the absence of any firm, final report from the Constituent Assembly after a number of years, provided the occasion for the imposition of military rule in 1954; and the basic conflicts between the religious fundamentalists and the secularists continue to this day, though the West-East conflict has at least been settled by *force majeure* with the successful secession of East Pakistan in 1971 to form the new state of Bangladesh, following confused political and military events that ended only with the intervention of the Indian army against the forces of the central Pakistan government in East Pakistan. The point remains, however, that a state founded (as in the case of Ireland, Pakistan, and Israel) or intended to be rebuilt (as in the case of Iran, after the overthrow of the Shah's regime) upon a religious ideal may sensibly decide to incorporate that ethic directly into the constitutional system itself, as a fundamental premise or *Grundnorm* limiting and controlling state action and policy for the future.

This was the course followed by the Ayatollah Khomeini's 'assembly of experts,' dominated by the Muslim clergy, in preparing their new 175-clause constitution which was adopted by referendum vote in December 1979, in replacement of the 1906, nominally 'Belgian'-style monarchical constitutional system under which the Shah's regime had purported to operate. Article 5 of the new constitution institutionalized the position of 'supreme guide' of the country: the country and its government were, thereby, to be directed by a 'man known for his qualities of courage, honesty, knowledge, wisdom, and who had never committed crimes or delicts.' This role which, in the Shiite sect, devolved upon the Twelfth Imam who disappeared 1,100 years ago, was to be entrusted, in his absence, to his earthly representative, the imam of the time (understood to be the Ayatollah Khomeini, though not indicated by name in Article 5). In the absence of such a personality, the new constitution specified, the country would be governed by a college of religious dignitaries and experts in Islamic law. The new constitution gave the 'supreme guide' a sweeping range of governmental powers, including the right to name the judges of the highest courts and the commanders of the armed forces. A key clause in the new constitution was Article 12 making the Jafari Asna Ashari brand of Shiism the state religion of Iran.

The direct incorporation into the constitutional charter itself of a specific religious creed as the official state religion, or at least a guide to official state conduct, has not, however, been the more general course of western constitutionalism, which has tended to remain, historically, as determindedly value-neutral in ethical-religious terms, for purposes of the constitutional charter. Western constitutional systems as a whole have thereby been facilitated in their peaceful adjustment to the changing tides of religious sentiment and religious passion.

Sometimes, as a pre-condition of an exercise in constituent power – occasionally imposed or sanctioned by some external power – a state may be compelled to pay deference to some transitory political exigency. The Japanese, as a pre-condition to the return of political sovereignty after their military defeat in the Second World War, had to accept the celebrated 'anti-war' stipulations in their new, democratic constitutional charter. It was a constitutional *donnée* established by the American military government of Japan which was operating, in the post-Second World War occupation era, on somewhat simplistic notions of historical causation with the resultant thesis that, to prevent war in Asia in the future, it was necessary permanently to disarm the Japanese. Within a scant few months, even, of the official promulgation of this new, American influenced if not American inspired, constitutional charter, it was already perceived by American occupation officials, preoccupied with the new threats of the cold war, that the very categorical and unequivocal constitutional provisions requiring that 'the Japanese people forever renounce war as a sovereign right of the nation,' and requiring, even more, that 'land, sea, and air forces, as well as other war potential, will never be maintained' (constitution, Article 9), would be a major practical impediment to the new American policy of building a western defence position in Asia, against the Soviet Union and emergent Communist China, that would be firmly centred upon Japan and have Japanese participation. The constitutional lessons to be drawn from these 'renunciation of war' provisions of the new, post-war Japanese constitutional charter are legion. It is not wise to snub a defeated enemy by insisting on having such nationally humiliating stipulations recorded in permanent form in their constitutional charter: the defeated enemy of today may be the ally of tomorrow, and it is better to show more public magnanimity. Again, it is not sensible to try to resolve today's temporary problem by creating a long-range solution in permanent, constitutional form: today's happy remedy may be tomorrow's continuing burden that you then have to live with as gracefully as possible.

Finally, and as a matter of the more general science of constitution-making, it may be not merely inconvenient, but also a direct invitation to recourse to more extreme, extra-constitutional methods, to make one's constitutional charter too rigid, in terms, in the sense of being incapable of amendment except by some quite extraordinary and difficult constitutional process. The new, post-war Japanese constitution, as an extra institutional guarantee of the immutability of its resolutely 'democratizing' principles, provided that its text could only be amended by two-thirds majority votes in each house of the national Diet (legislature), followed by a majority vote of the people in a popular referendum (constitution, Article 96). What happened with the 'anti-war' provisions of the new constitution was that they were taken to heart by many new political groupings in the post-war period – pacifist groups, radical leftists, anti-American organizations – so that it proved effectively impossible for successive, pro-United States governments in Japan to muster the necessary legislative majorities to initiate projects of constitutional amendment formally repealing the 'anti-war' sections. An alternative, rather more comprehensive governmental strategy was then developed, in the early 1960s, of devising a programme of general constitutional reform and novation which might include, inter alia, the repeal of the 'anti-war' sections. In spite of the enormous intellectual prestige attaching to this latter project, which was undertaken by a special cabinet commission, headed by a distinguished scholar and jurist, Kenzo Takayanagi, and in spite of the impressive research in Japanese and comparative legal literature undertaken by the commission, the project was still-born because becoming embroiled in the wider political debate over Japanese foreign policy and its defence implications. A partial, practical solution to the more immediate issue of Japanese participation in any generalized western defence programme in East Asia was achieved by the creation of a limited Japanese 'home defence' force which, by administrative interpretation, was accepted as not offending the spirit or letter of the 'anti-war' provisions of the constitution.

A further objective of the Takayanagi Commission – secondary, at least in the minds of the government appointing the commission, to repeal of the 'anti-war' sections and general structural changes – was the amelioration of the literary style and drafting of the existing constitutional charter. According to a popular canard, it had been drafted first in English, in General MacArthur's military occupation headquarters, and only subsequently rendered into Japanese by presumably unsympathetic translators. It is stated, in any case and for whatever reason, to be cast in a somewhat inelegant Japanese. This special, purely literary objective also sundered with the more general failure of the Takayanagi Commission. One lesson that can be drawn from this particular episode, and from the subsequent evident lack of concern of Japanese scholars and specialists and the general public with the prose style of the post-war constitution, is that when a constitutional system is already a going concern and when the law-in-books of the constitutional charter really does amount to constitutional law-in-action, one can get along very well without worrying too much about casual literary lapses or awkwardness in one's constitutional drafting and without feeling the need to offer honorific gestures or provide complimentary expressions in one's constitutional charter. The pursuit of the constitutionally trifling or insubstantial on the part of constituent assemblies or constitutional advisers generally, suggests that one is concentrating upon the purely symbolic in order to divert attention from one's inability or unwillingness to discuss the genuine issues of constitutional-governmental power and its location and exercise: *who* wields power, and through *what* institutions and processes?

The more general lesson, already referred to, from the Japanese 'anti-war' sections affair concerns the balance between flexibility and rigidity within a constitutional system. The constitutional charters of the early French revolutionary era generally contained stipulations, in advance, as to their minimum duration before any constitutional revision could be made. The first of these charters, the Constitution of 1791, rendered very difficult the process of constitutional amendment, with the result that, for practical purposes, it could not be revised before ten years; and yet the constitutional charter itself was only applied for a little less than a year. After the Constitution of 1793 (the Convention) which was, in fact, never applied because of the war emergency, the Constitution of 1795 (the Directory) established a process of constitutional revision extending over nine years: this disposition led directly to a coup d'état and the Constitution of 1799 (the Consulate), the model of the Abbé Sieyès' 'short and obscure' constitutional charter. Thereafter the process of constitutional change, involving the change from consulate to consulate-for-life in 1802, and from consulate-for-life to empire in 1804, secures its own legitimation, not a priori but ex post facto by way of plebiscitarian approval. The prime lesson drawn by French jurists from the rich and varied events of the revolutionary and Napoleonic eras – reinforced by the experience of the Republic of 1848 and the Second Empire – is as to the vanity of attempting to legislate the immutability of constitutional charters by a priori verbal stipulations in the charter itself. Societies change, and the constitutions developed in response to their needs must either change with them or disappear altogether: it is better to have such constitutional changes occur *within* the existing constitutional rules of the game, and so these rules should be matter flexible enough to encourage their use and not the resort to purely extraconstitutional methods. The constitution of the Third French Republic – the collection of organic laws of 1875, in contrast to the constitutions of 1791, 1793, 1795, and 1848 – rendered very easy indeed the revision of the constitution: it sufficed to have an absolute majority in each house of parliament, followed by a similar absolute majority in the two houses meeting together. Not surprisingly, such constitutional changes as were demonstrated as needed could be made directly, by the front door, without any need for coups d'état; and the constitutional system of 1875 lasted, accordingly, until the French military defeat of 1940. The Constitution of the Fourth Republic of October 1946 opted, nevertheless, for a somewhat more rigid process of constitutional revision – a two-thirds majority in the lower house of parliament; or a three-fifths majority in each of the two houses; or a simple majority in the lower house, followed by a popular, referendum vote (constitution, Article 90). It was in strict conformity with these provisions that the two houses of parliament voted, in 1958, the undertaking of a revision of the constitution and notably of Article 90 itself, the eventually resulting constitutional draft being submitted to popular referendum and becoming, after such popular approval, the constitution of the Fifth Republic. The Constitution of 1958 does not depart too substantially from the 1946 processes: constitutional amendments may be made by *either* an initiative of the president of the republic approved by a three-fifths majority of the two houses of parliament meeting together, *or* a project of revision approved by each of the two houses of parliament and then approved by a popular referendum (constitution, Article 89). The practical process of constitutional revision, as a matter of law-in-action, has undoubtedly been facilitated, however, by the existence of Article 11 of the constitution, permitting the president of the republic to submit to direct, popular referendum any project of law 'bearing on the organization of the public powers.' This article was successfully utilized by President de Gaulle in 1962 to modify those sections of the constitution of 1958 dealing with the election of the president of the republic by providing henceforward for direct election by universal suffrage (the Conseil constitutionnel refusing to intervene, on the demand of the presiding officer of the upper house of parliament, to rule on the constitutionality of this by-passing of Article 89). A more ambitious recourse by President de Gaulle, in 1969, to the Article 11 procedure (in effect, by-passing the Article 89 procedures once again), so as to introduce a new regionalization of French administration and so as to reduce the powers of the upper house of parliament, failed because it failed to secure popular approval at the ensuing referendum vote. The abortive 'regionalization' reform was strongly attacked by President de Gaulle's political opponents as being 'illegal,' because of its by-passing of the ordinary (Article 89) procedures governing formal amendment of the constitution. It was just as strongly defended by the president and his supporters as being in the spirit of the constitution, and so 'constitutional' in the full sense of the word. Unless the failure of the 1969 Gaullist 'regionalization' project should create a constitutional bias against recourse to Article 11 for the future, the conclusion must be that the Constitution of the Fifth French Republic is flexible, as a matter of law-in-action, and that it can be amended, quickly and easily, within its own pre-defined constitutional rules.

Some other constitutional systems – the constitution of the United States, for example – opt much more for a rigid constitution, involving extraordinary majorities or procedures, in a multi-step process. Article 5 of the American constitution provides for the initiation of proposals for constitutional amendment by two-thirds majorities in each house of the federal legislature (Congress), and for ratification of those proposals by majority votes by the legislatures of three-fourths of the member-states of the federal system (or by popular conventions in three-fourths of those member-states). (An alternative step for initiation of proposals for amendment is by way of a constitutional convention, which is to be convoked by Congress on the demand of the legislatures of two-thirds of the member-states of the federal system: in this case, too, the stipulated requirements as to ratification by three-fourths of the State legislatures, or by conventions in three-fourths of the states, apply.) Understandably enough, the difficulties in building such extraordinary legislative majorities in Congress at the initiation stage have meant that amendments to the United States constitution have been few and far between, over the years. If one leaves out the Bill of Rights (the first ten amendments to the constitution) adopted in 1791 as a result of well understood agreement or consensus existing at the time of the adoption of the constitutional charter itself in 1787, and the 11th and 12th amendments adopted about the same time (1798 and 1804, respectively), one must then go to the aftermath of the Civil War and the period 1865-70 for the 'Reconstruction' 13th, 14th, and 15th amendments. Only a handful of amendments – eleven in all – have been adopted since, including the rather odd 18th ('Prohibition') Amendment in 1919, and the 21st Amendment that repealed it in 1933. The way of change, with the American constitution and indeed with other common law-derived constitutional systems having difficult or complex processes of constitutional revision, has been, rather, by other more informal processes – developing constitutional custom and convention ripening, over the years, into firm constitutional rules: administrative glosses on the charter involving, sometimes, seeming departures from its strict letter; and, finally, judicial interpretation which, increasingly, takes on a legislative role as if the judges, *faute de mieux*, have decided to fill the revealed gaps in the constitution and continually to adjust the text of the charter to changing societal conditions and demands.

5

The principal antinomies of contemporary constitution-making: the presidential executive or government by assembly

The dilemmas of policy choice for contemporary constitution-making – the alternative institutional-machinery choices, and their practical political consequences so far as these latter can be scientifically calculated, and their probable social cost quantified in advance – are never more apparent than in the case of countries that have lived through at least several different constitutional systems. For whatever reasons change may now be sought from an old constitutional system to a new one – pressure of military defeat, political or economic revolution, or simple attrition of the old constitutional system and lack of corresponding will or simple capacity for creative adaptation to new community demands and needs on the part of the reigning political elite – there will be a certain element of trial and error inherent in the experience of the old constitutional system. Ideally, one profits from one's past mistakes; and lessons will therefore be sought to be learnt from the empirical evidence of past events, and appropriate constitutional remedies developed for the future. This continuing historical, dialectical development can be well demonstrated, in the case of the United States, in the transition from the original Articles of Confederation to the Constitution of the United States of 1787; in the case of France, most strikingly, in the successive revolutionary era constitutions, and, in more recent times, in the differences between the constitutions of the Third, Fourth, and Fifth French Republics; in the case of West Germany, in the interplay between the imperial federal constitutional system of 1871, the Weimar system of 1919, and the Bonn system of 1949; in Switzerland, in the movement from the constitution of 1848 to that of 1874. We can see it also in post-decolonization societies like Nigeria, in the reaction from an immediately post-independence, 'received,' British constitution to the eventual, post-civil war, American-style constitution of 1979.

But even with continuing constitutional systems like that of the United States after 1787, or Canada, or Great Britain, where, on the surface, nothing very much may seem to change in the constitution over prolonged periods of time, we may find that, nevertheless, at the level of constitutional law-in-action, there have been great, pendulum-like swings in interpretation and practical application and operation of the constitutional systems. The changes with these latter constitutional systems may be the more sweeping and pervasive because less apparent in terms of formal amendments to the constitutional charter as written and because occurring by way of constitutional custom or convention, or executive, administrative, or judicial construction.

This interplay between alternative constitutional models or stereotypes at the constitutional drafting stage, and between alternative constitutional 'policies' at the application stage, and the institutional checks and balances or 'correctives' attempted in the light of past felt constitutional experience, can best be examined and appraised in specific fields.

The legislature in western constitutional history has historically been the prime instrument for the achievement and concretization, in legal-institutional form, of popular sovereignty. In the political vindication, in late seventeenth-century English constitutional development, of Locke's conception of the social contract binding alike on the ruler and his subjects, it was the parliamentary forces that triumphed over monarchical executive power; just as in the preceding constitutional struggle, of the early and middle century, it had been the parliament, as the main political arena for the landed gentry, that had overcome Royalist, prerogative executive claims. In French constitutional development, a century later, Rousseau's ideas led logically and inevitably, in the early revolutionary constitutions, to that notion of government by assembly that has survived, in varied forms, in French constitutional history up to the present day.

The equation of the legislature with the expression of popular will – the rendition, both symbolically and practically, of popular sovereignty – is easily possible when the executive power in the state is purely hereditarily devolved, as was the case, certainly, with the Stuart kings in England or the ancien régime in France. It may be possible to make a similar argument, by extension, where the executive is indirectly elected or selected, as was the intention, for example, with the United States constitution as originally drafted, or with the English system of government before the rise of the modern political party system when the prime minister was still 'the king's man' and able to govern by presiding over a loose cabal of political forces in the parliament. It is hardly possible so to argue, of course, when the principal executive office in the state is filled by direct, nationwide ballot, either in terms of express constitutional provisions as under the Fifth French Republic, or the modern American constitutional law-in-action; and perhaps also as under the modern British and Commonwealth parliamentary systems where, with the transformation of the party system, the prime minister and opposition leader have become genuine masters of their own political houses and the general elections thus take on something of a plebiscitarian character as between rival leaders.

However static the relationships between the main organs of government under the original prescriptions in the abstract constitutional charters that were conceived so often in another age – the law-in-books, in the terms of sociological jurisprudence – every constitutional system that is normative and not nominal, and thus really operational as 'law-in-action,' reveals a constant shifting of functions and powers between legislature, executive, and courts at the level of constitutional law-in-action, depending in part on the accidents of intelligence and personality of the particular incumbents of those offices at particular times, and in part on the play of more long-range political forces.

Thus the American constitution, as originally drafted, directly incorporated Montesquieu's triadic division and separation of governmental powers, based on his original misreading of early eighteenth-century English constitutional government; and the elaborate checks and balances in the American constitution are designed to protect and reinforce that system. The American presidential executive is obviously a stronger institution, vis-à-vis the other co-ordinate institutions, the legislature and the courts, when it is filled by a dynamic, charismatic leader of the character, for example, of Jefferson, Andrew Jackson, Lincoln, Theodore Roosevelt, Woodrow Wilson, or Franklin Roosevelt. And the courts, by the same token, when faced with weaker executives and a congress swayed – as it often was – by populist impulses, were able easily to persuade themselves to fill the gap in governmental powers and to assume an activist, legislative role. In the period of the so-called gilded age, from the 1890s on to the great economic depression of the late 1920s and early 1930s, a conservative majority on the so-called 'Old Court' was able effectively to impose its own preferred socio-economic philosophy – here, laissez-faire liberalism – against legislative majorities at both the federal and the state levels. Those who could no longer control the legislatures looked to the courts as guardian of their special interests, in spite of the early admonition by the Supreme Court itself that 'For protection against abuses by legislatures the people must resort to the polls, not to the courts' [*Munn* v *Illinois* 94 US 113, 134 (1876)]; and in spite of the great Mr Justice Holmes's reminder, in his dissent in the *Lochner* case, that the majority opinion of the court in that case was rendered 'upon an economic theory which a large part of the country does not entertain' [*Lochner* v *New York* 198 US 45, 75 (1905)].

With the beginning of President Franklin Roosevelt's first term as executive in 1933, there followed four years of battle between a strong president and a strong court majority, until, after his re-election in November 1936, a fortuitous switch of votes within the court and the accidents of judicial deaths and retirements enabled the strong presidential executive to build its own court majority. Here we see the switch, in the American separation of powers, from strong court to strong president, and at a later stage, beginning under the Truman administration, and coming to a head under the Eisenhower administration, a switch in emphasis and weighting back to a strong legislature (Congress). The succeeding strong presidencies of the Kennedy, Johnson, and first Nixon administrations were replaced, in the second Nixon administration, in spite of the landslide presidential re-election of 1972, by an increasingly assertive and quarrelsome legislature in the light of the various Congress-based, 'Watergate' enquiries that sometimes seemed to be directed as much against the institution of a strong presidency as against the particular incumbent of presidential office at that time. The cyclical character of these swings and shifts in the location of effective governmental power under the American system suggests that the personality factors – the casual elements of individual ambition or individual malice and certainly of individual political savoir faire – have been as decisive in these developments as institutional elements inherent in the American constitutional system itself. There were, however, some congressional leaders in the Watergate period who clearly felt that long-range trends in American society – in particular, the development of the mass communication media, and the large-scale financing of American presidential election campaigns – had combined to produce a situation where the presidency had come to dominate the other, supposedly co-ordinate, organs of government to the point of producing a dangerous imbalance in the American system of government. There was, it must be noted, a certain element of 'special pleading' and ad hominem argumentation on the part of some of the principal political and professional critics of the presidency during the Watergate period: some of those who loudly decried the perils of an allegedly 'imperial presidency' in the Nixon era had been, not so long before, among the staunchest advocates of a 'strong presidency' in the eras of Presidents Roosevelt, Truman, and Kennedy. But apart from its purely internal, partisan political, 'American' aspects, the Watergate derived debate over the nature and character of the American presidency directed attention not merely to whether some basic governmental restructuring might not be needed to try to preserve or restore some pre-existing internal balance as between the different American governmental institutions, but also to even more fundamental questions of the desirable limits of government as a whole vis-à-vis the individual citizen.

It proved to be quite common for some contemporary critics of the Nixon presidency and of the abuses of presidential executive power committed during the Nixon term to sigh publicly for a British and commonwealth-style parliamentary executive for the United States in the claim that that would mean a diminution of executive powers and a consequent 'redressing of the balance' of the American governmental system with the return of the substance of community decision-making to Congress and the courts and away from the Presidency. Such a Utopian vision of a newly transformed, parliamentary-style American presidency perhaps suffered from the initial defect of being based upon an image of the British and Commonwealth parliamentary executive that was already many years out of date and no more than the law-in-books even at the time of its first postulation as a description of the late nineteenth-century English constitutional system. Even at the level of law-in-action, however, it tended to ignore cardinal features of British and Commonwealth constitutionalism that serve to make the prime minister a legally far less inhibited and fettered decision-maker than the American president, hemmed in as the latter is by so many and so varied constitutional checks and balances. Key elements of the American president's powers are legally exercisable only with the subsequent confirmation or ratification of the legislature: the presidential nomination of cabinet ministers, supreme court and other federal judges, senior civil servants, and ambassadors is subject to confirmation by the upper house or senate, while the presidential treaty-making power is subject, in its exercise, to ratification by an extraordinary, two-thirds majority in the Senate. Not merely is the British and commonwealth prime minister free from any such constitutional or practical limitations on his policy-making, but he has, in addition, and quite unlike the American president, that most powerful of all sanctions with which to coerce and control a recalcitrant or fractious legislature – namely the power (which, by constitutional custom or convention, seems now effectively exercisable at the discretion and timing of the prime minister, without need to show constitutional cause therefore, of dissolution of the legislature and of compelling of its members thereby to submit themselves to fresh parliamentary election. In the case of an effective bicameral legislature, as in Australia, the prime ministerial power of dissolution extends, under appropriate circumstances, to the simultaneous dissolution of both houses of the legislature. The delicate balance of governmental powers under the American constitutional system would have been transformed and the presidency dramatically strengthened at the expense of Congress if the president were ever given the power, like a British and commonwealth prime minister, to compel the elected members of Congress to submit themselves, at any time of the president's own choosing, to fresh elections! It is difficult to avoid the conclusion that the fact of the members of congress being immunized by their constitutionally fixed and unalterable terms of office from the risk of facing fresh legislative elections – in the case of a third of the senators, because of the staggering of Senate elections, for as long as six years – played its part in facilitating the revolt of members of both houses of Congress against the presidential executive power, so soon after the president had been re-elected in 1972 with a near record majority in the Electoral College. In any case, the postulated (Watergate era) example of an omnipotent, 'Imperial' executive would seem, on all the empirical evidence, to have been less true of the contemporary American presidency than of the contemporary British and commonwealth prime ministership. The American legislature has, in fact, by comparison both to the standard British and commonwealth legislatures and also to the modern continental European legislatures, not merely the very specific countervailing controls over the executive established in the name of constitutional checks and balances, but also quite extraordinary powers of investigation and review, and some would say of harassment, of the actual conduct of the presidential executive office – investigatory powers for which there is no express constitutional warrant but which have been successfully asserted over the years by successive congressional standing committees and committees of inquiry. Part of the political dominance of the American legislature today stems from fixed legislative terms, independent of possible curtailment or control through exercise of any executive power of dissolution. Another element is that the American legislature, in contrast to so very many other legislative bodies, is an effective bicameral legislature, with greater power and dignity residing in the upper house or Senate whose members can claim their own undoubted political mandate through their direct, popular election on a statewide basis. Indeed the Senate, because of the length of the term of office of its individual members and the sheer political and economic power of some of the state-wide constituencies that the individual senators represent, enjoys an effective power and prestige hardly paralleled in any other legislative system today.

One is tempted to make equations between the constitutionally 'strong' role of Congress vis-à-vis the presidency, in terms of the United States constitution, and the constitutional powers of the legislature vis-à-vis the executive in France, in the renewed 'government-by-Assembly' era of the

Third French Republic and to a considerable extent also under the post-Second World War Fourth French Republic. But the effective powers of the French legislative assemblies under the Third and Fourth Republics were often less a consequence of the positive law of the respective constitutional charters than a reflex of the intrinsic weaknesses of the other organs of government of the day, and were thus not really an affirmative commentary on the inherent capacity to govern or the practical efficacy in community decision-making of the legislative arm of government. Being immunized from any threat of presidential executive dissolution of the legislature, by constitutional custom or convention flowing from the historic example of President MacMahon's politically unfortunate user of that positive law power in the earliest years of the Third Republic, the loose political coalitions in the legislative assemblies of both the Third and the Fourth Republics were free to concentrate on the making and unmaking of governments until Prime Minister Edgar Faure's successful revival of the power of dissolution in 1955. The Gaullist Fifth French Republican constitution of 1958, by contrast, made a most determined bid to break with the constitutional tradition of 'government by assembly,' and with the weak executive authority and consequent weak community decision-making power that that inevitably implied; this was reinforced in 1962 by the adoption, at President de Gaulle's instance, of a constitutional amendment involving a conscious return to another and earlier style in French constitutionalism – namely, plebiscitarian democracy, as expressed in direct popular election of the presidential executive. In its actual exercise under Presidents de Gaulle, Pompidou, and Giscard d'Estaing, the Fifth French Republic's presidential executive has clearly meant a very strong executive authority and a very decisive executive leadership and direction of major community policy-making, with the political role of the legislature drastically weakened in compensation.

The constitutional system of the Fifth French Republic, in contrast to that of both the Third and Fourth Republics where the president was simply a nominal, titular head of state for all practical purposes, concentrates the weight of its executive power in the president. There is, in effect, a system of dual executive power – the president of the republic and the prime minister – but the prime minister is designated by the president (Article 8), and where the president's party or coalition of parties commands a majority in the lower house of the legislature, as has been the case from the coming into force of the Fifth Republic until the present day, the prime minister remains the president's man, deputed by him to carry out his executive programme through the legislature. The potential for a political, and hence a constitutional, impasse remains, of course, if ever the president, who is now popularly elected for a seven year term, should lose his majority support in parliament during the course of his presidential term – a situation that could conceivably arise in so far as the parliamentary elections do not coincide with the presidential elections, and follow the individual, geographical constituency model rather than the more nearly plebiscitarian, *scrutin de liste* system. A president of the republic, in that case, would seemingly either have to name a prime minister politically acceptable to the parliamentary majority and thus lose much of his own presidential power to a revived 'responsible' parliamentary executive, or else continue with his own preferred choice as prime minister and court constant frustration of his legislative programme. In this aspect, at least, the Fifth French Republic was framed in General de Gaulle's own personal image of a strong president who would be dominant in relation to parliament. It all illustrates the dangers inherent in constitutional drafting to meet a special political case that may not be repeated in the future; and it is perhaps fortunate for the political stability of the Fifth Republic that the dual executive power, by the luck of the ballot and the coincidence to date of presidential and parliamentary majorities, has always been able to function in tandem. Otherwise we would surely have seen a bicephalic constitutional system, operating in permanent conflict.

The Bonn Constitution of 1949, in reaction to the experience under the Weimar Constitution of 1919 where the president of the republic, by virtue of his election by direct popular vote (Article 41), could claim a direct political mandate from the people and so the constitutional right to function as an effective, and not merely a titular, head of state – in contrast to the chancellor and cabinet who were named by the president (Article 53) – deliberately set out to eliminate the plebiscitarian, 'strong executive' aspects of the presidency in the post Second-World War constitutional system. In the last years of the Weimar Republic, before the Nazi regime came to power in 1933, President von Hindenburg had made and broken successive governments or maintained them in power notwithstanding their loss of the confidence of the legislature, by effectively using his presidential power to dissolve the legislature (article 25) and also the so-called 'emergency' powers under the constitution (article 48). In historical retrospect, it was felt that this had constituted an abuse of presidential executive authority and had paved the way for the Nazi takeover; and so the corrective, under the Bonn Constitution of 1949, was to reduce the presidential office to a titular head-of-state role by drastically limiting its powers and also by substituting indirect, parliamentary election (Article 54) for the Weimar system of direct popular election. Effective executive power thus returned, under the Bonn constitution, to the chancellor and cabinet.

6

Constitutional antinomies: centralization and decentralization: federalism, regionalism and devolution

The *federal* idea – the notion of constitutional charter as being a compact between a number of hitherto sovereign constituent units – finds its historical origins in the Articles of Confederation adopted by the breakaway states in British North America for purposes of their war of independence against Britain. It owes something, obviously, to Locke and Rousseau and the notion of government as a social contract between sovereign and citizens, with the contract, however, now territorialized in geographical terms in the confederal constitutional association. And it also owes something to embryonic international law concepts of the treaty as a binding agreement or contract between different sovereign states. The difference between the Articles of Confederation, in force between 1777 and 1787 and considered, in historical retrospect and in the light of the lessons of the revolutionary war years, as connoting weak and divided executive authority, and the Constitution of the United States of 1787 was that the latter created a genuinely new and distinct political-governmental authority – no mere contractual alliance of states, in which the original contracting parties might retain a legal right to withdraw from or dissolve the contract or to vary its fundamental terms (*Staatenbund*), but a sovereign legal personality in its own right (*Bundesstaat*). Some plural-constitutional associations to be formed later than the American federal system of 1787 – the Austro-Hungarian Dual Monarchy of 1867; the North German Federation of 1867; even the European communities under the Treaty of Rome of 1957 – might more nearly correspond, both in law and also in terms of political realities, to limited contractual alliances between states rather than to true federal states.

The basic antinomies of federal constitutionalism are revealed, dramatically, in the historical unfolding of the whole European integration movement after the Second World War: *first*, in the differing attitudes towards a possible extension of the membership of the communities from the original 'six' continental European countries whose governments, in the 1950s, largely shared the same Christian Democratic values, so as to include 'outsiders' like Great Britain – an extension which President de Gaulle, as an integral European, always opposed as involving a weakening of the 'European' component of the movement; and, *second*, in the intellectual conflict as to whether the new Europe should remain a '*Europe des patries*'-style, league of sovereign, independent states, as President de Gaulle also favoured, or else allow itself to become progressively 'federalized' through its member-governments' acquiescing in the increasing exercise of effective decision-making powers by the new, supra-national European organs or institutions set up within the legal communities.

We can see the same constitutional dilemmas within some already existing federal systems. Canada, for example, might find it good practical politics to adjust an original federal constitutional system to something less than that, as some Quebec leaders might argue, to a 'two nations,' contractually based, association between Quebec and English-speaking Canada, in response to rising pressures of latter-day French-Canadian nationalism. But, beyond these examples, the classical federal constitutional system, by definition, calls into being a new sovereign personality at international law, that is separate and distinct from the governmental units from which it may have stemmed.

English constitutional authorities – from Lord Bryce who viewed the classical federal system as no more than a transitory step on the way to constitutional-governmental unity, to Laski who already, at the time of the outbreak of the Second World War, saw the era of federalism as being over, conceived of federalism as essentially a temporary constitution-making expedient adopted by colonial authorities like imperial Britain for purely pragmatic considerations for the devolution of power within the empire. Dicey himself viewed federalism as connoting weak government, legalism, and conservatism, and hence as unsuited to the needs of the modern state. What is certain is that, under the exigencies of two world wars and the great economic depression of the early 1930s, the classical federal systems – the United States, Canada, and Australia – all responded to the conceived imperatives of social and economic planning, and increasingly centralized community decision-making powers in the central or federal government at the expense of the member-states of the federal system and, if necessary, in despite of the words of the constitutional charter or some generations of settled constitutional interpretation by the courts. The rise of social democratic ideas, and often of left-of-centre political parties which both accepted the need for social

and economic planning and found the central government as a more access-
ible and convenient vehicle for that than a number of disparate and often
politically conservative units or member-states, also assisted the trend to
centralization within the classical federal systems. The centripetal governmental trends of the 1930s and the 1940s thus came to acquire, by a
combination of factors, a seeming quality of historical inevitability. One
French-Canadian jurist, taking note of the executive and judicially inspired
centralizing trends in the contemporary Canadian federalism, in contrast to
the earlier, more pluralist weighting given to it by the judicial committee of
the privy council, the highest appellate tribunal of the old British Empire and
British Commonwealth, was moved to remark that Lord Keynes had become the modern father of Canadian confederation.

In more recent years, both the necessity and also the historical inevitability
of centralizing of power in the classical federal state have come into question.
Where centralizing of power occurs today, it is very often a quite conscious
act of political will on the part of the executive decision-makers concerned,
and not simply an unthinking surrender to the deadhand control of past
history or the supposed constitutional maxims or absolutes stemming there-
from. Thus, in some of the recently decolonized countries like India and
Nigeria that either adopted or else 'received' British-style federal systems on
the attainment of independence and self-government, classical federalism is
seen as an essentially 'Anglo-Saxon' constitutional-governmental form that
is not necessarily suited for application in non-Western countries that want
very quickly to move through the stages of economic growth. The marked
centralization of governmental power in Nehru and Gandhi India has rapidly
transformed the original Indian federal system in a way going well beyond
the more measured constitutional development in the older, classical federal
systems, so that India must rank today as a quasi-unitary state. If the process,
in India, has been by organic growth in response to central government planning imperatives, it has taken the fires of civil war to produce essentially the
same result in Nigeria, after the disastrous Biafra conflict of the late 1960s,
and the suspension of the original, post-decolonization, British Empire-style
federal constitution.

In contrast to the experience of these post-decolonization 'new' countries
with their 'received' western federal constitutions, some of the older, classical federal states are themselves manifesting signs, already, of a governmental wish to devolve power, or at least to involve the constituent units or
member-states more fully in the federal decision-making process. 'Co-operative federalism' has become the new watchword, with emphasis upon joint
federal-state programmes, both as to policy-making and as to policy admini-

stration. Within Canada, though the term has become a constitutional bête noire for many people since reflecting current French-Canadian aspirations for national self-determination, the notion of a 'special constitutional status' for Quebec (and indeed, for the other, English-speaking provinces if they care to opt for it) is already reflected in the reality of federal-provincial joint, co-operative decision-making in the complex field of immigration – operating, here, as a gloss upon the original federal constitutional charter of 1867. Such inter-governmental arrangements, conceived ad hoc in response to concrete problem-situations of federal governance, reflect the new pragmatism in federal-provincial relations and the recognition that co-operation not competition must henceforward be the governing principle in the approach to community solving of complex problems going beyond any one level of government. It may be a socially less costly form of political problem-solving, where the federal system concerned is built, according to the accidents of history and past military defeats and forced cessions of territory, upon the non-voluntary transfer of the allegiance of discrete and different civil populations from one nation-state to another, and where, in consequence, political fractionalism and threats to 'national unity' are rampant with the contemporary resurgence of minority claims to national self-determination in their own right.

Acknowledgment that even a federal, plural-constitutional system may have in-built, static elements inherent in the notion of the federal system as a 'compact' between original, 'founding' states – constituting contractual relations between those states themselves, and between those states on the one hand and the newly created federal government on the other – is to be seen in the more imaginative developments in regard to the 'third level' of government (municipal, local government) in modern or continually self-modernizing federal systems like that of West Germany and the United States. Though municipal government is not mentioned, as such, in the United States constitution, there was a proud history of local, town government in the pre-revolutionary era, particularly in New England; and this tradition, and also the supervening political reality of the development of the large urban centres and population concentrations, suggested the merits of not continuing to treat the municipalities as the mere creatures or legal instruments of the governments of the member-states of the federal system. That might be true as a matter of abstract constitutional theory; but today the concept of constitutional 'Home Rule' for municipalities, with an autonomous sphere of law-making competence entrenched in the municipal charter itself and with power on the part of the municipalities to amend that charter themselves, is widely accepted in the United States as is the correlative notion of financial 'Home Rule' – meaning, here, an area of direct taxation power reserved to the municipalities in their own right, or at least a guaranteed, term-of-years, percentage quota for the municipalities from more general state tax revenues. In West Germany, with the Bonn Constitution of 1949, similar principles of constitutional and financial 'Home Rule' for the municipalities – reflecting, in some measure, modern American constitutional developments and practice – are accepted and applied, the provisions for financial 'Home Rule' being even more specific and detailed and resting in part on quite elaborate tax sharing agreements involving all three levels of government (federal, *Land* (state), and municipal). The Bonn constitution, drawing upon older German history as to the special, privileged status of the old Baltic, Hanseatic cities, elevates two of them – Hamburg and Bremen – to the constitutional rank of member-states (*Länder*) of the federal system, on an equal basis to the other *Länder*; and a somewhat similar constitutional disposition is made for the city of West Berlin, though for special, post-Second World War historical considerations in that case.

Other, non-federal constitutional systems, including specifically and historically long centralized states like Great Britain and France, are making at least symbolic gestures towards decentralization of administration or devolution of decision-making power on a local or regional basis, in response to demands for political autonomy on the part of geographically based minority cultural-linguistic groups. These demands are perhaps understandable enough in the case of more recently unified states like Italy, or of the countries of central Europe that so often claimed and were granted, in the successive peace treaties and in the name of 'natural frontiers,' pockets of racial-linguistic minorities that they never succeeded in culturally assimilating over the years. It is the more surprising in the case of France, which largely completed the process of national unification within its present territorial frontiers and the creation of a strongly centralized administration to maintain that political unity by the seventeenth century and the time of Richelieu, and in the case of Great Britain, which seemed to have solved its 'Welsh problem' by the fourteenth century and its 'Scottish problem' with the Union of 1603 and with the ruthless suppression of the rebellions of 1715 and 1745, and which finally rid itself of the geographically largest part of the 'Irish problem' with the grant of independence to Roman Catholic southern Ireland immediately after the First World War. The contemporary revival of picturesque local nationalist groups is to be seen within France – in Britanny, Occitanie, and Corsica, with sporadic resort to direct action, civil disobedience, and terrorist acts – and within Great Britain in the emergence of the Welsh and the Scottish nationalist political parties which have campaigned for regional governmental autonomy in the British general elections and thereafter, as elected members and pressure groups, inside the House of Commons. The ever-festering Northern Irish question remains as a leftover from the larger Irish problem that was only partially and incompletely resolved with the grant of independence to the Irish Free State and the successor Republic of Ireland in the political settlement of the 1920s and the 1930s – the still more infinite complexity of the minority within the minority to whom one has finally granted national self-determination on a regional basis. In the larger western European context, the political resurgence of regionally based, cultural autonomy or self-determination groups in France and Great Britain is paralleled by the Flemish-Walloon racial-linguistic conflict in contemporary Belgium; and it all occurs at a time of steadily augmenting, transnational, 'European' thinking in all main western European countries, translating itself in the institutionally based approach to supra-national political and economic integration of western Europe, on a pragmatic, step-by-step basis. What we are seeing today, in fact, is a coexistence of two distinct and different, and on the surface mutually opposing, governmental trends in western Europe – the centripetal and the centrifugal. The centripetal trend corresponds to the impetus in community decision-making towards political and economic problem solving on an increasingly larger, transnational or continental, even worldwide basis; and the European communities movement today is simply the most notable expression of that fact. At the same time, and by way perhaps of compensation for the consequential increasing diminution of the role of the conventional nation-state, there seems to be a re-discovery of particularist, ethnic-cultural identities and roots within that nation-state, long buried or suppressed by the original centralizing drives that welded that nation-state together in the first place. This resurgence of ethnic-cultural particularism and the assorted responses by troubled central governments within the existing nation-state are what we mean by the new constitutional pluralism. Those governmental responses seem too often timid and half-hearted, and partial only, even where, as in the case of Wales and Scotland, they amount to the offer of the grant of regional autonomy through regional parliamentary assemblies endowed with limited law-making competences; and perhaps this is one of the reasons why they have not been able to command substantial majority support at the public referenda held upon them. In any case, nationalism – the key political imperative of the nineteenth century that was so cruelly perverted between the two world wars and that then seemed to be in decline and discarded after the Second World War – has now become respectable again and is achieving special constitutional-institution recognition, even at a time when the pressures for supra-national integration and association on a regional basis have never been stronger.

7

Constitutionalism and 'extraordinary powers': the concept of constitutional emergency

All constitutional systems recognize, in measure, the maxim *salus populi suprema lex*, though the tendency to do so explicitly, with express mention in the constitutional charter itself, is a modern one.

In British constitutionalism, the two world wars were marked by the introduction, in statutory form, of the concept of emergency, whereby parliament delegated to the government, for the duration of the war and under the Defence of the Realm Acts, the most sweeping law-making and law-applying powers, including, of course, preventive detention. It had been an older British constitutional tradition to suspend, by legislation, the application of the Habeas Corpus Act in time of war or emergency; and then, in order to make assurance doubly sure, to adopt a retroactive indemnity act, conferring immunity on administrators for their actions, at the time of conclusion of the war or emergency. In 1942, at the height of the Second World War, the British courts sanctioned this concept of emergency powers overriding ordinary constitutional processes, by the decision in *Liversidge* v *Anderson* ([1942] AC 206) which upheld the executive's own determination of the existence of a state of emergency against legal challenge.

The concept of constitutional emergency powers, overriding ordinary constitutional principles and processes, was applied by successive British colonial administrators in imperial India; and it was in essence those same preventive detention laws inherited from imperial, British India that Prime Minister Indira Gandhi applied to her political opponents during the internal conflicts of the mid-1970s, long after, of course, decolonization, independence, and self-government had been achieved for India. After the president of India, as titular head of state, had, at Prime Minister Gandhi's request, in June 1975, issued a proclamation of emergency under Article 352 of the constitution, and a further presidential order under Article 359 of the constitution suspending the enforcement of the fundamental rights sections, part III of the constitution, and in particular Article 14 (equality before the law), Article 21 (protection of life and personal liberty), and Article 22 (protection against arrest and detention in certain cases), the Supreme Court of India followed the example of the British courts before it in declining to intervene in the cases of the arrest of opposition politicians and their being held in preventive detention for many months without being charged. The Supreme Court, in *Additional District Magistrate, Jabalpur* v *Shivkant Shukla* in 1976 [AIR 1976 SC 1207], refused to issue habeas corpus during the period of the presidential order under Article 359, thus in effect leaving it to the ordinary political processes and the eventual federal general elections of March 1977 (which resulted in the overwhelming defeat of the Gandhi government) to correct any alleged abuses of executive power during the period of the emergency proclamation.

The British government traditionally justified its special, emergency exceptions to the ordinary constitutional principles and processes, on the score, first, of political necessity, and then of the existence of a continuing tradition of constitutional government and of respect for the constitutional 'rules of the game' as a guarantee against abuses. Other older, established constitutional systems like that of the United States, while not formally incorporating such a concept of emergency powers in terms and in the constitutional charter itself, nevertheless recognize or accept it in practice. In United States jurisprudence, the concept of emergency powers is reached by broad judicial construction and tolerance of expanded executive or legislative power in time of war and emergency, and by the judicial acceptance, in particular, that constitutional guarantees such as the First Amendment free speech guarantee are not constitutional absolutes but are to be weighed against other, countervailing interests and against a concrete fact setting. In Mr Justice Holmes' words, in the *Schenck* case in 1919: 'the character of every act depends upon the circumstances in which it is done ... The most stringent protection of free speech would not protect a man in falsely shouting fire in a theatre and causing a panic' [*Schenck* v *US*, 249 US 47, 52 (1919)].

On the whole, the United States Supreme Court has, over the years, applied fairly strict standards to the presidency and Congress in their invocation of emergency as a justification for sweeping extensions in their powers; but this has not prevented injustices like the Japanese-American cases, where the massive deportations from the west coast and internment during the Second World War were, in retrospect, clearly unrelated to any legitimate wartime need. A somewhat cognate example, involving citizens of Japanese origin during the Second World War, occurred over the border in Canada with equally unfortunate results; and in Canada, again, in 1970, the executive clearly acted hastily on insufficient fact finding, and thus massively over-reacted, in submitting hundreds of French-Canadian intellectual and public leaders to preventive detention, on the fear (unfounded, as it turned out) of existence of a widespread popular conspiracy behind the kidnapping of the British consul in Montreal and a Quebec cabinet minister by political terrorists.

The Weimar Constitution of 1919, conceived and elaborated during a period of political crisis following military disaster, the downfall of the old imperial regime, and civil violence in the streets between right-wing and left-wing extremists, specifically incorporated an 'emergency' section – Article 48 – into the constitutional charter itself. This authorized the president of the republic – 'if the public safety and order in the German state [were] considerably disturbed or endangered' – to take the necessary measures towards their restoration, with the help of armed force; and to this end, to suspend wholly or in part a number of the provisions of the constitutional Bill of Rights, including the guarantees of freedom of the person and of the home, freedom of communication, freedom of speech and opinion, freedom of assembly, freedom of association, and freedom of property. The president of the republic might also, in terms of Article 48, use armed force to compel a member-state (*Land*) of the federal system to fulfil its obligations under the constitution or under federal laws – a power actually invoked by President von Hindenburg in July 1932, at the instance of Chancellor von Papen, to suspend the state government of Prussia and to occupy its government buildings by the army, and to install a federal government administration in place of the deposed state government. This act of presidential executive power – the so-called *Preussenschlag* – was upheld against legal challenge by the German supreme court in a judgment of October 1932. The presidential powers under Article 48 of the Weimar constitution were, in terms of Article 48 itself, subject to notification to the lower house of the federal parliament (Reichstag) and to invalidation, if need be, at its demand. A special order on the protection of the republic proclaimed in June 1922 by the then president of the republic, Ebert, after the assassination of two prominent cabinet ministers, and which allowed for strong measures against anti-constitutional elements and also set up a special court for the adjudgment of acts of violence against the state, subsequently had to be adopted as a formal amendment to the constitution as it clearly conflicted with a then existing provision of the constitution (Article 105) against the creation of special courts.

The Bonn Constitution of 1949, in the conscious reaction of its drafters to the 'strong executive' aspects of the Weimar constitution and their conceived facilitation of the Nazi takeover of power in 1933, is extremely circumspect as to making provision for emergency powers. One direct provision in the constitutional charter of 1949 relates to the somewhat special concept of a 'state of legislative emergency,' defined as cases of disagreement between the federal cabinet and the federal legislature (Article 81). Under certain circumstances, the federal president may, on the request of the cabinet and with the approval of the federal upper house (Bundesrat), declare a state of legislative emergency if the federal lower house (Bundestag) rejects a bill despite the fact that the cabinet has declared it to be urgent. In such circumstances, Article 81 allows the adoption of the bill on the approval of the federal upper house alone, though it is stipulated that the constitutional charter itself may neither be amended, nor repealed or suspended, under this provision. Article 91 of the Bonn constitution contains certain stipulations as to the averting of dangers to the existence of the federal system or a member-state (*Land*) including a power of the federal government to place the *Land* police forces under its own instructions and to commit federal armed forces and also to issue instructions to the *Land* governments: such federal orders are to be rescinded 'after the removal of the danger' or upon the request of the federal upper house (Bundesrat). The stylistic links to Article 48 of the Weimar constitution are clear, but the teeth in the Weimar provisions are not present in the corresponding Bonn provisions. Articles 81 and 91 of the Bonn constitution have not had to be employed, the limited danger that might be thought by some to have been created by the urban terrorist groups of the 1970s having been demonstrated as perfectly capable of control by normal constitutional rules and processes, without recourse to exceptional, 'emergency' powers.

There was added to the Swiss constitution, after the Second World War and by popular initiative, an emergency clause amendment (Article 89-*bis*) authorizing a majority of members of both houses of the federal legislature to enact decrees. This provision, adopted in 1949, was an outcome of the emergency periods of both world wars, when both the federal legislature and the federal executive found it necessary to exercise more extensive powers than provided for in the constitution. The constitutional amendment was designed to limit such federal emergency power by defining the conditions of its user: any such decrees were to be ones of 'general application, whose entry into force admits of no delay,' and where they conflicted with the constitution they had to be ratified by popular vote and by the member-states of the federal system (cantons) within twelve months or else lose their validity.

It is difficult to avoid the conclusion that the ultimate tests of the invocation of emergency powers are political and not constitutional ones. Every constitutional system will claim them if it feels the need arises, and this whether or not the constitutional charter expressly authorizes them or not: they are to be implied from the existence of the state itself. The courts seem unlikely *not* to sanction the invocation of such powers; and will, predictably, give executive-legislative power the benefit of the doubt, at least as long as the claimed emergency exists. The constitutionalization of emergency powers would thus, realistically speaking, involve the control and limiting of the manner and mode of their actual user and, if need be, retrospective retribution for their abuse – after the event.

8

Man and the state: the 'Open Society' and affirmative action

Modern constitutional systems almost universally include a formal bill of rights, or at least a catalogue of postulated fundamental human freedoms which the state obligates itself as being bound to protect and extend wherever possible by its own executive and administrative action. The archetype for the formal constitutional bill of rights, written into the constitutional charter itself, is the American Bill of Rights, adopted, as to its first twelve articles, almost contemporaneously with the Constitution of the United States of 1787; and supplemented by the important 13th, 14th, and 15th ('Reconstruction') amendments in the late 1860s, immediately after the ending of the American Civil War. Two important antinomies exist as to constitutional bills of rights today: *first*, as to their content, and the question whether such catalogues should be limited to the 'classical,' *liberal*-democratic constitutional freedoms, or whether they should not, in addition, venture boldly into the 'newer,' *social*-democratic claims; and *second*, as to whether they should be given 'teeth' by the provision of concrete, institutionally based machinery for their application and enforcement even against recalcitrant governments.

The second antinomy leads us also into another, lesser problem that is largely disposed of, for better or for worse, by contemporary practice in constitution-making: if one's society, or at least its political élite, has a sincere and genuine commitment to human freedoms, is it constitutionally necessary, or even more effective, to concretize that commitment into a formal constitutional bill of rights, rather than leaving the protection of human rights to the self-discipline and self-restraint of the executive itself. A full century of British constitutional thinking, from the late nineteenth century onwards and as expressed, particularly, in the constitutional writings of the celebrated A.V. Dicey, rallied firmly to the notion that this area of constitutional law, above all others, is empty rhetoric unless it is firmly rooted in the intellectual attitudes and the practices of authoritative decision-makers – cabinet ministers, civil servants, judges – and unless it is also firmly supported by public opinion. Dicey's concept of the 'rule of law' finds its expression in the ordinary decisions of the ordinary courts of the land, and its practical outlet in the settled administrative attitudes and outlook – the received traditions – of the governing class. The rule of law is thus, at the same time, a reflection of the national *Zeitgeist* and an important component of it. Hence, according to this reasoning, there is no need for a formal constitutional bill of rights; and its presence might even be counter-productive in lulling people into a false sense of security and into a relaxation of their own self-vigilance. The British themselves, for historical reasons, do not have a constitutional bill of rights: their complex constitutional system had evolved in its main outlines before either written constitutional charters or written bills of rights had become intellectually fashionable. The constitutional charters of the self-governing countries of the 'old' British Empire and Commonwealth – Canada, Australia, the Union of South Africa – being drafted in the late nineteenth or early twentieth century, in the heyday of British constitutional prestige and influence in their countries, follow the British example and eschew formal bills of rights or even attempts at catalogues of human rights. The Union of South Africa constitution of 1909 did have some special constitutional provisions as to voting rights for non-whites; but that was part of the imposed constitutional settlement (*Grundnorm*) at the time of devolution of self-government and dominion status within the empire, and in any case was ignored or overridden when the political crunch came in the 1930s and again in the early 1950s. Canada, in 1960, adopted a statutory bill of rights that, having regard to conceived constitutional problems and the need to secure a general political consensus (including French-Canada) prior to the effecting of a formal constitutional amendment, was never entrenched in the constitution: perhaps residual 'British' constitutional attitudes against formal constitutional bills of rights helped the Canadian government's decision not to try to entrench the bill, and it has had, in any case, a fairly modest history of judicial application since its adoption in statutory form.

The point is clear that there is no area of comparative constitutional law where the gap between the law-in-books and the law-in-action is greater than in regard to constitutional bills of rights. They are the paradigm of the distinction between purely *nominal* and genuinely *normative* constitutional provisions, adopted too often for reasons of political window-dressing without any serious thought of implementing them in day-by-day political action.

They become, too often, part of the rhetoric of constitutional law, incapable of controlling the rise of authoritarian regimes or controlling the basic facts of power. Yet, the trends in constitutionalism and constitution-making today are clear: constitutional bills of rights are part of the approved charter models, and are to be found, for example, in the post-Second World War, post-decolonization constitutions of the former British territories in Asia, Africa, and the Caribbean. Dicey's battle against the abstract, a priori codes is lost, and the battle must shift, instead, to guaranteeing effective institutional machinery or constitutional checks and balances for the enforcement of those bills of rights provisions.

The prime instrument for the application of the American Bill of Rights has been the United States Supreme Court; but it has also been supported by an army of ancillary agencies, originally largely of a private character, dedicated to the raising of issues of claimed violations of political and civil rights before the courts. These bodies – starting off as voluntary, private interest groups and associations specialized according to their own particular sectional, religious, or ethnic-cultural affiliations – have carried the burden, and also the enormous expense, of civil liberties litigation before the United States Supreme Court over the years. One need only mention the American Civil Liberties Union, the National Association for the Advancement of Coloured Peoples, the Jehovah's Witnesses, to indicate their political and social range and appeal. In more recent years they have been joined by official, governmental agencies like the civil rights division of the federal Justice Department. Their role has been crucial in the development of a civil rights strategy, on a continuing and, if necessary, highly selective, case-by-case basis over the years, on key political and social tension issues like urban housing, public education, and, not least, voting rights. As such, they have operated in tandem with the United States Supreme Court: Jeremy Bentham's maxim that law is not made by judge alone, but by judge and company – meaning, here the civil rights litigation special interests groups – was never truer than in this area. The modern jurisprudence on the ambit and application of the First Amendment, free speech guarantee, or the Fourteenth Amendment, criminal due process guarantee, would have hardly emerged so clearly and consistently without their activist intervention in sponsoring and promoting cases before the court.

In other countries where equivalent special interest groups do not exist to the same level of professional-legal sophistication, the recourse to the courts as the remedy for enforcement of claimed political and civil rights is hardly likely to be so effective. These countries have managed to get by, perhaps, because their social problems have not been as pervasive or farreaching or intense in their potential for community violence in the absence of legally based solutions as in the United States. The contemporary flirtation with constitutional palliatives like the Scandinavian institution of the ombudsman seems appropriate only in the case of bland societies that can duplicate the ethnic-cultural homogeneity and social cohesiveness of the Scandinavian originals. The office of ombudsman has, by definition, no teeth in it, but must rest on friendly persuasion and publicity for its sanctions against alleged abuses. Is this not, after all, a restatement of Dicey's truth that political and civil rights reflect the *Zeitgeist*, and must depend on governmental self-restraint for their effective application and enforcement? Dicey was, of course, himself writing for a bland society that had achieved social cohesiveness, at least among its political élite. Is it necessary to improve on Dicey for a bland society? Once one goes beyond this, however, the search for some more elaborate and systematic institutionally based guarantees – whether by way of a supreme court actively applying a constitutionally entrenched bill of rights, or a specialized administrative law court or Conseil d'Etat acting as watch-dog over the executive and the civil service in their practical application of constitution and statute law, or even a standing investigatory committee of the legislature armed with powers to compel testimony by government officials and the production of government documents – becomes compelling and urgent.

The first main question mark as to basic relations of man and state, as sought to be detailed in a constitutional bill of rights, goes to the actual contents of that bill. The American Bill of Rights, as part of a constitutional charter adopted before the close of the eighteenth century, limits itself to what we may call, without apology, classical, liberal-democratic constitutional freedoms. These are the freedoms that emerged from the protracted political struggles between king and parliament in England in the seventeenth century, and from the succeeding battles over the limits of newspaper reporting and publication in England in the eighteenth century. They are, in essence, Dicey's later common law rights of Englishmen, reduced to written constitutional charter form. We would today classify them as the 'open society' freedoms, since they are designed to keep the political processes free and unobstructed, by removing any unnecessary clogs upon the free expression of political ideas or their dissemination. As such, the 'open society' freedoms reflected the political values and outlook of the cultivated élite who made up the constituent assembly that drafted the American Constitution of 1787 and the Bill of Rights that so closely accompanied it. If at times during the so-called Gilded Age of American capitalism the American Bill of Rights seemed synonymous with the maintenance of political and economic laissez-faire, through the 'liberty of contract' notion that successive United States Supreme Court majorities persisted in reading into the 5th and the 14th amendments 'due process of law' clauses, as a device for striking down maximum hours of labour and minimum wage laws, and social reform legislation generally, that prolonged trend in constitutional jurisprudence was eventually reversed by the court itself in 1937; and the presidential power of nomination of judges to the court, subject only to senate confirmation, was soon used, as it was constitutionally intended to be used, to produce an entirely new supreme court majority more reflective of presidential, and thus of popular, predilections for governmental social and economic planning at that time. It is the very openness of the Bill of Rights, in fact, with the facility thereby offered for incorporating changing political conceptions of the state and its role in society peacefully and pragmatically into the ordinary constitutional law-making processes, that perhaps explains as much as anything else the basic durability of the American constitutional charter. The eternal verities are the 'open society' values – not the temporary social or economic preferences of the time and place, like the aberrant and fortunately short-lived 18th (Prohibition) Amendment. Emerging new political élite groups have therefore been able to accommodate themselves most easily, over the years, within the contours of the 'rules of the game' laid down in the existing constitutional system.

The 'open society' values are perhaps predicated, for their successful political operation, upon the existence of political parties and political and social pressure groups with the necessary professional sophistication and technical skills successfully to compete in what Holmes called the 'market place of ideas,' with other countervailing parties or pressure groups. Does this require a certain combative, aggressive disposition; and does it maximize the opportunities thereby for the economically or educationally privileged? Minority religious groups like the American Jewish community, and minority ethnic groups like the Italians, the Germans, or the Scandinavians, have had no trouble in crossing the various hurdles in the way of their upward mobility. More recently politically conscious ethnic minority groups, however, like the Mexican-Americans and the Negroes, have not had the same obvious success, and the issue now raised is whether 'affirmative action' – meaning, here, positive governmental intervention to redress an evident extreme imbalance in terms of social and economic opportunity and access, therefore, to constitutional values – is not warranted. Such 'affirmative action' poses obvious challenges to the 'open society' values as substantially interpreted by the United States supreme court over the years: the contradiction is between a constitutional right in the abstract and the existence of that right in the concrete which may imply a very substantial social, economic, or educational base as a pre-condition to its effective user. It is not surprising that the first legal confrontations over this issue – notably in the challenge to the constitutionality of *numerus clausus*-type, affirmative quotas provided for members of educationally disadvantaged minorities seeking preferred admission to university graduate-professional schools, ahead of educationally better qualified candidates from the more privileged majority ('reverse discrimination') – have been long drawn-out and bitter and, in their actual judicial resolution, not always fully persuasive intellectually. They can be viewed, however, as community attempts, using 'judge and company' (the Supreme Court, activated by interest-group sponsored litigation), to make sure that the constitutional Bill of Rights really is constitutional law-in-action, in meaningful contemporary societal terms. 'Reverse discrimination' thus becomes today yet another legal stratagem or device for translating constitutional rights from the level of law-in-books to law-in-action.

In the *Bakke* case, decided by the United States supreme court in 1978 [*Regents of the University of California* v *Bakke*, 438 US 265 (1978)], the University of California Medical School at Davis had reserved a specific quota of places in its first year class to minorities students, in pursuance of a special university programme to aid black students. This quota plan was legally challenged as being violative of the United States constitution's 14th Amendment 'equal protection' clause, on the argument that race could not properly be used as a criterion of admission nor racially preferential quotas established. Prominent Jewish community organizations, responding to the Jewish community's own experience, in past years, with exclusionary policies or negative quotas, based on race or religion, in academic admissions, joined in filing briefs supporting the constitutional challenge to the University of California programme. The constitutional challenge itself was upheld by the United States Supreme Court; but court majority, in its composition and also its actual grounds of decision, reflected the major philosophical conflicts inherent in the case and in the attempt to redefine more traditional, 'open society'-style conceptions of constitutionally based 'equal protection' to accord with contemporary societal pressures. The decision was only rendered by a five to four vote, with no single, clear ground of majority decision (*ratio decidendi*), four of the five majority judges deciding on narrow statutory construction grounds and the fifth (Mr Justice Powell) deciding on cognate, 'strict scrutiny' grounds.

On the other hand, the post-independence Indian constitution, as a modern legal document and one devised, moreover, for a plural society in which vast differences in social status, education, and economic wealth and opportunity clearly existed between different communities and classes, reflects the basic antinomy between the older 'open society' values and the more contemporary 'affirmative action' thinking on constitutional equality in the constitutional text itself. Article 14 (equality before law), Article 15 (prohibition of discrimination on grounds of religion, race, caste, sex, or place of birth), Article 16 (1) and (2) (equality of opportunity in matters of public employment), and Article 29 (2) (protection of interest of minorities) reflect more the classical 'Anglo-Saxon' (British and American) attitudes on constitutional equality. However, these provisions are balanced by Article 15 (4), inserted in the constitution by special constitutional amendment in 1951, specifically authorizing the state to make 'any special provision for the advancement of any socially and educationally backward classes of citizens or for the Scheduled Castes and the Scheduled Tribes,' and by Article 16 (4) specifically authorizing the state to provide for 'the reservation of appointments or posts in favour of any backward class of citizens which, in the opinion of the State, is not adequately represented in the services under the State.' Again, the directive principles of state policy, reflecting the newer, social democratic constitutional thinking rather than the older, laissez-faire liberal values, create an affirmative duty on the part of the state, in terms of Article 46, to 'promote with special care the educational and economic interests of the weaker sections of the people, and, in particular, of the Scheduled Castes and the Scheduled Tribes, and [to] protect them from social injustice and all forms of exploitation.'

Article 15 (4), as already noted, was inserted into the Indian constitution by way of constitutional amendment in 1951 as a direct result of, and in order to overcome, a very early Supreme Court of India decision to the effect that Article 46, as a directive principle, could not overcome Article 29 (2), a fundamental right, and that the reservation of seats on communal grounds therefore violated Article 29 (2), the constitution not being intended to protect the interest of the backward classes in the matter of admission to educational institutions (*State of Madras* v *Champakam Dorairajan* [AIR (1951) SC 226]). The patent conflict between Articles 16 (1) and (2) of the constitution, and Article 16 (4), could not, however, be disposed of on such special, intrinsically technical, legal arguments. In *State of Kerala* v *N.M. Thomas* [AIR (1976) SC 490], the Supreme Court of India had to pass upon a state of Kerala plan designed to favour Scheduled Castes and Tribes employees by exempting them from the obligation of passing the regular departmental tests required for promotion within the civil service, in this case promotion from lower division to upper division clerk. The constitutional challenge was based upon Article 16 (1) ('equality of opportunity for all citizens in matters relating to employment or appointment to any office under the State'), with the argument that Article 16 (4) ('reservation of appointments or posts in favour of any backward class of citizens ... not adequately represented in the services under the State') did not apply. Within the Supreme Court of India majority which upheld the state of Kerala plan, vestiges of the original philosophical contradictions, existing at the time of adoption of the constitution and manifest in its text, seemed to remain. While one majority judge, Mr Justice Beg, justified the Kerala plan, in terms as a conditional or partial reservation in favour of backward classes under Article 16 (4), the four other majority judges preferred to uphold the Kerala plan directly under Article 16 (1) as a valid protective discrimination, designed to ensure equality of opportunity for all citizens and not being hit by Article 16 (2), thus avoiding the necessity for ruling on any notional conflict between the two different approaches to equality represented in Articles 16 (1) and 16 (4).

The more direct approach to the problem, of course, is the solution, only partly achieved in the case of the Indian constitution because of the inherent contradictions within the constitutional Bill of Rights provisions themselves and also the effective antinomy between the Bill of Rights and the directive principles already referred to, of incorporating the newer social and economic rights, with their implication of an affirmative community responsibility for redressing imbalances between different races, classes, or groups within the community, directly into the constitutional charter itself. The Stalin Constitution of 1936, in its chapter on fundamental rights and duties of citizens, ventured into these fields with stipulations on the right to work (Article 118), the right to rest and leisure (Article 119), the right to maintenance in old age and also in case of sickness or disability (Article 120), and the right to education (Article 121); though it was, perhaps, a little arch in accompanying the right to freedom of speech and freedom of the press by an express stipulation as to 'placing at the disposal of the working people and their organizations printing presses, stocks of paper ... ' (Article 125). These socio-economic rights are essentially reproduced in the Brezhnev Constitution of 1977 (Articles 39 to 45), with a right to housing added for good measure (Article 44). The positive action aspects of Soviet constitutional doctrine are evidenced again in all these articles, as, for example, in the injunction in the housing article that the state shall assist co-operative and individual housing construction, and make fair distribution, under public control, of housing space allotted in accordance with the implementation of a programme for the construction of well appointed housing, and also by low apartment rents and charges for municipal services. The more obviously rhetorical or picturesque aspects of the freedom of speech and the press article

(Article 125) in the Stalin Constitution of 1936 have been toned down in the new Brezhnev Constitution of 1977, though the substantive element in the earlier constitutional provision is still preserved (Article 50). They emerge again, however, somewhat quaintly perhaps, in the chapter on fundamental rights and duties of citizens (Articles 44 to 59) of the Constitution of the People's Republic of China of 1978, where citizens are guaranteed, as part of freedom of speech and of the press, the right to 'speak out freely, air their views fully, hold great debates and write big-character posters.' The social and economic rights articles in the People's Republic charter closely parallel those in the Brezhnev charter, no doubt reflecting the common source in Marxist-Leninist abstract philosophical doctrine and certainly not drafting eclecticism and the conscious borrowing or copying from the one constitutional text to the other. The standard western criticism of such socio-economic rights, as constitutional charter express stipulations, is that they may be no more than passing political tastes and preferences, which do not merit the relative permanence of being enshrined in a constitutional charter. They are the sort of stuff that only become really meaningful when 'operationalized' in governmental economic planning programmes; yet their popularity as expressions of contemporary community aspirations and yearnings should not be underestimated, and constitution-makers may therefore find it difficult to exclude them, today, from their constitutional catalogues of human rights.

An ever more difficult conceptual problem – at least for constitution-makers brought up in western, liberal, 'open society' notions of constitutional rights, including 'equality before the law' – is whether, and how, to strike a balance between individual rights and asserted 'collective' or group rights having a common ethnic-cultural base. This basic antinomy or conflict is manifested very strikingly today in the claims by French Canadians for constitutional self-determination within their 'home' province of Quebec, involving the maximizing of French-Canadian cultural-linguistic interests within Quebec and ultimately also French-Canadian economic interests so far as these are argued to have been repressed or downgraded, over the years, by an economically dominant minority within the province – the entrenched, English-speaking, 'Anglo-Saxon' economic élite. The legislative attempts by two successive Quebec governments, of quite different political ideologies, to make French the official language and also the language of work in Quebec – by the Bourassa government in its Bill 22 of 1974, and the Lévesque government in its Bill 101 of 1977 – have been argued as designed to correct or reverse that situation in the interests of the French-Canadian majority within Quebec; but both Quebec laws have had to run the gauntlet of a determined 'guerrilla war' campaign of harassment before the courts, launched by members of the English-speaking minority, who have invoked the older, classical, individual, 'open society' constitutional values against the assertedly newer, collective or group values. The problem, qua constitutional problem, shades off into broader questions of federalism and regional devolution as constitutional-governmental mechanisms for conceding, on a geographically decentralized base, political self-determination to national minorities within the one, ethnic-culturally plural, state. Once national self-determination has been constitutionally conceded on a regional or provincial basis within a federal state, there may remain a still further problem of minority enclaves within the region or province itself. This problem is one that arises not merely within the province of Quebec but also within the three cultural-linguistic regions of Belgium under the Pact of Egmont accord of 1977. Classical, 'Anglo-Saxon' thinking and practice on federalism does not offer very many suggestions for solution for refined problems of this nature. The 'open society' values, rigorously applied in constitutional terms, seem to lead inexorably to the assimilation and disappearance of the original ethnic-cultural minorities, both the provincially based ones and also the smaller minorities within the provincial minority. For ethnic-cultural minorities that wish to retain their national identity, even after absorption into a larger, plural state, the solution may have to be to break out of 'Anglo-Saxon' constitutional stereotypes and to experiment boldly with models drawn from other constitutional systems – the special, group or ethnic, political representation that was such a marked feature, for example, of the electoral systems of the multiracial Austro-Hungarian Empire in its constitutional apogee from 1867 to 1918, or, conceivably, a system of proportional (*scrutin de liste*) representation (partial or whole) of the sort that one finds in continental European electoral systems and practice at various times and especially in West Germany under the current 'Bonn' constitutional system.

9

Political representation: direct and indirect elections: individual and group representation

The detailed rules of political representation are not normally included in a constitutional charter itself. The reasons for this are in part historical and in part aesthetic. The historical reasons have to do with the fact that, at least until recent times, constitutional charters have generally limited themselves to definition of the main governmental decision-making institutions and establishment of their relationships inter se. The aesthetic reasons go to issues of style and balance in constitutional drafting: electoral rules normally require a certain amount of detail in their elaboration in order to be operational, and it is better not to clutter up a constitutional charter with them. They are best dealt with separately, in special statutes, which can be more readily and easily amended than a constitutional charter, as fashions and tastes as to political representation change (as they demonstrably do, from time to time).

The constitution of the United States, as originally adopted in 1787, did include certain ground rules as to political representation: the principle of minimum representation of each state of the federal system in the lower house of the federal legislature (Article I (2) 3) and also the age and citizenship qualifications of candidates for election (Article I (2) 2); the principle of equal representation of each state in the federal Senate and of delegation of the senators from each state by the relevant state legislature, and the length of term of office of such senators (Article I (3) 1); and the principle of election of the federal president by an electoral college composed of members selected from each state in correspondence to the total number of members of the federal Senate and the lower federal house from each state (Article II (1) 2). These provisions, as originally adopted, have been modified, through time – in part by direct constitutional amendment, and in part by binding constitutional custom engrafted upon the text of the constitution – in ways reflecting the more general historical trends in democratic constitutionalism. Thus, the members of the federal Senate, viewed originally as delegates from the state legislatures, have been chosen, since the adoption of the 17th Amendment to the constitution in 1913, by direct popular election within their respective states, and can thus claim a direct popular mandate in their own right. This is in accord with the historical trends, from 'aristocratic,' hereditary or nominated upper houses, through 'oligarchic,' indirectly selected houses, to popularly elected legislatures. Some vestigial remnants still remain – the hereditary British House of Lords, the nominated Canadian Senate, and even, perhaps, those indirectly elected upper houses that are a characteristic of modern French constitutionalism; but their powers are either scrupulously defined and limited, as in France, so that no colour of a claim to a political mandate can arise in opposition to the popularly elected lower house, or else, as in Great Britian and Canada, they exercise a prudent political self-restraint in the face of modern, representative democracy, to the point where, for practical purposes, their powers may be said to have disappeared by constitutional attrition through the development, in modern times, of a constitutional custom or convention to that effect. Even the election of the American president, clearly intended, historically, to be a reasoned, deliberate act on the part of the constitutionally stipulated electoral college (Article II (1) 2, and constitution, 12th Amendment, adopted 1804), has by now become a purely automatic, non-discretionary function, with the electoral college members from each state committed to the popular majority vote cast within their states at the presidential elections. There have been suggestions for a constitutional amendment recording this developed, constitutional law-in-action in postitive law, constitutional form, and also for correcting certain other anomalies; but this seems unnecessary in view of the highly developed constitutional practice amounting by now to a custom or convention of the constitution.

More substantial, however, is the issue of political representation in relation to claims to ethnic-cultural or group identity – whether of race, colour, language, or religion. The Anglo-American constitutional tradition, in accordance with 'open society' ideals already adverted to, has been to deny the principle of 'particular' representation, on the score that this is ultimately politically divisive and productive of inter-group tensions or conflicts. Group representation, in the 'Anglo-Saxon' countries, tends to be left to the accidents of political geography, and to the casual, accidental facts of concentrations of particular ethnic-cultural minority or similar discrete and insular groups in particular areas of the country. The system of single-member geographical constituencies and the first-past-the-post voting system favoured by the Anglo-Saxon countries, may thus occasionally operate to produce some leavening of the overall national majority, ethnic-cultural, linguistic, or religious patterns, by yielding area based minority or group representation – even if it were not historically intended to do that but designed simply to secure a stable, two-party system of government. In fact, in the case of Canada, the concentration of French-speaking citizens in the province of Quebec has ensured the presence of a continuingly solid bloc of French-speaking members of the federal lower house, albeit operating on the basis of the national political parties (essentially, the national Liberal party) and not, as yet, of a distinctively regional, 'Quebec' party. It works less well, in Canada, with other minorities that are rather more loosely dispersed throughout the country: though the Ukrainian Canadians in the western provinces may have effectively broken through into the political processes, this is not true, as yet, of the Chinese Canadians or the Italian Canadians, or, certainly, the native Indian peoples in Canada. In the United States, though more determinedly upwardly mobile minorities – the Jewish, Italian, and Polish minorities in the big cities, for example – seem to have achieved national political representation in proportion, more or less, to their numbers, the non-white minorities, demonstrably, have not, and this in spite of the existence of express constitutional stipulation designed to remove any legal barriers or clogs to their effective exercise of voting rights.

The 15th Amendment to the United States constitution, adopted in 1870 as the last of the three post-civil war 'Reconstruction' amendments, declares that: 'the right of citizens of the United States to vote shall not be denied or abridged by the United States or by any State on account of race, colour, or previous condition of servitude,' and it confers on the federal legislature power to enforce that provision by federal legislation. Although the first post-civil war federal legislatures moved to implement this guarantee, reaction to the claimed excesses of federal reconstruction in the defeated southern states and a desire to bring political reconciliation between North and South soon led to the attrition of this constitutional principle. This attitude of federal non-intervention and political and legal laissez-faire in voting matters was assisted by the United States Supreme Court's jurisprudence. For the court, ever reluctant to intervene in great political *causes célèbres* and conscious of the effective limits to its own office and to its own capacity for community policy-making as an only indirectly created organ of government, where the two popularly elected organs, Congress and the presidency, refused to act to correct claimed abuses, applied the doctrine of 'political questions' to render voting questions non-justiciable and therefore beyond its own legal powers to review. The manifest abuses of the political processes and the manifest inequities of electoral laws voted by legislative majorities within the state houses in their own interests and in the knowledge that they were free from constitutional scrutiny by the courts brought, in time, their own delayed political reaction by the courts.

The Supreme Court as late as 1946 had refused to intervene against the gerrymandered federal electoral districts within the state of Illinois [*Colegrove* v *Green* 328 US 549 (1946)]. But, very soon, the new notion began to emerge that judicial self-restraint or deference to the legislature, as the popularly elected organ of government, must be predicated upon the legislature's being, in fact, a bona fide 'representative' body. Mr Justice Stone, in 1938, had launched the idea of the court's affirmative duty to keep the political processes open and free and unobstructed, by removing any unnecessary clogs upon their operaton [*U.S.* v *Carolene Products Co* 304 US 144, 152 n 4 (1938)]. In *Gomillion* v *Lightfoot* in 1960 [364 US 339 (1960)], the supreme court invoked the 15th Amendment to the constitution to invalidate a state reapportionment plan that would have denied almost all the Negro voters within the city of Tuskegee, Alabama, their pre-existing municipal vote by removing them from within the city's limits. It was, however, *Baker* v *Carr* [369 US 186 (1962)] that permitted voters to challenge the apportionment of electoral districts for state legislatures, by ruling that such issues were justifiable and that voters had the necessary legal standing to sue. This landmark decision opened the flood-gates to constitutional litigation designed to effect more equitable and more 'representative' legislative apportionment systems for both federal and state elections. This was achieved as to equality of federal congressional electoral districts in *Wesberry* v *Sanders* in 1964 [376 US 1 (1964)]; and as to state legislatures (and in the instant case a state upper house), in *Reynolds* v *Sims*, decided in the same year, from which the 'one man, one vote' doctrine evolved [377 US 533 (1964)].

The implications of this new court jurisprudence were immense, not merely for ensuring fair political representation systems in both federal and state politics, but also for the court's own work-load and its claims to specialist expertise. Courts can annul manifestly unjust electoral laws, but unless they are prepared themselves, in effect, to sit as electoral boundary commissions, they must either rely on the goodwill and desire to co-operate in good faith of the relevant federal or state legislature or else accept the temporary substitute of elections-at-large on a statewide basis for federal or state elections as the case may be. A constitutional amendment – the 24th Amendment – adopted in 1964 at the time the landmark, activist-interventionist decisions on voting laws were being rendered by the Supreme Court, indicated affirmative will to co-operate on the part of both the federal legislative majorities that formally initiated it as a constitutional amendment and the state legislative majorities that ratified it as a constitutional amendment. The 24th Amendment struck down the 'poll tax,' – a device historically adopted in many of the states, after the Civil War, as a means of restricting or controlling access by Negro voters to the electoral rolls – and gave the federal legislature power to enforce that interdiction, if necessary, by appropriate legislation. Of course, part of the complexity of the problem of political representation, in the United States, comes from the fact that the members of the federal lower house and the federal Senate are elected in each state according to state electoral laws. The federal constitution, and amendments such as the 15th and the 24th and federal laws passed in direct furtherance of these, may establish controlling norms, but they hit the problem only partially or piecemeal. Hence the importance of the supervisory, monitoring role now being assumed by the Supreme Court of the United States in regard to fairness of electoral laws.

'Affirmative action,' directed to the advancement of minority group interests, gave rise, as already noted in the general field of political and civil rights, to a concept of a constitutionally licit 'reverse discrimination.' Applied to the specific field of political representation and electoral systems, this has generated even more intriguing notions – 'benign gerrymandering,' for example, when the electoral system is based not on general electoral lists (as in some continental European countries), to which some form of ethnic-cultural, religious, or general racial quota could be annexed as part of a proportional representation system, but on fixed geographical constituencies, as is the general rule in the United States. In *United Jewish Organizations, Inc.* v *Carey* [430 US 144 (1977)], the United States Supreme Court, by a seven to one majority, upheld a legislative reapportionment of New York state electoral districts in New York City in which the evidence indicated that the boundaries of new electoral districts had been drawn up with the deliberate intent of creating non-white (Puerto Rican and Negro) racial majorities as a means of maximizing such non-white representation in the state legislature as a whole. The effect of the state's 'affirmative action' on behalf of the Puerto Rican and Negro voters, however, was significantly to diminish the value of the voters of another minority group, the Hasidic Jewish community of Brooklyn whose voting strength, originally concentrated with the one state Assembly (lower house) and the one state Senate seat, was now dissipated by being split between several Assembly and Senate districts. This seriously eroded the Hasidic Jewish community's political influence, and effectively deprived them of the opportunity to elect their own representatives to the state legislature, hence their constitutional challenge before the courts. The

United States Supreme Court majority opinion, written by Mr Justice White, was based directly on the federal Voting Rights Act of 1965, designed to implement the 15th Amendment to the constitution and focusing on the position of racial minorities with respect to their effective exercise of the electoral franchise. Mr Justice White found that 'neither the Fourteenth nor the Fifteenth Amendment mandates any *per se* rule against using racial factors in districting and apportionment'; while Mr Justice Brennan, in a specially concurring opinion, embraced the notion of 'benign discrimination' which, in his view, might be 'permissible because it is cast in a remedial context with respect to a disadvantaged class rather than in a setting that aims to demean or insult any racial group.' By the logic of the court majority opinions in the *Hasidic Jews* case, however, political representation is to be seen less as a direct relationship between the elected representative and the individuals who are resident in his particular geographical constituency – the rationale of the geographical constituency approach to political representation – than as a more complex and plural relationship in which the elected representative is seen, also, as representing specific ethnic-cultural or racial groups. Mr Justice White noted, in his opinion for the court majority, that the white voter in effect consigned, by the reverse discrimination-style reapportionment, to a district likely to return a non-white representative would be 'represented, to the extent that voting continues to follow racial lines, by legislators elected from majority white districts'; while Mr Justice Brennan, in his concurring opinion, suggested that 'to the extent that white and non-white interests and sentiments are polarized ... petitioners still are indirectly 'protected' by the remaining white Assembly and Senate districts.'

We are a long way now, of course, from classical, 'traditional' concepts of role of the courts in the general political processes. The courts become committed, inevitably, to a very refined and difficult form of social engineering, in which, apart from the philosophical conflicts involved in the two different, antinomic views of constitutional 'equality,' the strains on the judges' own specialist legal training and expertise become severe, electoral sociology not normally being part of the armoury of judicial skills. All this would suggest the merits, for the future, if 'affirmative action' in behalf of racial minorities and their political representation in federal and state legislatures is to continue to be an accepted political imperative, of considering also approach to the problem from the front door. Perhaps at-large representation, with proportional representation principles applied at the same time, could be considered, for the future, as a partial supplement at least to the standard, single-member, geographical constituency based approach to political representation at both the federal and the state levels.

Representation by group is not, as we have noted, an 'Anglo-Saxon' principle of representation, save, perhaps, for some politically unfortunate experiments in the case of non-white or multiracial countries of the old British Empire and Commonwealth. The provision of separate electoral rolls for blacks and for 'coloured' (mixed blood) persons, inserted into the constitution of the newly self-governing Union of South Africa, formed by the British government in 1909 out of the two former British colonies and the two recently defeated Boer (Dutch) republics (South Africa Act 1909, sections 35 and 152), may have stemmed from special historical factors in the British colonies existing prior to the Boer War, but could not veil the fact that the new, self-governing British dominion thereby created in 1909 conferred political power upon a white (British and Boer) minority within a much larger, non-white society. These so-called 'entrenched' voting provisions were replaced in the 1930s and the early 1950s by other provisions that provided for separate political representation in other, special assemblies, for non-whites; but these were viewed as largely token in character, and were soon caught up in the larger political conflicts over separate political and social development (apartheid) for non-whites.

In the Indian subcontinent, the principle of separate, group representation, according to racial or religious ties, was applied by British colonial administrators in the pre-Second World War tentative ventures in constitutional devolution within the British Imperial framework. The search for the *right* principle of political representation for a multiracial society such as imperial India, which was divided by race, religion, and caste questions as well as its opposition to British rule, was complex and difficult; the gestures towards group representation by the British administrators preparing constitutional devolution were viewed by the predominantly Hindu, majority Congress party as an imperial government tactic of 'divide and rule'; and the Congress party, resolutely modernizing and secular in its orientation, thereupon rejected the principle of group representation – 'the blight of communalism' – in the name of majority rule. On the other hand, once the British decision to decolonize and withdraw from the Indian subcontinent was made in 1946, the Hindu, Congress party obduracy in rejecting communal representation and in insisting upon simple majority rule probably made inevitable the schism within the original Constituent Assembly and the breakaway of the minority, Muslim delegates and their setting up of their own separate constituent assembly. Would a more consciously pluralist approach to constitution-making, including plural system of political representation, have helped to avert the breakdown in the original constituent assembly and hence the political fission of the post-decolonization India subcontinent into the two separate and independent states of India and Pakistan? Nothing in British imperial experience allows any confident answer. It can be said, however, that in more assured and stable western societies, having some considerable historical experience of existing in a multiracial context – the old Austro-Hungarian Empire, for example – separate representation by race was a recognized principle for facilitating entry by ethnic minorities into the political processes; and though the Austro-Hungarian Empire finally collapsed in the military disaster of the First World War, all the evidence suggests that the principle of separate ethnic representation was an integrating, rather than a disruptive or divisive factor. The new multiracial federal states formed outside the 'Anglo-Saxon' world and its juridical traditions – Yugoslavia, for example, whose richly 'eclectic' legal traditions include some partial borrowings from the Habsburg Empire, apart from the more obvious post-Second World War Communist influences – do try to reconcile, in their latest drafts, the geographically based federal principle with the nationalities based federal principle; but these experiments, interesting and innovatory as they are from the comparative constitutional law viewpoint in their new approaches to political representation, are too recent to permit of empirical evaluation at the level of law-in-action. Belgium, by contrast, in responding to the awakened Flemish national self-determination movement, appears to have easily opted for the geographically federal approach to constitutional novation rather than for experiments in new approaches to electoral laws and plural political representation within the original, essentially unitary constitutional system inherited from 1830.

In the continental European countries, the interest in conscious adjustment of the electoral laws in aid to political pluralism, and the concomitant awareness of the necessary linkage between constitutional institutions and the system of political representation and voting in the development of a democratic polity, are clear. The French, in the Constitution of 1791, included detailed prescriptions as to electoral rights and voting rules within the constitutional charter itself. The more recent constitutional charters – those of the Third, Fourth, and Fifth Republics for example – tend to leave these questions to the domain of ordinary statute law, the latter two limiting themselves to specification of high level, general principles only, such as election by universal suffrage and with a system of direct election for the lower house and indirect election for the upper house (constitution of the Fourth Republic, Article 6: constitution of the Fifth Republic, Article 24). The French Revolution arrived very early at the principle of universal (male) suffrage, and this in the Constitution of 1793 (the Convention); the same charter introduced the principle of direct election in single-member, geographically based constituencies of approximately equal size. Thereafter, the antinomy in French approaches to political representation has been between the geographically based, single-member constituency approach and the more general, *scrutin de liste* voting system, based upon each political party's establishing its own list of candidates for larger, plural-member constituencies created upon the great administrative *départements* on which French government and administration has been organized since the first Napoleon's era. Within both these approaches there has been frequent variation between requirements of absolute majority or simple plurality for purposes of election, and between the principle of a single round of balloting only and two rounds of balloting, with the second round limited to the highest candidates on the first ballot and obviously facilitating the making of electoral alliances and vote transfers between the two rounds. And there has also been considerable flirtation and experimentation with the system of proportional representation, which the *scrutin de liste* system – certainly when limited to a single ballot – effectively implies. What emerges from the French electoral system history, since the origin of the Third French Republic, is a large element of political calculation, looking to the effects of proposals for change upon the composition of the legislature and the party system within it, and ultimately upon the character and stability of the parliament based executive government. The first elections for the National Assembly of 1871, constituted after the fall of the Second Empire, were largely based upon a revived electoral law of 1849, instituting, for these purposes, a *scrutin de liste* system within each administrative *département*, with a simple plurality (not an absolute majority) sufficient for election and (effectively) a single round of balloting only. However, in 1873, the monarchical majority within the National Assembly amended the electoral system in one very important respect: being divided, within itself, among the two rival royalist factions and the remaining Bonapartist group, the monarchical majority voted to impose an absolute majority, instead of simple plurality, at the first ballot, in order to give themselves the possibility of forming electoral coalitions against the republicans at the second ballot. It was, again, a purely tactical move by the monarchical Right, within the National Assembly, that amended the electoral laws once more, in 1875, to re-establish a single-member constituency system with two rounds of balloting, looking to expected electoral advantages to the Right. Thereafter, the posthumous influence of Gambetta and the strength of the forces of the Left in the National Assembly brought, in 1885, a further electoral reform re-instituting the system of 1873, the *scrutin de liste* system, with absolute majority at the first ballot and simple plurality at the second ballot. In 1889, there was a return to the single-member constituency system, with two rounds of balloting, and this lasted for thirty years until the end of the First World War. The year 1919 saw a return to the *scrutin de liste*, but under rather complex rules that seemed designed to achieve, through the two ballot system, a form of proportional representation corresponding more or less to the popular vote within each *département*. In 1927, there was a return to the classical single-member constituency system, with two ballots, which lasted until the downfall of the Third Republic in 1940. The Fourth French Republic saw a return to the *scrutin de liste* once more, the two successive election laws of 1945 and 1946 establishing a direct regime of proportional representation, based upon the *départements* as the constituencies and excluding a second ballot.

What is one to make of this seemingly bewildering, and certainly rather rapid succession of French electoral law amendments and reforms, alternating between the two poles of single-member constituencies and election by absolute majority, and the *scrutin de liste* based upon the larger, multi-member, departmental constituencies and proportional representation? Generally speaking, the *scrutin de liste* system favours autonomy of the various political parties: they choose the list of candidates for their own party and thus effectively decide whom they will send to the legislature and whom they will exclude. It gives the political party bureaucrats or managers a substantial control over the elections and, ultimately, of the governments formed from the political parties in the legislature. French commentators praise the *scrutin de liste* system, whether employed with a system of pure majority vote or direct proportional representation, as assuring the cohesion of parliamentary majorities. The significant departures from the *scrutin de liste*, proportional system – with the electoral laws of 1875 and 1927, for example – are explained upon particular circumstances leading to a failure to impose some unity and coherence in the major trends in electoral opinion: in the early and the mid-1870s, in the fractionalism within the monarchical forces, creating the risk that the majority, Right-wing parties could not prevail over the Left-wing forces in the general elections; and in the mid-1920s, in the alliance of convenience aspects of the Cartel des Gauches of the mid-1920s where a coalition formed by radicals and socialists against their common adversary, the Bloc National of Poincaré, presented irreconcilable elements, in actual government, due to their mutually contradictory social and economic conceptions. Under these circumstances, the *scrutin de liste* proportional system may seem automatically to favour coherent minorities at the expense of divided majorities; and this is why the Right-wing forces in the 1870s, and the Left-wing forces in the mid-1920s, both turned their backs on it at a period when they both felt divided but without, however, believing that they had lost their overall majority in public opinion throughout the country – a situation that, in fact, turned out to be the case and so frustrated the basic purpose of the electoral law changes that they sponsored.

The return, under the electoral system of the Fourth French Republic, to the *scrutin de liste* based proportional representation system, in its most explicit form, is to be explained by the electoral 'management' aspects which that system favours, particularly with its blocked lists and its single ballot: it means, effectively, a considerable reinforcement of the influence of the organized political parties and their bureaucracies, with their control of the party lists and thus of the candidates who would be elected. This was a condition not unpleasing to the dominant political forces in the Fourth Republic, after the failure of General de Gaulle's post-liberation, 'strong' presidential executive based constitutional initiative.

However, if the proportional representation system leads to coherent, rigid and influential political parties, in numbers superior to two but sufficiently limited, nevertheless – as one French authority remarked – it also involves, ineluctably, the necessity to build majorities in the legislature and thus governments by coalition; and there is the difficulty in putting together these coalitions, the number of possible combinations being limited. This tends, in the end, to compromise the homogeneity of governments and the coherence of their policies. It is also true that the proportional system carries the risk of bringing successive legislatures of almost identical composition, thereby creating obstacles to the mounting of dramatic new changes in direction in public policy, even where these are patently urgent and necessary. This form of intellectual attrition was particuarly noticeable in the case of the Fourth French Republic by the mid-1950s: its political leaders had run out of ideas and initiatives, and were quite incapable of resolving major policy dilemmas like the Algerian civil war. When the Fourth Republic constitutional system gave way to the Gaullist inspired Fifth Republic of 1958, and the government-by-Assembly constitutional notions of the earlier era gave way to a strong presidential executive at last, the *scrutin de liste* proportional representation system which had admirably served the political interests of the legislature based leaders of the Fourth Republic reverted once again to a single member-constituency, absolute majority, two ballot electoral system as a means of facilitating a clear, decisive electoral choice and thus of building a firm 'presidential majority' in the legislature – a condition that has, in fact, effectively prevailed since the outset of the Fifth Republic, when a coalition in support of the president of the republic's programme has always controlled the legislature.

The constitution-makers of the Weimar Republic of 1919 effected, as we have seen, a somewhat uneasy combination of the two different models of executive government – the parliamentary executive and the presidential executive. The internal contradictions in the constitutional system created by the interactions of these two are perhaps responsible, far more than the electoral system, for the downfall of the Weimar Republic; but the electoral system established under the Weimar Republic also had its own contradictions, involving the balancing of the idea of creating a strong, stable parliamentary (governmental) majority and the idea of reflecting all segments of electoral opinion in the legislature itself. Article 22 of the Weimar constitution established the principle of universal, equal, direct, and secret election, on the part of all men and women over twenty years of age, but included in its stipulations the requirement of election by proportional representation, leaving the details to be implemented by federal legislation. This was a major concession to the principle of representative democracy in its purest form, which thus prevailed over countervailing electoral modes directed, rather, to governmental efficacy.

The Weimar electoral system is set out in detail in a statute of 1920 which created thirty-five large electoral districts within Germany, related to considerations of geographical region and to relative population balance, and with a majority of them having over a million voters apiece. The system of proportional representation was extremely complex, being intended to ensure – as, in fact, resulted – as faithful a reflection as possible of diverse electoral opinion. It involved, in addition to the thirty-five regional districts in which seats were allocated according to the percentage of votes obtained by each political party list, a further, larger, notional, 'federal' district in which votes were carried over from the regional districts and seats allocated between the parties in exact proportion to the number of votes they had received throughout the nation. While there were some limitations established requiring achievement of a minimum number of votes before a party could participate in the allocation of seats from its list, the overall result of the Weimar electoral system was a marked proliferation of parties and a highly fractionalized legislature as a consequence. The proportional representation system, applied through the thirty-five regional districts, ensured the domination of the party leaders who selected the lists of candidates, and thus a bureaucratization of the political parties and their programmes, and a corresponding diminution of the intellectual quality as well as the political authority of the elected members. It meant, in the end, a triumph of mediocrity in the parliamentary parties, and this was undoubtedly one of the contributing factors to the failure of the traditional parliamentary forces effectively to combat the revolutionary forces of the Right and of the Left when the crises came. The multiplicity of minor parties, and the small numbers of seats that most of them could command, also rendered peculiarly difficult and painful both the building of governmental coalitions and also their maintenance once they had gained office. The frequency of governmental, ministerial crises was hardly assuaged by the frequent recourse to the power of the president of the republic, under Article 25 of the constitution, to dissolve the Reichstag, the lower house of the federal legislature, and compel fresh general elections. Used half a dozen times, it rarely restored the government which had sought the dissolution from the president, and, for the most part, merely aided the revolutionary parties of the Right and the Left which were far better organized to re-group the increasing number of politically frustrated, discontented, and alienated groups in the community. The solution finally found by Chancellor Brüning in 1930 of governing with a minority ministry, in spite of the resistance of the Reichstag, through the device of emergency decrees issued by the president of the republic in reliance on the constitutional emergency powers under Article 48 of the constitution, staved off the economic and political crisis, in some way, until 1932, but progressively lost the democratic base for the government and paved the way, after the short-lived interludes of the von Papen and von Schleicher quasi-authoritarian regimes, to the Hitler takeover. The successive ministerial crises of the Weimar years, and the electoral system which had facilitated the proliferation of the parties and so contributed to the governmental instability, have to be balanced, in terms of evaluation of the constitutional lessons from the Weimar Republic, against the special constitutional role played by the president of the republic as 'guardian of the constitution.'

The use made by President Hindenburg of the Article 48 emergency powers under the Weimar charter to counteract the multiplication of ministerial crises led on, in fact, to the 'Man-on-horseback'-style presidential executive, allied as it was to the president's being elected by direct, universal suffrage and so having his own, presidential political mandate. This was, in any case, the major constitutional lesson attributed by the Bonn constitution-makers of 1949 to the bitter experience of the Weimar years. And so, with the formation of the new federal democratic constitutional system, out of the wreckage of the Hitler years and the experience of the post-war Allied military occupation, it was not thought necessary to retreat altogether from the idea of a *scrutin de liste* proportional representation electoral system; and it is therefore retained for fifty per cent of the seats in the lower House of the federal legislature. The details are governed by ordinary federal statute (Bonn Constitution of 1949, Article 38), such statute law also containing provision for mitigating the worst consequences of a multiparty system such as produced by the proportional system of allocation of seats under the Weimar constitution, in stipulating that a party must receive a certain minimum percentage of the overall popular vote before it is eligible to participate in the proportional allocation of seats. This statutory rule was designed to discourage the rise of 'splinter' parties and to ensure a certain stability in the party political structure – in the result, in West Germany today, two major parties of the Right and Left respectively, with a third, minor, centrist party usually holding the balance of power in the federal lower house and so able to determine the choice of government by throwing its own votes in coalition.

Upper houses, where they still exist today, and where they are not constitutional anachronisms created on a hereditary or purely nominee basis, are often selected on an indirect electoral basis as under the Third, Fourth, and Fifth French Republics; or they may be for vestigial, historically derived considerations, delegates of the governments of the member-states of the federal system, as in the case of Germany under the imperial federal constitutional system of 1871, the Weimar Constitution of 1919, and the Bonn Constitution of 1949. Their powers, in compensation, tend to be limited either in terms, in the constitutional charter, or by long developed constitutional custom and convention as in the case of older constitutional systems like those of Great Britain and Canada. In the case of Great Britain, longtime customary, conventional constitutional law was even rendered into written, statutory constitutional law with the passage, after the budget troubles of the years 1909-11, of the Parliament Act of 1911 drastically limiting the powers of the House of Lords vis-à-vis the House of Commons. Where upper houses are elected by direct popular election, as in the case of the United States Senate since the 17th Amendment to the constitution was adopted in 1913, or as in the case of the Australian Senate where the system of direct popular representation now includes proportional representation on a statewide (province) basis, they can point to their own constitutional legitimation in their own right, in accordance with the best modern ideas on constitutionalism. If their own constitutional term of years should exceed that of the lower house, as is the case with the United States Senate, they may well, because of their wider, statewide political constituency, claim a political mandate and actually exercise a political power considerably exceeding that of the lower house.

This was, in fact, the attitude adopted by the Australian Senate in the constitutional crisis of 1975 when, rejecting arguments that British and general commonwealth experience, constitutional custom and convention today required an upper house to defer to the lower house's will, it voted to reject the federal budget introduced by the Whitlam government and already passed by the lower house. This senate exercise of an undoubted positive law power, in the constitution-as-written, brought on a fresh constitutional crisis (the so-called Kerr-Whitlam affair) when the governor-general (head of state), rejecting further arguments that British and general commonwealth constitutional custom and convention required the governor-general, as a strictly appointive official, to defer to the advice of the prime minister of the day, dismissed the Whitlam government and replaced it by the opposition parties to whom the governor-general promptly granted a dissolution of parliament and fresh general elections.

10

Control of constitutionality: judicial review, and government by the judiciary

The concept of a judicially based, institutional control of constitutionality – literally, an ultimate constitutional power of the courts to pass on executive and legislative actions and to rule on their compatibility or otherwise with the constitutional charter's express terms and also with more general notions of constitutionalism – carries the necessary implication that executive and legislative authority will accept such court rulings and co-operate loyally and in good grace in their practical implementation. The roots of this concept go back to English common law legal history, and the early seventeenth-century struggles between the common law judges and royal executive (pre-rogative) power, when Sir Edward Coke drew upon Bracton and eloquently reminded King James I that though the king was not under any man he remained, nevertheless, 'under God and the Law.' Common law based, natural law ideas of the limits of governmental power vis-à-vis the citizen, 'received' in the American colonies through writers such as Blackstone and popular at the time of the American Revolution and the Declaration of Independence from Great Britain in 1776, were undoubtedly influential in the landmark decision by Chief Justice Marshall of the United States Supreme Court in 1803, in *Marbury* v *Madison* [1 Cranch 137 (1803)], asserting the power of judicial review of the constitution – in this case, the constitutionality of federal executive action. The power of judicial review is not formally sanctioned or even mentioned in the constitution of the United States. It could no doubt be argued as being a logical consequence of the constitutional doctrine of the separation of powers, borrowed indirectly from Montesquieu and more or less written into the Constitution of 1787 with the separate definition of the powers of executive, legislature, and judiciary and with some specification of the relationships of those governmental organs inter se. But a fullscale debate on the power of judicial review, if it had taken place at the time of the drafting and adoption of the Constitution of 1787, would undoubtedly have led to consideration of the establishment of still further constitutional checks and balances, as a countervailing power to use or abuse by the judiciary of that power in relation to the other, co-ordinate organs of government, the executive and the legislature. This would possibly have implied including in the constitutional charter an express executive-legislative power to vote impeachment (removal from office) of the judges, and for avowedly political reasons – for example, the political character of their constitutional decisions – and not simply legal reasons such as the failure to maintain 'good behaviour' which the constitutional charter, as adopted, modestly specified (constitution, Article III (1)). Perhaps if Chief Justice Marshall's decision in *Marbury* v *Madison* had involved a direct political confrontation with the executive – as it happened, Marshall's former political opponent, President Jefferson – in the instant case, there might have been occasion for the executive to try to move to limit the judges' power by extending the constitutional notion of judicial 'good behaviour' to require also 'political' good behaviour. As it was, Chief Justice Marshall, a masterly politician in his own right, read a moral lecture on good government to the incoming Jefferson administration, asserted the power of judicial review with an eye (no doubt as intended) to the future, and then declined jurisdiction in the instant case and so avoided any immediate, direct political conflict with President Jefferson. Thereafter, in the more than thirty years of service remaining to him on the Supreme Court, Chief Justice Marshall never again challenged the constitutionality of a presidential executive action or a statute enacted by Congress. By the time of Marshall's departure from the court in 1835, the power of judicial review, asserted for the first time in *Marbury* v *Madison*, had become generally accepted as part of the constitutional system by the legal profession and public, as well as the executive and legislative authority.

The institution of judicial review of the constitution, developed in the United States and becoming a common-place of the American constitutional law-in-action by the latter half of the nineteenth century and becoming, at certain periods in the twentieth century, the key arena of constitutional inter-action and conflict and the key source of community policy-making (here, judicial law-making) in regard to major social or economic problems, soon finds constitutional analogues in other countries and other constitutional systems partially or wholly influenced by the American experience. In the old British Empire, judicial review originates as an imperial, British instrument of control over the dependent colonial empire overseas. An imperial, judicial tribunal sitting in London – the Judicial Committee of the Privy Council –

composed of judges appointed ad hoc by the imperial government, functioned during the nineteenth and twentieth centuries (until its jurisdiction
over the British Empire and Commonwealth countries was largely abolished), as final appellate tribunal having ultimate decision over all questions
of private and public law within the empire, including of course constitutional questions. This imperial jurisdiction of the Privy Council, vis-à-vis
the overseas colonial empire, presented no particular problems of British
political and legal theory. The juridical foundations of the empire were pyra-
midal, in Roman law fashion: ultimate legal sovereignty resided in the imperial government in London, and whatever authority it might devolve to the
self-governing dominions or colonies within the empire and later commonwealth remained, in terms of strict legal theory, revocable and always subject
to scrutiny or review as to the substance, but also the manner and mode, of
any decisions. When, after 1926, in the era of what became known as
'Dominion status,' the self-governing countries within the empire and
emerging commonwealth began to assert their own autonomous, local root
of legal sovereignty or *Grundnorm*, and when, finally, after the Second World
War, those same countries began to solidify the legal break with Great Britain and to abolish, by their own legislation, the erstwhile jurisdiction of the
Privy Council in relation to their own statutes or executive acts and the
decisions of their own courts, the original, historical, imperial roots for judicial review of their constitutions – as exercised by the Privy Council as an
instrument of empire – had long since been forgotten. Thus local supreme
courts, within those self-governing countries of the old empire and commonwealth, had grown accustomed to judicial review and to judicial control of
constitutionality, and never bothered to stop to question its raison d'être or
its constitutional justification today in the post-imperial, post-decolonization
phase. One might argue, in British constitutional terms, that judicial review
had by now, through use and practice, long since become part of those countries' own domestic constitutional law, in the form of constitutional custom
or convention. It is not difficult to speculate that the local judges liked what
they saw, and what they had themselves been doing in the past as lesser or
intermediate courts subject to appeal to the Privy Council, and that they
enjoyed the intellectual opportunities that would be presented, hence-
forth – after the abolition of the appeal to the Privy Council – by their sitting
in the new capacity of final appellate tribunal exercising judicial review of the
constitution in their own right. Undoubtedly, within the self-governing
countries of the old British Empire and Commonwealth, latter-day political
developments establishing a local, non-imperial, constitutional root and
justification for judicial review of the constitution were reinforced by the

widespread 'reception' of American constitutional ideas and the popularity of the American Supreme Court, as the first waves of commonwealth students began to flock to the great American graduate law schools immediately before and after the Second World War. By the late 1940s and the early 1950s, when the appeal to the Privy Council in London was being largely swept away by local statutes, the American Supreme Court – in its post-1937, Roosevelt image – was already established for commonwealth law professors (and increasingly, also, for commonwealth judges) as the apogee of a liberal, policy-making institution – the philosopher-king turned judge.

Outside the commonwealth, American influence immediately after the Second World War was much more proximate and direct. Newly defeated Germany and Japan, submitted to the enforced discipline of foreign military occupation and saddled by decisions of those same foreign military occupation powers with the total moral burden of war guilt, were constrained to adopt 'democratic' constitutions as a pre-condition to restoration of political and legal sovereignty and acceptance, thereafter, into the western political-military alliance systems. This meant, of necessity, fairly rapid exercises in constitution-making, and a certain deference to the constitutional ideas of the western occupation powers who would, after all, in the end be making the decision on restoration of sovereignty. But it did not involve any necessary, servile acceptance of those occupation powers' constitutional stereotypes, or any purely mechanical constitutional-eclecticism: to imply this is to underestimate the degree of political manoeuverability and capacity to improvise on the part of the recently defeated 'enemy states,' as the western powers sought desperately to consolidate their own strength and gain new allies for the then current east-west 'cold war' conflicts. American constitutionalism happened, at that particular time in the immediate post-Second World War era, to be in a period of great confidence in its own inherent problem-solving capacities and of optimism for the future; and the prestige of American constitutional institutions, and of the Supreme Court in particular, was literally unparalleled outside the United States. American experience was always the first to be consulted in constitution-making of that era, and American institutions became natural models for one's own domestic needs. In that sense, the 'reception' of American constitutional experience and ideas – in West Germany and in Japan after the Second World War – was logical and inevitable, and also essentially voluntary on the part of the local constitution-makers, particularly as to the constitutional role and possibilities of the courts.

In the case of West Germany, there were certainly some indigenous, local, civil law, *German* roots for judicial review of the constitution prior to the adoption of the new post-war Bonn Constitution of 1949. The Weimar Republic Constitution of 1919 introduced the notion of a special constitutional jurisdiction over constitutional disputes within a member-state (*Land*) of the federal system, or between different member-states, or between the federal government and a member-state (Weimar constitution, Article 19); and a special federal supreme court, the Staatsgerichtshof, was given jurisdiction to deal with such conflicts (Articles 19, 108). These provisions of the Weimar constitution were closely modelled on the older, imperial federal Constitution of 1871 which it had replaced; except that under the Constitution of 1871, jurisdiction over such federal conflicts and their resolution was entrusted to the upper house of the federal legislature (Constitution of 1871, Article 76). The Weimar constitution therefore made a constitutional breakthrough in introducing the principle of *judicial* control of such federal constitutional conflicts, though the absence of jurisdiction over conflicts within the federal government itself (see Weimar constitution, Article 19) made for a serious gap in the Weimar constitutional system, since disputes between different federal organs (the president, the chancellor, the two houses of the federal legislature), rather than federal-*Land* or inter-*Länder* disputes, turned out to be the real points of political confrontation in the Weimar Republic. Nevertheless, in the major constitutional conflict of July 1932, when the federal president invoked Article 48 of the constitution and the constitutional doctrine of emergency powers to suspend the government of the *Land* of Prussia and replace it by a federal administrator and to occupy the Prussian government offices by federal army units, the Staatsgerichtshof was, in fact, promptly seized of the matter by the deposed Prussian government and by another *Land*, Bavaria. The Staatsgerichtshof decision on this constitutional crisis – the so-called *Preussenschlag* – was mixed: the court confirmed the removal of the Prussian ministers from the exercise of their office, but declared that a formal dismissal of them could not constitutionally be made by the federal president under Article 48 (2) of the constitution. In the immediate result, the court decision changed nothing in the practical political situation, though it remained as constitutional precedent for the post-Second World War Bonn constitution-makers, in their attempt to build a democratic constitutionalism including judicial control of constitutionality. The Bonn Constitution of 1949 in fact goes substantially beyond that limited Weimar precedent. In several key articles (Bonn constitution, Articles 92 to 94), it establishes a special federal constitutional court (Bundesverfassungsgericht) and gives it jurisdiction over a catalogue of matters, covering disputes within the federal government (inter-organ disputes), federal-*Länder* conflicts, inter-*Länder* conflicts, and also complaints raised by private citizens concerning alleged violation of their constitutional rights. This last category has turned out to be an enormous source of constitutional litigation before the court, in response, in part, to the very extensive and detailed bill of rights adopted as the opening nineteen articles of the Bonn constitution and also the the keen public interest in civil liberties after the Second World War. The happy coincidence of the presence of several very strong judicial personalities, well schooled in comparative (and especially Anglo-American) constitutional jurisprudence, in the early, formative years of the West German federal constitutional court after 1951, plus the active involvement of all major political parties in the judicial appointment processes which, under the unusually felicitous provisions of the Bonn constitution, has ensured a genuinely multi-partisan court, have combined to give the court an unusual prestige and authority, extending both to the general public and the other organs of the federal government. The court was thus enabled, at important stages in the development of West German democracy in the 1950s and 1960s, to take a lead in resolving political and social conflicts not otherwise readily soluble under the ordinary executive and legislative processes – in voting and electoral problems, and in disputes over public television, for example.

In Japan, very much more than in the case of West Germany, the decision to introduce judicial review of the constitution in the post-Second World War 'democratic' constitution appears to be a fairly direct response to the pressures and counsel of the American military occupation officials. The 'MacArthur constitution,' self-evidently from its language, phrasing, and styling, owes so much to American constitutional ideas that it is not surprising to find an explicit constitutional statement of the power of judicial review – in effect, a rendering, in positive law form, of the power that the United States Supreme Court has effectively exercised, as a matter of constitutional custom, since Chief Justice Marshall's landmark decision in *Marbury* v *Madison* in 1803. Article 81 of the Japanese Constitution of 1946 declared: 'The Supreme Court is the court of last resort with power to determine the constitutionality of any law, order, or official act.'

The Japanese Supreme Court decided very early – in the *Suzuki* case decision in 1952 – that its power under Article 81 extended, like the power of judicial review exercised by the United States Supreme Court, to the decision of constitutional issues arising in concrete legal disputes between specific parties, and that it had no power to render constitutional opinions in the abstract, outside the fact-setting of concrete cases. With the power of judicial review and its manner of judicial exercise thus confirmed, the Japanese Supreme Court entered upon a very busy first decade of constitutional jurisprudence, putting aside older, pre-war precedents whereby the old Privy Council, established under the imperial Constitution of 1889, had rendered what amounted to abstract, advisory opinions on constitutionality. Constitutional review in the more contemporary, 'American' sense of constitutional case-law was thus rendered for the first time under the Constitution of 1946. The Supreme Court, beginning its work in 1947, soon ventured on the tentative elaboration of a civil liberties jurisprudence that owed a good deal to 'received' American constitutional ideas; and it also undertook the judicial testing of the 'renunciation of war' section (Article 9) of the constitution which General MacArthur's advisers had insisted on inserting in the new Japanese constitution – improvidently, as it turned out, from the rapidly supervening American and general Western military needs for a strong Japanese military presence in aid of common defence objectives in the Far East in the cold war era. By contrast, the second decade of the Japanese Supreme Court's work – the 1960s – seemed much quieter in court terms, no doubt because of the far more prosperous general economic climate of Japanese society. The military security treaty crisis of 1960 may be viewed, in retrospect and in this context, as a 'rite of affirmation of the legitimacy of the Constitution of Japan and of the necessity for political sensitivity to its demands, rather than as a revolutionary threat to the constitutional order,' the anti-security treaty effort being drained of enthusiasm by the shift to other outlets for political activism such as student contestation within the universities in the late 1960s and preoccupation with consumer questions. There was also, in the decade of the 1960s, a popular concern, reflected in the court's case load, with environmental protection and its impact in institutional terms in national-local governmental relations; a separation (or alienation) of citizens from their political parties, and a corresponding concern – not fully admitted, perhaps, by the Supreme Court – with electoral representation; and finally some mounting public criticisms, on ideological grounds, of the judiciary, culminating in the ineffective public petition launched by over two thousand members of the legal profession in the late 1960s seeking the impeachment of Chief Justice Ishida of the Supreme Court.

For the foreign student, there are some key questions concerning the operation of the judicial process in review of constitutionality in Japan after the Second World War. If the actual adoption of judicial review of the constitution in the Constitution of 1946 is a response to American pressures or at least the influence of American constitutional ideas, how much does the actual, empirical, working record of judicial review in Japan since 1947 owe to those 'received' American substantive constitutional ideas; how much to an original post-*Meiji*, 'received' German and general continental European civil law influence; and how much to indigenous, national, Japanese conditions and experience, including the contemporary exigencies of Japan's own post-industrial society? All of these elements are clearly present in the case-by-case development of constitutional jurisprudence by the Japanese Supreme Court since 1947. The Japanese Supreme Court decisions, to the outside observer at least, do seem to read as more German than American in their logical development and reasoning; in their literary formulation; and in the relative modesty and restraint shown in the adumbration of special or dissenting opinions, there being, here, a conscious avoidance of judicial 'Byzantinism' that seems to owe very much to continental European 'collegial' judicial traditions. This may be assisted, however, by the numerical factor of the rather larger court membership – fifteen judges in the case of the Japanese Supreme Court. Though the judges, appointed by the government of the day as vacancies occur, must be at least forty years old and retire at seventy, most of them, in keeping with the Japanese traditional respect for age, seem to be appointed very late in life and so hold office for only a few years, thus facilitating a rapid turnover in judicial personnel and making the elaborate statutory provisions for review of appointments at periodic intervals somewhat otiose. Lastly, and in comparison with supreme courts in other countries, the Japanese judges' decisions of the 1960s, particularly on civil liberties cases, look pragmatic rather than absolutist in any libertarian sense, and somewhat conservative in the end result – closer to the Chief Justice Burger-led majority on the United States Supreme Court of the 1970s than to the liberal activist court majorities of the Roosevelt and later eras in the court's history.

EROSION OF THE LEGITIMACY OF JUDICIAL REVIEW

In retrospect, the two decades after the Second World War appear as a golden era in western, and (as in the case of societies like Japan and India) western derived or western influenced, constitutionalism. In spite of all the external challenges of the cold war that dominated international relations over that time, strong and vibrant constitutional democracies took root in defeated West Germany and in Japan; and there was a general confidence in the possibilities of human improvement or betterment, under law, in the expanding economies of the western post-industrial societies as a whole. Translated into legal-institutional terms, this seemed to mean a technocratic society successfully reconciling science and humanism through the key intellectual élite group of the judges, applying the principle of judicial legislation or judicial policy-making on great issues of community tension. In the context of the times, the judicial arm of government appeared to be more rational and more equipped with 'right reason' and civil courage than the executive and legislative arms. It was not altogether by accident, one may suggest, that the high-water mark of judicial review in western or western influenced societies was attained in the 1950s. In the United States, for example, both Congress and the presidency were dragging their feet noticeably in race relations matters, and it was left to the court, *faute de mieux*, to take the political giant step in desegregation of education in the grade schools involved in the long drawn out case of *Brown* v *Board of Education* in which judgment was finally rendered in 1954. In West Germany and Japan, the political generations exercising government in the early years of the new, democratic constitutional systems of the post-Second World War era were often seared or tainted by their political experiences and associations during the wartime period and the years leading up to the war: the judges, in a certain sense, were above the battle and uncorrupted, morally or psychologically, by the crisis years, and therefore better equipped than anyone else to lead the way to a genuinely democratic constitutional law-in-action. In fact, the jurisprudence of the West German federal constitutional court and of the Japanese Supreme Court in those early years stands as a model of liberal constitutionalism, imaginative and forward looking in its policies and its application.

Since that time, judicial authority and judge-made law as a solution to social problems have been in partial retreat throughout the western world. Key retirements, like that of the great comparative jurist and philosopher Gerhard Leibholz, in the case of West Germany, or key political errors of judgment like the failure to broaden or 'federalize' the process of appointment of judges to the Canadian Supreme Court while there was still time before the Quebec 'Quiet Revolution' had run its course, no doubt have played their part. But the International Court of Justice in The Hague has had, over the decade of the 1970s, only a handful of cases on its docket, in striking contrast to the richness and fullness of the work of its predecessor in the inter-war years, the Permanent Court of International Justice. The principle of judicial settlement of international disputes, once a cardinal element in the western approach to international relations in general and to settlement of international disputes in particular, is now in fairly general disrepute or discarded, a consequence in part, but only in part, of what non-western and especially Third World countries conceive, rightly or wrongly, as the court's 'self-inflicted wounds' – great political *causes célèbres* like the *South West Africa, Second Phase* decision of the World Court, rendered in 1966 by an eight to seven majority on the second, tie-breaking vote of the (western) president of the court. Only the High Court of Justice of the European Communities, among the major final appellate tribunals, seems to evidence the creative vitality of judicial power to be found so generally in the immediate post-war years, though even that court evidences intellectual conflicts, internally, between a small activist group of judges and a more substantially 'strict constructionist' judicial majority.

A major part of the problem is clearly the contemporary breakdown of confidence in the post-industrial society and the disappearance of that sense of direction and movement for the future that is a precondition of wise judicial policy-making on any consistent, long-term basis. The threatened disappearance or impairment of the pre-existing constitutional consensus or *Grundnorm* in the case of Canada, or the current challenges to the social-market-economy societal consensus in the case of West Germany, or the general decline of public faith in governmental institutions (including, necessarily, the courts) in the United States in the Vietnam War and Watergate periods are perhaps no more than indices of this more general and constitutional malaise of our times.

The problem becomes one of the legitimacy of judicial review today, viewed in constitutional-legal terms certainly but also in ultimate political terms. The *constitutional* legitimacy of judicial review may be more open to question in countries like those of the old British Commonwealth where the institution of judicial review is not formally made part of the positive law of the constitution, and when it has simply been successfully asserted by the judges, over the years, without effective counter-challenge by executive-legislative authority, and when, by definition, the judicial function is assertedly neutral and only technical (non-political) criteria are to be considered in the selection and appointment of judges. By contrast, the *constitutional* legitimacy of judicial review is hardly subject to doubt where it is established, as such, in the constitutional charter itself, as in the case of West Germany and Japan, or else recognized by long-standing constitutional custom, as in the case of the United States. The constitutional legitimacy of judicial review is reinforced, in the case of several of these countries, by the open incorporation into the political processes of the business of selection of judges for the ultimate constitutional tribunal – *indirectly*, in the case of the United States, with the provision for federal Senate confirmation of executive (presidential) nominations of judges to the court (US constitution, Article II (2) 2); more *directly*, in the case of West Germany, with the provision for election of the judges of the federal constitutional court, for a non-renewable term of years, by the federal legislature, one half of the judges being elected by the lower house and one half by the upper house (Bonn Constitution of 1949, Article 94 (1)).

The *political* legitimacy of judicial review, however, seems open to challenge in either case, where executive-legislative authority insists on referring to the courts, for judicially based solution, great political *causes célèbres*, or where judges themselves insist on rushing in and accepting jurisdiction in great partisan political conflicts where even angels prudently fear to tread. In issues like the segregation of schools and race relations cases generally, in the 1950s, even though the political and social problem, on some views, was properly the constitutional responsibility of the other two arms of government, the United States Supreme Court, acting in default of affirmative executive-legislative action, still operated against a background of an overall, nation-wide consensus – overriding local, regional pockets of opinion – in favour of ending segregation. Where such general societal consensus exists, the courts can effectively venture upon sustained judicial policy-making; where it does not yet exist, the courts may perhaps more sensibly make an ally of time and apply the lessons of judicial self-restraint, in recognition of the undoubted political limits to the judicial office. It is, however, difficult to obtain an unbiased, objectively scientific view of the political legitimacy of judicial review, so many of the scholarly appraisals turning out to be yet more exercises in political special pleading. Those academic critics who castigated the 'conservative' anti-Roosevelt judicial majority on the United States Supreme Court up to 1937 and who called for an end to 'government by the judiciary' and to the hegemony of the 'Nine Old Men' made a complete constitutional volte face only a few years later when the new Roosevelt majority on the court started to implement a liberal activist jurisprudence: these erstwhile critics of the court began discovering the constitutional virtues of judicial activism, and calling for affirmative judicial legislation to fill the gaps in executive and legislative policy-making and so to achieve a democratic constitutionalism. It must also be recognized that, once launched upon judicial policy-making on great issues of social tension, the courts may find themselves involved in community problem-solving of great complexity and difficulty, requiring considerable technical expertise and skills in social fact-finding which judges, in contrast to members of the executive and the legislature, are often neither equipped for nor have the staff resources, in depth, to investigate thoroughly. The school-bussing cases, involving the compulsory transfers of grade school children from one school district to another, as a means of achieving racial 'balance' in the schools and so, in the court's view, meeting the mandate of the American constitution's 14th Amendment 'equal protection' clause, are just such an example of the challenges and effective limits of specialist, technical judicial expertise in complicated community problem-solving exercises; and, by the same token, the cases involving the 'reverse discrimination,' affirmative action quotas for under-privileged racial minorities, in graduate professional schools, seem to require applied sociological skills, in depth, that judges normally do not have. We have come a long way from the day when a judge committed to the principle of judicial activism and affirmative judicial legislation on social problems could implement the canons of sociological jurisprudence through a vaguely intuitive, purely impressionistic approach to society and its ills. Are there some social problems today that are so complex and difficult that they are, in fact, better left to the far more richly endowed executive commissions of enquiry or legislative task forces, in preparation for the drafting of statutory measures for presentation to the legislature?

AN ALTERNATIVE CONVENTION FOR CONTROL OF CONSTITUTIONALITY: THE LEGISLATIVE COMMITTEE, OR COUNCIL

The Conseil constitutionnel, created under the 1958 Constitution of the Fifth French Republic, has some historical links to the Comité constitution-nel of the immediately post-Second World War Fourth French Republic. However, that earlier institution hardly operated in practice so that, to a very real extent, the present Conseil constitutionnel is, in comparative (time and space) constitutional terms, sui generis. It is, in any case, having regard to main contemporary foreign analogues, neither an American supreme court nor a West German Bundesverfassungsgericht, the more strictly juridical functions of these foreign institutions being, to some extent at least, assumed in France by the Conseil d'Etat and the Cour de Cassation.

The constitution of the Fifth French Republic, in reaction to the supposed weakness of the Fourth French Republic which, in the 1950s, had seemed to disintegrate into the unstable regime of rapidly changing parliamentary majorities that had brought the Third French Republic to a standstill by the time of the French military defeat of 1940, had tried to establish a new equi-librium between legislative and executive institutions, and to correct that supremacy of parliament which had come to dominate French constitutional practice after 1870. In the spirit of the Gaullist constitution-makers of 1958, the prime role of the new Conseil constitutionnel was to prevent any return to parliamentary dominance over the executive.

In the event, those expectations of 1958 have hardly been fulfilled. If the constitutional system of the Fifth French Republic, as actually written in 1958, is characterized by an equilibrium of forces between the three main institutions – the president of the republic, the prime minister, and parlia-ment – the switch, in 1962, to election of the president of the republic by direct popular vote with the consequent direct political mandate that that confers, plus the happy coincidence of presidential and parliamentary majorities after 1958, have ensured the emergence of a very strong executive authority, reflected in the personalities, prestige, and authority of the three presidents elected since that time – de Gaulle, Pompidou, and Giscard d'Estaing. There has hardly been any need, in consequence, for the Conseil constitutionnel to try to assert itself as a countervailing power to intransigent parliamentary majorities. Its role has been a somewhat modest one, although there is an emerging tendency – facilitated by the enlargement of the court's jurisdiction in 1974 so as to permit any group of sixty members of the lower house of parliament or sixty senators to seize the Conseil of a constitutional question – for the Conseil to proceed to the control of executive policy-making by passing on the compatibility or otherwise of projects of legislation with more general constitutional stipulations. In this category fall the Conseil's ruling on the legalizing of abortions, made in 1975 at the instance of members of the government majority in the lower house of parliament; the 1976 ruling on the amendments to the general statute on the status of civil servants; the 1977 ruling on police powers of search and seizure; and perhaps the 1975 ruling on the application of the constitutional principle of self-determination (Article 53) to the proposed secession of the Comores.

On 20 December 1979, the Socialist party group in the lower house took advantage of the 1974 amendment to the Conseil's statute permitting any group of sixty members of the house to invoke the Conseil's jurisdiction, to launch (in company with the presiding officer of the lower house, M. Chaban-Delmas, a prominent Gaullist party member) a challenge to the constitutionality of the Barre government's finance (budget) law. The constitutional issue was a complex procedural one, not going to the substance of the budget law itself. A general ordinance adopted in 1959 had required that budget laws be in two parts, the first establishing the general conditions of financial equilibrium and the second comprising the actual voting of credits. The Barre government had been defeated in parliament on the *first* part of its budget law; but it had then proceeded to parliamentary adoption of the *second* part of the budget law, utilizing Article 49 (3) of the French constitution whereby, if the matter is treated as one of 'confidence,' the measure is considered as adopted unless a motion of censure against the government is carried within twenty-four hours. The Conseil constitutionnel, within four days of receiving the constitutional complaint, ruled on 24 December 1979 that the budget law did not conform to the constitution. The constitutional vice, as indicated, was not one of substance, but of procedure – the conditions under which the budget was adopted, or, more exactly, the chronology of the vote. The governmental corrective to the Conseil constitutionnel ruling was immediately to convoke parliament and to have adopted, on 27 December 1979, a law authorizing the government to collect, in 1980, already existing taxes. The Conseil constitutionnel, being seized again of the issue by the necessary number (sixty) of Communist and Socialist members of the house, ruled on 30 December 1979 that the law authorizing the government to collect, in 1980, the already existing taxes conformed to the constitution. This ruling allowed the government to carry on until such time as parliament could be convoked again in regular session, early in 1980, to consider the Barre government's budget project. What was involved in this whole affair of the Barre government's budget was not any real 'crisis of regime'; for in fact, and aided in part by the promptness with which the Conseil constitutionnel ruled in favour of the 'corrective' action adopted by the Barre government after its first ruling of unconstitutionality, the government was able to extricate itself relatively easily and quickly from the resultant impasse. It was simply a reminder to the government of its general obligation to observe already existing, well defined procedures in the approach to law-making. The political significance is that the Conseil constitutionnel, on the demand of members of the legislature, did not hesitate to invoke its constitutional arbitration role against the executive, in relation to a governmental measure as notionally fundamental as the budget.

The Conseil is not, in its composition and membership, a judicial or even a strictly legal body. (Do issues of constitutional law, with the high 'policy' notions that they involve, absolutely require a legal training for their wise resolution?) The Conseil has nine regular members, a third of whom are named by the president of the republic, a third by the speaker of the lower house of parliament, and a third by the presiding officer of the Senate (Article 56 of the constitution). Since the three designated nominating officers (and particularly the president of the senate) have not always been of identical personal or political sympathies, this has ensured some degree of political mix though not, be it noted, any great political contestation. Some of the members of the Conseil have been lawyers – several professors of law, and the occasional civil servant or magistrate from other tribunals – but to a considerable extent they have been either active or retired politicians (M. Pompidou prior to his presidency of the republic; M. Frey and M. Monnerville). Ex-presidents of both the Fourth and the Fifth Republics (Presidents Auriol, Coty, de Gaulle, as it turned out) were made ex officio life members of the Conseil under Article 56 of the constitution, though this condition has not been oppressive in operation, the ex-presidents having usually not exercised the right or else not lived long enough to be decisive; the other, regular members of the Conseil hold office for nine years, and cannot be renewed. The strictly consultative character of the Conseil – prior to the 1974 extension of the right to seize it of a constitutional question – is indicated in the 1958 constitutional definition of its jurisdiction; apart from the Conseil's role in the supervision of presidential elections and of referenda and in ruling on disputed parliamentary elections, and apart from *organic* laws (changes of the constitutional charter) which must be submitted to the Conseil before promulgation, ordinary laws would only reach the Conseil on the voluntary initiative of the president of the republic or the prime minister or the presiding officer of either house of parliament.

It is difficult to avoid the conclusion that the Conseil constitutionnel, notwithstanding the December 1979 *cause célèbre* of the Barre government budget laws, remains a largely embryonic institution, whose full constitutional potential in establishing an equilibrium of power between executive and legislative authority is hardly likely to be realized unless and until the popularly elected president of the republic is confronted, on some continuing or permanent basis, by a hostile majority of rival political parties or coalitions within parliament itself. In that case, we would have the potential of conflict and confrontation between two ideologically different political majorities and political mandates in the executive and the legislature, with the as yet unresolved, post-1958 issue of whether the president of the republic, in such circumstances, should continue to designate a prime minister in his own political image rather than one representative of the new parliamentary majority. In either event, the Conseil constitutionnel, having regard to the 1974 opening up of access to its jurisdiction, could well find itself at the centre of conflicts between the president of the republic and the prime minister, or between the president and his own preferred prime minister on the one hand and a politically hostile parliamentary majority on the other. That particular political scenario has not, however, occurred since the establishment of the Fifth Republic in 1958.

As a final point, the Conseil constitutionnel, as already noted, is not a court; and at a time when the high political aspects of *judicially* based constitutional review are under criticism in more than one American influenced contemporary constitutional system, the Conseil has a certain interest and importance as an alternative convention or model for the constitutional arbitrament of great political-governmental *causes célèbres*.

11

The limits and possibilities of contemporary constitutionalism

Constitutional government is under challenge or stress in very many parts of the world today. Western constitutional systems, with long traditions of power sharing and the peaceful accommodation of new social and economic forces, are being challenged by direct action, operating outside the ordinary constitutional 'rules of the game.' The organized anarchist, terrorist groups in West Germany and Italy today, challenging the existing 'system,' are somewhat more visible in their actions and their effects than the regionally based activist groups in Spain, France, and other countries that resort to direct action to publicize their regional causes and to pressure governmental action. Civic protest through civil disobedience and public flaunting of the law and legal processes, however, is also a part of ethnic-minority based protest action in many countries, and most notably in the United States in the Vietnam War 'protest' era. The implication is that the ordinary political processes open for constitutional change, and thus for the achievement of social and economic change, have become clogged – either becoming closed altogether or else hemmed in by time consuming and expensive procedures. In many non-western countries that inherited tidy, western-style constitutional charters on decolonization and independence, those 'received' constitutional systems have either been replaced by 'strong executive' constitutional models – thinly disguised constitutional versions of the 'Man on horseback' – or else suspended altogether in favour of frankly authoritarian regimes. These post-decolonization constitutional systems, often federal in structure and organization at the original point of departure on independence and self-government, have in many cases been rent by sectionalism, group fractionalism and regional alienation, leading to threats of political secession by force of arms and direct civil war.

THE SOCIO-ECONOMIC LIMITS TO CONSTITUTIONALISM

Is constitutionalism, which found its political apogee, in western society, during the predominance of political and economic laissez-faire ideas, inextricably linked with political liberalism to the point where it amounts to a barrier, today, to the effectuation of social democratic ideas, community planning, and the 'welfare state.' Certainly, the supreme court jurisprudence of the main western federal systems, and also of non-western federal systems such as post-decolonization India that were strongly influenced by 'received' western constitutional ideas, indicates a series of prolonged, last-ditch battles before the courts by economic special interest groups resisting governmental social and economic planning legislation, with the judges, in the earlier years at least, actively supporting the special interest groups and striking down the legislation trenching on their privileges. Those who could no longer control the legislatures did, indeed, look to the courts and the judges as guardians of their special interests. The history of United States Supreme Court jurisprudence up to the 'court revolution' of 1937 does, indeed, say something about the constitutional judiciary and the relatively narrow social groups to which they belonged and their restricted range of social sympathies; and it certainly suggests the need for broadening the recruitment of the constitutional judges, by opening up the processes of appointment to public scrutiny and by involving the legislatures as much as possible in the election or, at the very least, the confirmation of judicial candidates. The important thing, however, in relation to the jurisprudence of the 'Old Court' majority on the United States Supreme Court up to 1937, or, for that matter, the 'decentralized' weighting given by the Privy Council to the Canadian constitution from the close of the nineteenth century to the late 1930s, or the favouring of private property claims by the Indian supreme court majority in the first decade after decolonization and independence, is that it ended and was capable of being ended within the existing constitutional system and within the general context of the existing constitutional charter. The constitution was open-ended enough to allow of its continuing adaptation to changing societal conditions and demands, and to allow for a new content to be given to it as laissez-faire ideas ceased to correspond to dominant societal sentiment. The openness of constitutional systems to societal change is a key element in liberal constitutionalism, and it is no barrier in itself to social democracy. Perhaps the process of community transition could be assisted, in the case of new ventures in constitution-making, by constitutional bill of rights provisions that identify the new social and economic claims to sharing of wealth and social opportunity in addition to the classical liberal, 'open society,' freedom of speech and association and communication values; though there is always the risk of jelling as timeless constitutional absolutes the purely passing, temporary political claims of today and so, ultimately, of acting as a brake on social change and social progress.

Constitutional systems that rely less on the constitutional judiciary than on legislative majorities as solvents for community change have sometimes been tempted to try to reflect the newer societal demands for a more effective and more widespread community participation in social and economic decision-making, in concrete institutional terms in the constitutional charter itself. This is sometimes noticeable in continental European civil law ventures in constitution-making, for the influence of corporatist ideas of economic organization, involving management and labour syndicates in industry-wide associations, is much more pronounced in those countries than in the 'Anglo-Saxon' world. The Weimar Republic Constitution of 1919 consecrated a special final section of fifteen articles (Weimar constitution, Articles 151-65) to what it classified as 'Economic Life,' including detailed stipulations as to management-labour relations and wages and work conditions negotiations (Article 165). These provisions, in retrospect, stand out as among the more abstract, 'professorial' sections of the Weimar charter; and though they are partly, if much more economically, repeated in the Bonn Constitution of 1949 (see Bonn constitution, Article 9 (3)), the fact remains that this major area of community activity and community decision-making in social and economic matters has continued to be, under the Bonn system as under the Weimar system before it, a matter of non-public, or at least non-constitutional, private legal action. The federal constitutional court, under the Bonn system has, however, in recent years, helped to 'publicise' the matter to some extent by establishing peripheral or limiting principles as to private, entrepreneurial and syndical, action.

The Constitution of the Fourth French Republic of 1946 made its own special institutionally based gestures towards economic decision-making by authorizing the creation of an economic council which might be consulted by the legislature for advisory opinion in advance of projects of statute law, and by the cabinet, on an obligatory basis, on the establishment of a 'national economic plan having for object full employment and the rational utilization of material resources' (constitution of the Fourth Republic, 1946, Article 25). These provisions were repeated, in slightly more expanded form, in the Gaullist Constitution of the Fifth Republic of 1958, the council being renamed as an economic and social council but its essentially consultative, advisory character retained (constitution of the Fifth Republic, 1958, Articles 69-71). These French constitutional innovations remain, however, essentially embryonic developments – honorific gestures in recognition of the widened scope of community decision-making responsibilities, perhaps, but not changing the substance of that decision-making which could always count on civil service and expert economic advice prior to and in aid of decision, and certainly not, as a matter of constitutional law-in-action, bridging the gap between classical, liberal constitutionalism and the claimed new constitutional exigencies of the social welfare state.

THE ETHNOCENTRIC LIMITS TO CONSTITUTIONALISM

Is constitutionalism and the essentially western derived institutional models and practices in which it is historically rooted something that is peculiarly limited to western culture, in the sense that it cannot easily be exported to other, non-western societies with any reasonable prospects of its taking root there and becoming genuinely operational? All laws do reflect culture in certain measure, to the point that, within western constitutionalism itself, there are discernible differences of emphasis and degree between the English common law-derived and the continental European civil law-derived institutional models; and even within continental European civil law constitutionalism, the French experience shades off significantly from, for example, the German. We can meaningfully speak, therefore, of 'Anglo-Saxon' and continental European constitutional models, and, within these categories, of 'English' and 'American' models, and 'French,' 'German,' 'Swiss,' and 'Italian' models. The categories and sub-categories are the result of different national specialized legal and more general historical developments, and of differences in the timing and degree of 'reception' of original foreign legal elements – the Roman law, for example. To speak of an ethnic-cultural aspect to constitutionalism thus becomes meaningful and rational in this particular context. What is also true and demonstrable, however, in the light of comparative constitutional law experience, is that there is no necessary and inevitable ethnic-cultural barrier to the successful reception or transfer of particular constitutional institutions developed in the one society to another society, so long as the special social and economic and other basic historical conditions under which those institutions developed in the first society are already present in reasonable degree or at least can be expected to be present within a reasonable period of time in the second society. The special intellectual skills and aptitudes of the political élite group in the second, 'receiving' society are obviously crucial, of course. What is clear, in retrospect, is that some of the immediate, post-decolonization 'receptions' of constitutional institutions in newly independent Third World countries from the 'parent' European imperial powers – in the late 1940s, the 1950s, and the 1960s – were not particularly useful or scientific exercises in the sociology of law. Entered upon too hurriedly, perhaps, and undoubtedly in good faith, they sought to implant the institutions of essentially stable, politically bland, post-industrial societies in new countries that too often had not yet conquered the basic problems of mass education and that were still to go through even the earliest of stages of economic growth. There is something especially ironic in the attempt to export 'classical' federal constitutionalism – which requires, above all, enormous skills of pragmatism and political compromise for its continuingly successful operation, as recent Canadian experience shows – to the new, post-independence, multiracial societies of Asia, Africa, and the Caribbean. Strong executive decision-making was clearly needed to overcome the massive social and economic problems of the post-decolonization era, and the reconciliation with the strains and tensions of multi-culturalism required some more imaginative ventures in plural-constitutional models – perhaps drawing on earlier continental European models of plural-constitutional states where the institution of a strong central executive was maintained, by definition, as a condition of survival of the state. These post-decolonization classical federal states seemed to have failed rather more because of the weakness of their executive power than because of the centrifugal pressures of ethnic-cultural particularism, strong though these undoubtedly were. It is not surprising perhaps that Indian government, under Nehru and Madame Gandhi, though maintaining a British styled prime minister as the official head of government, evolved increasingly, at the level of constitutional law-in-action, into a 'strong executive,' presidential-type regime; or that Nigeria, having ended the disastrous Biafran Civil War with a military solution, should wind up the long period of post-war reconstruction by the adoption, in 1979, of an American presidential model, federal state. The attempt is there, in any case, to reconcile in constitutional form the twin, often directly competing imperatives of a strong central executive and the deference to regionally based, ethnic-cultural particularism. It is a change from the authoritarian 'Man-on-horseback' model of direct military rule; and the military leaders in Nigeria, in handing back civilian government on this basis, seem to have chosen a far more promising constitutional model for their present needs than the immediate post-decolonization, classical federal model (British Empire, polite export variety).

It remains to add that sometimes the post-decolonization, 'received' European constitutional charters for the new Asian and African countries seem to place too much emphasis on abstract civil and political rights, as such, and not enough on the correlative obligations of the citizen in what is, after all, in strictly juridical terms, a right-duty relationship. The expensive and sophisticated, special interests groups-based, constitutional litigation before the Supreme Court is a trademark of contemporary American and also much contemporary 'older' commonwealth constitutionalism. There are, however, in the United States and the 'older' commonwealth countries, enough countervailing social pressures upon the political processes to ensure that urgent community decisions are in fact made, in spite of any delays created by such litigation. Sometimes, however, in the post-decolonization constitutional development of certain new countries – India and Nigeria at certain periods of time, for example – one has the impression, almost, of a constitutional litigation neurosis, with too many lawyers invoking too many high prerogative writs to frustrate or obstruct executive or legislative decisions on pressing community problems. Perhaps, the necessary constitutional balance could be provided by a more effectively working, plural political party system and the discipline and mutual give and take that that implies; but in the absence of any evident widespread sense of political self-restraint as to rushing to the court house door to launch a guerilla war against decisions of the elected government, the temptations will be considerable, as post-decolonization commonwealth experience has shown, for those governments to by-pass the constitutional charter based guarantees and, if need be, the constitutional court system, by legislating by decree through invocation of a constitutional 'emergency powers' doctrines. The French constitutional charters, 'export variety,' for the post-decolonization societies of the former French Empire and French Union, seem to have by-passed very many of these special constitutional problems by going directly to a strong presidential executive – Gaullist-style, of course, after 1958, on the model of the Constitution of the Fifth French Republic.

THE POLITICAL LIMITS TO CONSTITUTIONALISM

This question takes us back directly to the nature of the political élite in any society, and its inherent problem-solving capacities. Some of the problems of post-decolonization constitution-making, in the Third World countries, clearly stemmed from the character of the 'succession' political élite to whom the parent European imperial state had handed over political sovereignty, and its representativeness, or lack of it, in nationwide terms, in the new succession state. Where the succession élite was drawn from only one geographical region of the new country, or from one dominant communal or tribal group, no amount of technical legal sophistication in constitutional drafting, and no federal charter, however carefully balanced in institutional terms, could expect to succeed in veiling the naked facts of power and to keep a basically non-representative constitutional system together in the face of all the centrifugal pressures.

On the other hand, the political élite and its political maturity and judgment can also be expected to be tested in the case of an existing constitutional system that has successfully met the test of time, over a considerable period of years. The task of decision-makers, in such case, is to maintain a continuing societal consensus in support of the constitutional system, by identifying points of social and economic tension in timely fashion and making appropriate balancing with other, countervailing interests, and adjusting the constitution accordingly. The problem-solving capacity of the élite consists in its ability to recognize social conflicts and to make the necessary political compromises and the correlative constitutional changes – *before* those conflicts reach a pathological stage involving resort to extra-constitutional, direct action.

The political limits to constitutionalism are thus a product of the two distinct elements, usually in mutual and reciprocal interaction: the constitutional system, as such – its degree of openness to new political ideas or ideologies, and also its intrinsic qualities of creative adjustment or change, without too much expenditure of energy or social cost, to rapidly changing societal expectations and demands – and the political élite – its ability to be seen as legitimate or representative, and also its inherent intellectual flexibility and ability to apprehend and respond to new problems in timely fashion. No constitutional charter could have, perhaps (to paraphrase a United States Supreme Court judge of yesteryear), saved Louis XVI or Marie Antoinette. On the other hand, no government, however intelligent and forward-looking and representatively established, can be expected to operate successfully with an archaic or rigid charter that imposes serious practical obstacles to much needed community decisions for change. Poland may well have been doomed, politically, in the late eighteenth century because of the pressures of external events, but the institution of the liberum veto certainly speeded it along the road to disaster.

A principal task and responsibility of a constitutional-governmental élite, therefore, becomes one of anticipating and correcting in advance the attrition or decay of the constitutional system. Constitutional systems must always include an in-built quality of change; and constitutionalism itself becomes not merely the substantive values written into the constitutional charter, but the actual processes of constitutional change themselves. That is why constitutional style – the respect for the constitutional rules of the game, and their respect in the spirit as well as in the letter – becomes so important in the ultimate evaluation of a constitutional system.

12

Some rules of constitutional-prudence for contemporary constitution-makers

The celebrated constitutionalist of the French Revolution, a priest with the developed political skills of survival in dangerous times, is known for his constitutional aphorisms, or general canons of wisdom for those charged by political leaders with the task of drafting a new constitutional charter. The Abbé Sieyès generalized against a background of his own personal, unusually rich and varied experience in constitution-making and constitutional drafting over the first decade of the Revolution, which produced four distinct and different constitutional charters, each intellectually well conceived and elaborated, in only eight years. The Abbé Sieyès' aphorisms were the product of direct, firsthand, trial-and-error experience. While that learning was certainly French, it was also eclectic since drawing very fully on the writers and philosophers – Montesquieu and Rousseau for example – and on foreign examples thought to be especially relevant in the French Revolutionary context of the 1790s – the American Declaration of Independence of 1776, the original Articles of Confederation of 1779, and, finally, the Constitution of the United States of 1787, adopted only two years before the outbreak of the French Revolution itself.

The canons of constitutional-prudence that follow are linked, by direct ties of consanguinity, to the Abbé Sieyès' aphorisms, but try to update and extend these in the light of all the empirical experience since the time of the French Revolution and in many seemingly disparate legal systems.

Rule 1 Keep the constitutional charter short. A constitution is neither a municipal ordinance on sewers and drains, nor a master planner's detailed blueprint for a new community welfare programme.

Rule 2 Keep the language of the charter clear and non-technical. The charter is intended to be read and understood by ordinary citizens, and not simply by constitutional specialists and supreme court judges.

Rule 3 Avoid flights of oratory in the constitutional charter. A constitution should not be made an excuse for a party *pronunciamento*, or, for that matter, for honorific gestures and 'complimentary expressions.'

Rule 4 Keep the charter neutral, or at least open-ended in political-ideological terms (particularly in bill of rights provisions). Otherwise the charter may become too closely identified with the transient fortunes of a particular political party or pressure group, and rise and fall with them.

Rule 5 Do not try to solve too many and too specific, purely temporary and short-range, problems in the charter. A constitution is not a railway excursion ticket, good for one journey only, on one particular day and to one particular place; but is intended to endure, if not for the ages then at least for a certain term of years.

Rule 6 Actual constitutional drafting is, in the end, a professional legal exercise. If the constitutional draughtsman does not himself have a direct political mandate – coming, for example, from his own direct popular election as a member of a constituent assembly – then he should be clear, always, as to the limits of his professional drafting mandate and, if necessary, seek fresh political instructions from the political arm of government. Constitution-making is not an excuse or licence for the constitutional drafter to go on a personal ego trip: he should respect his technical mandate and its political limits.

Rule 7 A pre-condition for any politically viable exercise in constitution-making is a prior political consensus – on the part of the society for which the constitutional charter is intended, or at least its dominant political élite – as to the main goal values and policies of that society for the future. If that prior societal consensus does not exist, the constitution-maker may have to exercise self-restraint and return his brief to the political decision-makers.

Rule 8 Where a sufficient, but not a substantial or comprehensive societal consensus exists – a tolerable accommodation or coexistence of the rival forces within the society – the constitution-maker may feel justified in going ahead nevertheless. In that case, he should resist all the temptations to try to draft the 'Sermon on the Mount,' but, instead, make an ally of time and operate modestly and limit himself to those constitutional areas where significant societal consensus does exist. This would suggest less a single constitutional charter, adopted in one blow, than a series of specific, and limited, organic acts adopted successively, and over a period of years, as the opportunity presents itself.

Rule 9 A constitutional charter should never try to act in vain or to legislate the politically or socially impossible. Do not make the constitutional charter so rigid or difficult to change by the ordinary modes of constitutional amendment that you invite people to try to change it by extra-constitutional means and direct action, or else to ignore it altogether.

Rule 10 Law cannot exist in isolation from society. The text of a constitutional charter should have a lapidarian quality, or in-built element of generality that facilitates its continuingly creative adaptation, through time (by judicial interpretation and executive-administrative application – apart from formal amendment), to changing societal needs and expectations.

Rule 11 Be cautious in your borrowings from other constitutional systems, developed for other societies. Remember the principle of the non-transferability of constitutional institutions. What works beautifully in another society may turn out very badly, or at least quite differently and unexpectedly, when translated to your own society, since the underlying political, social, and economic conditions may be quite different between that other society and your own.

Rule 12 Even seemingly limited, piecemeal constitutional change may have far-reaching and unexpected consequences within a constitutional system. Remember the principle of the interdependence of constitutional institutions. Transform any one institution and you have to expect reciprocal effects and interactions upon the other institutions of government and the system of constitutional checks and balances generally.

Rule 13 Don't forget the *extra*-constitutional rules that effectively condition or limit the application of a constitutional charter. Change in a society's basic electoral system and electoral laws may be at least as important as change in any of the key governmental institutions (executive, legislature, or judiciary) in building or maintaining democratic constitutionalism. It may also, according to the principle of the 'digestibility' of proposals for constitutional change, be more than enough for any society that is already a going concern to absorb fully and successfully into its existing constitutional system at any one time.

Rule 14 Do not place too great a 'Trust for Salvation' in constitutional drafters. No constitutional charter can save a sick society! Always take into account the human element in constitutional decision-making and application. Drafting a new constitutional charter can never be a substitute for wise political action – the exercise of the ordinary skills of political compromise, and respect for the constitutional 'rules of the game.'

Rule 15 Where, as in the case of a newly independent, developing country or a one-party state, political exigencies may dictate the adoption of a didactic, programmatic constitutional charter, it would seem prudent to separate the postulation of ideological objectives, which are normally either quickly achieved or else quickly overtaken by events and historically dated, from the establishment of the institutional machinery and processes and procedures of government which, in contrast, are likely to have more long-range operation and utility. This can sensibly be achieved by enacting the general principles or programme in their own special statute, separate and distinct from the charter defining the politically more neutral, machinery provisions of the constitution.

Appendix

Extracts from major constitutional charters

United States of America
Articles of Confederation (drafted 1777, ratified 1781)
Constitution of the United States of America (adopted 1787)

France
Declaration of the Right of Man and the Citizen (26 August 1789; incorporated in the constitution of 1791; adopted again by the Preambles of 1946 (Fourth Republic) and 1958 (Fifth Republic))
Constitution of the Fifth Republic (4 October 1958)

Germany
Constitution of the German Reich (Weimar Constitution, 11 August 1919)
Basic Law of the Federal Republic of Germany (23 May 1949)

Japan
Constitution of Japan (promulgated 3 November 1946)

India
Constitution of India (adopted 26 November 1949, entered into force 26 January 1950)

Soviet Union
Constitution (Basic Law) of the Union of Soviet Socialist Republics (published 8 October 1977)

China
Constitution of the People's Republic of China (adopted 5 March 1978)

European Communities
Treaty of Rome (signed 25 March 1957, entered into force 1 January 1958)

United States of America

Articles of Confederation (drafted 1777; ratified 1781)

THE ARTICLES OF CONFEDERATION AND PERPETUAL UNION

BETWEEN THE STATES OF NEW HAMPSHIRE, MASSACHUSETTS BAY, RHODE ISLAND AND PROVIDENCE PLANTATIONS, CONNECTICUT, NEW YORK, NEW JERSEY, PENNSYLVANIA, DELAWARE, MARYLAND, VIRGINIA, NORTH CAROLINA, SOUTH CAROLINA, GEORGIA

Article 1 The style of this confederacy shall be 'The United States of America.'

Article 2 Each State retains its sovereignty, freedom and independence, and every power, jurisdiction, and right, which is not by this confederation expressly delegated to the United States, in Congress assembled.

Article 3 The said states hereby severally enter into a firm league of friendship with each other for their common defence, the security of their liberties and their mutual and general welfare; binding themselves to assist each other against all force offered to, or attacks made upon them, or any of them, on account of religion, sovereignty, trade, or any other pretence whatever.

Article 4 The better to secure and perpetuate mutual friendship and intercourse among the people of the different states in this union, the free inhabitants of each of these states, paupers, vagabonds, and fugitives from justice excepted, shall be entitled to all privileges and immunities of free citizens in the several states; and the people of each State shall have free ingress and regress to and from any other State, and shall enjoy therein all the privileges of trade and commerce, subject to the same duties, impositions, and restrictions, as the inhabitants thereof respectively; provided, that such restrictions shall not extend so far as to prevent the removal of property, imported into any State, to any other State of which the owner is an inhabitant; provided also, that no imposition, duties, or restriction, shall be laid by any State on the property of the United States, or either of them.

If any person guilty of, or charged with treason, felony, or other high misdemeanor in any State, shall flee from justice and be found in any of the

United States, he shall, upon demand of the governor or executive power of the State from which he fled, be delivered up and removed to the State having jurisdiction of his offence.

Full faith and credit shall be given in each of these states to the records, acts, and judicial proceedings of the courts and magistrates of every other State.

Article 5 For the more convenient management of the general interests of the United States, delegates shall be annually appointed, in such manner as the legislature of each State shall direct, to meet in Congress, on the 1st Monday in November in every year, with a power reserved to each State to recall its delegates, or any of them, at any time within the year, and to send others in their stead for the remainder of the year.

No State shall be represented in Congress by less than two, nor by more than seven members, and no person shall be capable of being a delegate for more than three years in any term of six years; nor shall any person, being a delegate, be capable of holding any office under the United States, for which he, or any other for his benefit, receives any salary, fees, or emolument of any kind.

Each State shall maintain its own delegates in a meeting of the states, and while they act as members of the committee of the states.

In determining questions in the United States, in Congress assembled, each State shall have one vote.

Freedom of speech and debate in Congress shall not be impeached or questioned in any court or place out of Congress: and the members of Congress shall be protected in their persons from arrests and imprisonments, during the time of their going to and from, and attendance on Congress, *except for treason*, felony, or breach of the peace.

Article 6 No State, without the consent of the United States, in Congress assembled, shall send any embassy to, or receive any embassy from, or enter into any conference, agreement, alliance, or treaty with any king, prince, or state, nor shall any person, holding any office of profit or trust under the United States, or any of them, accept of any present, emolument, office or title, of any kind whatever, from any king, prince, or foreign state; nor shall the United States, in Congress assembled, or any of them, grant any title of nobility.

No two or more states shall enter into any treaty, confederation, or alliance, whatever, between them, without the consent of the United States, in Congress assembled, specifying accurately the purposes for which the same is to be entered into, and how long it shall continue.

No state shall lay any imposts or duties which may interfere with any stipulations in treaties entered into by the United States, in Congress assembled, with any king, prince, or state, in pursuance of any treaties already proposed by Congress to the courts of France and Spain.

No vessels of war shall be kept up in time of peace by any State, except such number only as shall be deemed necessary by the United States, in Congress assembled, for the defence of such State or its trade; nor shall any body of forces be kept up by any State, in time of peace, except such number only as, in the judgment of the United States, in Congress assembled, shall be deemed requisite to garrison the forts necessary for the defence of such State; but every State shall always keep up a well regulated and disciplined militia, sufficiently armed and accoutred, and shall provide, and constantly have ready for use, in public stores, a due number of field pieces and tents, and a proper quantity of arms, ammunition and camp equipage.

No State shall engage in any war without the consent of the United States, in Congress assembled, unless such State be actually invaded by enemies, or shall have received certain advice of a resolution being formed by some nation of Indians to invade such State, and the danger is so imminent as not to admit of a delay till the United States, in Congress assembled, can be consulted; nor shall any State grant commissions to any ships or vessels of war, nor letters of marque or reprisal, except it be after a declaration of war by the United States, in Congress assembled, and then only against the kingdom or state, and the subjects thereof, against which war has been so declared, and under such regulations as shall be established by the United States, in Congress assembled, unless such State be infested by pirates, in which case vessels of war may be fitted out for that occasion, and kept so long as the danger shall continue, or until the United States, in Congress assembled, shall determine otherwise.

Article 7 When land forces are raised by any State for the common defence, all officers of or under the rank of colonel, shall be appointed by the legislature of each State respectively, by whom such forces shall be raised, or in such manner as such State shall direct; and all vacancies shall be filled up by the State which first made the appointment.

Article 8 All charges of war and all other expenses, that shall be incurred for the common defence or general welfare, and allowed by the United States, in Congress assembled, shall be defrayed out of a common treasury, which shall be supplied by the several states, in proportion to the value of all land within each State, granted to or surveyed for any person, as such land and the buildings and improvements thereon shall be estimated according to such mode as the United States, in Congress assembled, shall, from time to time, direct and appoint.

The taxes for paying that proportion shall be laid and levied by the authority and direction of the legislatures of the several states, within the time agreed upon by the United States, in Congress assembled.

Article 9 The United States, in Congress assembled, shall have the sole and exclusive right and power of determining on peace and war, except in the cases mentioned in the 6th article; of sending and receiving ambassadors; entering into treaties and alliances, provided that no treaty of commerce shall be made, whereby the legislative power of the respective states shall be restrained from imposing such imposts and duties on foreigners as their own people are subjected to, or from prohibiting the exportation or importation of any species of goods or commodities whatsoever; of establishing rules for deciding, in all cases, what captures on land or water shall be legal, and in what manner prizes, taken by land or naval forces in the service of the United States, shall be divided or appropriated; of granting letters of marque and reprisal in times of peace; appointing courts for the trial of piracies and felonies committed on the high seas, and establishing courts for receiving and determining, finally, appeals in all cases of captures; provided, that no member of Congress shall be appointed a judge of any of the said courts.

The United States, in Congress assembled, shall also be the last resort on appeal in all disputes and differences now subsisting, or that hereafter may arise between two or more states concerning boundary, jurisdiction or any other cause whatever; which authority shall always be exercised in the manner following: whenever the legislative or executive authority, or lawful agent of any State, in controversy with another, shall present a petition to Congress, stating the matter in question, and praying for a hearing, notice thereof shall be given, by order of Congress, to the legislative or executive authority of the other State in controversy, and a day assigned for the appearance of the parties by their lawful agents, who shall then be directed to appoint, by joint consent, commissioners or judges to constitute a court for hearing and determining the matter in question; but, if they cannot agree, Congress shall name three persons out of each of the United States, and from the list of such persons each party shall alternately strike out one, the petitioners beginning, until the number shall be reduced to thirteen; and from that number not less than seven, nor more than nine names, as Congress shall direct, shall, in the presence of Congress, be drawn out by lot; and the persons whose names shall be so drawn, or any five of them, shall be commissioners or judges to hear and finally determine the controversy, so always as a major part of the judges who shall hear the cause shall agree in the determination; and if either party shall neglect to attend at the day appointed, without shewing reasons which Congress shall judge sufficient, or, being present, shall refuse to strike, the Congress shall proceed to nominate three persons out of each State, and the secretary of Congress shall strike in behalf of such party absent or refusing; and the judgment and sentence of the court to be appointed, in the manner before prescribed, shall be final and conclusive, and if any of the parties shall refuse to submit to the authority of such court, or to appear or defend their claim or cause, the court shall nevertheless proceed to pronounce sentence or judgment, which shall, in like manner, be final and decisive, the judgment or sentence and other proceedings being, in either case, transmitted to Congress, and lodged among the acts of Congress for the security of the parties concerned: provided, that every commissioner, before he sits in judgment, shall take an oath, to be administered by one of the judges of the supreme or superior court of the State where the cause shall be tried, 'well and truly to hear and determine the matter in question, according to the best of his judgment, without favour, affection, or hope of reward:' provided, also, that no State shall be deprived of territory for the benefit of the United States ...

The United States, in Congress assembled, shall also have the sole and exclusive right and power of regulating the alloy and value of coin struck by their own authority, or by that of the respective states; fixing the standard of weights and measures throughout the United States; regulating the trade and managing all affairs with the Indians not members of any of the states; provided that the legislative right of any State within its own limits be not infringed or violated; establishing and regulating post offices from one State to another throughout all the United States, and exacting such postage on the papers passing through the same as may be requisite to defray the expenses of the said office; appointing all officers of the land forces in the service of the United States, excepting regimental officers; appointing all the officers of the naval forces, and commissioning all officers whatever in the service of the United States; making rules for the government and regulation of the said land and naval forces, and directing their operations.

The United States, in Congress assembled, shall have authority to appoint a committee to sit in the recess of Congress, to be denominated 'a Committee of the States,' and to consist of one delegate from each State, and to appoint such other committees and civil officers as may be necessary for managing the general affairs of the United States, under their direction; to appoint one of their number to preside; provided that no person be allowed to serve in the office of president more than one year in any term of three years; to ascertain the necessary sums of money to be raised for the service of the United States, and to appropriate and apply the same for defraying the public expenses; to borrow money or emit bills on the credit of the United States, transmitting, every half year, to the respective states, an account of the sums of money so borrowed or emitted; to build and equip a navy; to agree upon the number of land forces, and to make requisitions from each State for its quota, in proportion to the number of white inhabitants in such State; which requisitions shall be binding; and, thereupon, the legislature of each State shall appoint the regimental officers, raise the men, and clothe, arm, and equip them in a soldier-like manner, at the expense of the United States ...

The United States, in Congress assembled, shall never engage in a war, nor grant letters of marque and reprisal in time of peace, nor enter into any treaties or alliances, nor coin money, nor regulate the value thereof, nor ascertain the sums and expences necessary for the defence and welfare of the United States, or any of them: nor emit bills, nor borrow money on the credit of the United States, nor appropriate money, nor agree upon the number of vessels of war to be built or purchased, or the number of land or sea forces to be raised, nor appoint a commander in chief of the army or navy, unless nine states assent to the same; nor shall a question on any other point, except for adjourning from day to day, be determined, unless by the votes of a majority of the United States, in Congress assembled.

The Congress of the United States shall have power to adjourn to any time within the year, and to any place within the United States, so that no period of adjournment be for a longer duration than the space of six months, and shall publish the journal of their proceedings monthly; except such parts thereof, relating to treaties, alliances or military operations, as, in their judgment, require secrecy; and the yeas and nays of the delegates of each State on any question shall be entered on the journal, when it is desired by any delegate; and the delegates of a State, or any of them, at his, or their request, shall be furnished with a transcript of the said journal, except such parts as are above excepted, to lay before the legislatures of the several states.

Article 10 The committee of the states, or any nine of them, shall be authorized to execute, in the recess of Congress, such of the powers of Congress as the United States, in Congress assembled, by the consent of nine states, shall, from time to time, think expedient to vest them with; provided, that no power be delegated to the said committee, for the exercise of which, by the articles of confederation, the voice of nine states, in the Congress of the United States assembled, is requisite.

Article 11 Canada acceding to this confederation, and joining in the measures of the United States, shall be admitted into and entitled to all the advantages of this union; but no other colony shall be admitted into the same, unless such admission be agreed to by nine states.

Article 12 All bills of credit emitted, monies borrowed and debts contracted by, or under the authority of Congress before the assembling of the United States, in pursuance of the present confederation, shall be deemed and considered as a charge against the United States, for payment and satisfaction whereof the said United States and the public faith are hereby solemnly pledged.

Article 13 Every State shall abide by the determinations of the United States, in Congress assembled, on all questions which, by this confederation, are submitted to them. And the articles of this confederation shall be inviolably observed by every State, and the union shall be perpetual; nor shall any alteration at any time hereafter be made in any of them, unless such alteration be agreed to in a Congress of the United States, and be afterwards confirmed by the legislatures of every State.

These articles shall be proposed to the legislatures of all the United States, to be considered, and if approved of by them, they are advised to authorize their delegates to ratify the same in the Congress of the United States; which being done, the same shall become conclusive.

Constitution of the United States of America (adopted 1787)

PREAMBLE

We the People of the United States, in order to form a more perfect Union, establish justice, ensure domestic tranquility, provide for the common defense, promote the general welfare, and secure the blessings of liberty to ourselves and our posterity, do ordain and establish this Constitution for the United States of America.

Article I
Section 1 All legislative powers herein granted shall be vested in a Congress of the United States, which shall consist of a Senate and House of Representatives.

Section 2 The House of Representatives shall be composed of members chosen every second year by the people of the several States, and the electors in each State shall have the qualifications requisite for electors of the most numerous branch of the State Legislature ...

Section 3 The Senate of the United States shall be composed of two senators from each State, chosen by the legislature thereof, for six years and each senator shall have one vote ...

Section 8 The Congress shall have power to lay and collect taxes, duties, imposts and excises, to pay the debts and provide for the common defense and general welfare of the United States; but all duties, imposts and excise shall be uniform throughout the United States;

To borrow money on the credit of the United States;

To regulate commerce with foreign nations and among the several States, and with the Indian tribes;

To establish a uniform rule of naturalization, and uniform laws on the subject of bankruptcies throughout the United States;

To coin money, regulate the value thereof, and of foreign coin, and fix the standard of weights and measures;

To provide for the punishment of counterfeiting the securities and current coin of the United States;

To establish post offices and post roads;

To promote the progress of science and useful arts, by securing for limited times to authors and inventors the exclusive right to their respective writings and discoveries;

To constitute tribunals inferior to the Supreme Court;

To define and punish piracies and felonies committed on the high seas, and offenses against the law of nations;

To declare war, grant letters of marque and reprisal, and make rules concerning captures on land and water;

To raise and support armies, but no appropriation of money to that use shall be for a longer term than two years;

To provide and maintain a Navy;

To make rules for the government and regulation of the land and naval forces;

To provide for calling forth the militia to execute the laws of the Union, suppress insurrections and repel invasions ...

Article II

Section 1 The executive power shall be vested in a President of the United States of America. He shall hold his office during the term of four years, and, together with the Vice President, chosen for the same term, be elected, as follows ...

Section 2 The President shall be Commander in Chief of the Army and Navy of the United States, and of the militia of the several States, when called into the actual service of the United States; he may require opinion, in writing, of the principal officer in each of the Executive Departments, upon any subject relating to the duties of their respective offices, and he shall have power to grant reprieves and pardons for offenses against the United States, except in cases of impeachment.

He shall have power, by and with the advice and consent of the Senate, to make treaties, provided two-thirds of the Senators present concur; and he shall nominate, and by and with the advice and consent of the Senate, shall appoint ambassadors, other public ministers and consuls, judges of the Supreme Court, and all other officers of the United States, whose appointments are not herein otherwise provided for, and which shall be established by law: but the Congress may by law vest the appointment of such inferior officers, as they think proper, in the President alone, in the courts of law, or in the heads of departments ...

Section 4 The President, Vice President and all civil officers of the United States, shall be removed from office on impeachment for, and conviction of, treason, bribery, or other high crimes and misdemeanors.

Article III
Section 1 The judicial power of the United States shall be vested in one Supreme Court, and in such inferior courts as the Congress may from time to time ordain and establish. The judges, both of the supreme and inferior courts, shall hold their offices during good behavior, and shall, at stated times, receive for their services, a compensation, which shall not be diminished during their continuance in office ...

Article V
The Congress, whenever two-thirds of both Houses shall deem it necessary, shall propose amendments to this Constitution, or, on the application of the legislatures of two-thirds of the several States, shall call a convention for proposing amendments, which, in either case, shall be valid to all intents and purposes, as part of this Constitution, when ratified by the legislatures of three-fourths of the several States, or by conventions in three-fourths thereof, as the one or the other mode of ratification may be proposed by the Congress; provided that no amendment which may be made prior to the year one thousand eight hundred and eight shall in any

manner affect the first and fourth clauses in the Ninth Section of the First Article; and that no State, without its consent, shall be deprived of its equal suffrage in the Senate.

AMENDMENTS

Amendment I
Congress shall make no law respecting an establishment of religion, or prohibiting the free exercise thereof; or abridging the freedom of speech, or of the press; or the right of the people peaceably to assemble, and to petition the Government for a redress of grievances. [adopted 1791]

Amendment V
No person shall be held to answer for a capital, or otherwise infamous crime, unless on a presentment or indictment of a grand jury, except in cases arising in the land or naval forces, or in the militia, when in actual service in time of war or public danger; nor shall any person be subject for the same offense to be twice put in jeopardy of life or limb; nor shall be compelled in any criminal case to be witness against himself, nor be deprived of life, liberty, or property, without due process of law; nor shall private property be taken for public use, without just compensation. [adopted 1791]

Amendment X
The powers not delegated to the United States by the Constitution, nor prohibited by it to the States, are reserved to the States respectively, or to the people. [adopted 1791]

Amendment XIII
Section 1 Neither slavery nor involuntary servitude, except as a punishment for crime whereof the party shall have been duly convicted, shall exist within the United States, or any place subject to their jurisdiction.
Section 2 Congress shall have power to enforce this article by appropriate legislation. [adopted 1865]

Amendment XIV
Section 1 All persons born or naturalized in the United States, and subject to the jurisdiction thereof, are citizens of the United States and of the State wherein they reside. No State shall make or enforce any law which shall abridge the privileges or immunities of citizens of the United States;

nor shall any State deprive any person of life, liberty, or property, without due process of law; nor deny to any person within its jurisdiction the equal protection of the laws.

Section 2 Representatives shall be apportioned among the several States according to their respective numbers, counting the whole number of persons in each State, excluding Indians not taxed. But when the right to vote at any election for the choice of electors for President and Vice President of the United States, Representatives in Congress, the executive and judicial officers of a State, or the members of the legislature thereof, is denied to any of the male inhabitants of such State, being twenty-one years of age, and citizens of the United States, or in any way abridged, except for participation in rebellion, or other crime, the basis of representation therein shall be reduced in the proportion which the number of such male citizens shall bear to the whole number of male citizens twenty-one years of age in such State.

Section 3 No person shall be a Senator or Representative in Congress, or elector of President and Vice President, or hold any office, civil or military, under the United States, or under any State, who, having previously taken an oath, as a member of Congress, or as an officer of the United States, or as a member of any State legislature, or as an executive or judicial officer of any State, to support the Constitution of the United States shall have engaged in insurrection or rebellion against the same, or given aid or comfort to the enemies thereof. But Congress may by a vote of two-thirds of each house, remove such disability.

Section 4 The validity of the public debt of the United States, authorized by law, including debts incurred for payment of pensions and bounties for services in suppressing insurrection or rebellion, shall not be questioned. But neither the United States nor any State shall assume or pay any debt or obligation incurred in aid of insurrection or rebellion against the United States, or any claim for the loss or emancipation of any slave; but all such debts, obligations and claims shall be held illegal and void.

Section 5 The Congress shall have power to enforce, by appropriate legislation, the provisions of this article. [adopted 1868]

Amendment XV
Section 1 The right of citizens of the United States to vote shall not be denied or abridged by the United States or by any State on account of race, color, or previous condition of servitude.

Section 2 The Congress shall have power to enforce this article by appropriate legislation. [adopted 1870]

Amendment XVI
The Congress shall have power to lay and collect taxes on incomes, from whatever source derived, without apportionment among the several States, and without regard to census or enumeration. [adopted 1913]

Amendment XVII
Section 1 The Senate of the United States shall be composed of two senators from each State, elected by the people thereof, for six years, and each senator shall have one vote. The electors in each State shall have the qualifications requisite for electors of the most numerous branch of the State legislatures ... [adopted 1913]

Amendment XVIII
Section 1 After one year from the ratification of this article the manufacture, sale, or transportation of intoxicating liquors within, the importation thereof into, or the exportation thereof from the United States and all territory subject to the jurisdiction thereof for beverage purposes is hereby prohibited.
Section 2 The Congress and the several States shall have concurrent power to enforce this article by appropriate legislation.
Section 3 This article shall be inoperative unless it shall have been ratified as an amendment to the Constitution by the legislatures of the several States, as provided in the Constitution, within seven years from the date of the submission hereof to the States by the Congress. [adopted 1919]

Amendment XIX
Section 1 The right of citizens of the United States to vote shall not be denied or abridged by the United States or by any State on account of sex.
Section 2 Congress shall have power to enforce this article by appropriate legislation. [adopted 1920]

Amendment XXI
Section 1 The eighteenth article of amendment to the Constitution of the United States is hereby repealed.
Section 2 The transportation or importation into any State, Territory, or possession of the United States for delivery or use therein of intoxicating liquors, in violation of the laws thereof, is hereby prohibited.
Section 3 This article shall be inoperative unless it shall have been ratified as an amendment to the Constitution by convention in the several States,

as provided in the Constitution, within seven years from the date of the submission hereof to the States by the Congress. [adopted 1933]

Amendment XXIV
The right of citizens of the United States to vote in any primary or other election for President or Vice President, for electors for President or Vice President, or for Senator or Representative in Congress, shall not be denied or abridged by the United States or any State for reason of failure to pay any Poll Tax or other Tax. [adopted 1964]

France

Declaration of the Rights of Man and the Citizen (26 August 1789; placed at the head of the Constitution of 1791; put into force again by the Preambles of the Constitutions of 1946 (Fourth Republic) and 1958 (Fifth Republic))

The representatives of the French people, constituted in National Assembly, considering that ignorance, forgetfulness, or mistake as to the rights of man are the sole causes of the public misfortunes and the corruption of governments, have resolved to set out, in a solemn declaration, the natural, inalienable, and sacred rights of man, in order that this declaration, constantly present in the minds of all members of society, will recall to them unceasingly their rights and their duties; in order that the acts of legislative power and executive power, being capable at every moment of being compared with the goal of every political institution, may thus be more respected; in order that the claims of citizens, founded henceforward on simple and uncontestable principles, will turn always to the maintenance of the Constitution and to the common good, – in consequence, the National Assembly recognises and declares, in the presence and under the auspices of the Supreme Being, the following rights of man and of Citizen.

Article 1 Men are born free and remain free and equal in their rights. Social distinctions can only be founded on the general utility.

Article 2 The goal of every political association is the preservation of the natural and imprescriptible rights of man. These rights are liberty, property, security, and resistance to oppression.

Article 3 The principle of all sovereignty resides essentially in the Nation ...

Article 4 Liberty consists in being able to do everything that does not harm another; thus, the exercise of the natural rights of each man has only those limits that assure to the other members of society the enjoyment of the same rights ...

Article 5 The law has the right to forbid only those actions harmful to society ...

Article 6 The law is the expression of the general will ...

Article 7 No man can be accused, arrested, or detained except in the cases established by law and according to the forms it has prescribed ...

Article 9 Every man [is] presumed innocent until he has been declared guilty ...

Article 10 No one may be pursued on account of his opinions, even religious opinions, provided their manifestation does not trouble the public order established by law.

Article 11 The free communication of thoughts and opinions is one of the most precious rights of man; every citizen can thus speak, write, and print freely ...

Article 15 Society has the right to demand an accounting from every public official as to his administration.

Article 16 Every society in which the guarantee of rights is not assured, nor the separation of powers established, has no constitution at all.

Article 17 Property being an inviolable and sacred right, no one can be deprived of it, save when the public need, legally established, clearly requires it, and on condition then of a just compensation paid in advance.

Constitution of the Fifth Republic of 4 October 1958

Preamble The French people solemnly proclaim their attachment to the Rights of Man and to the principles of national sovereignty as defined by the Declaration of 1789, confirmed and completed by the Preamble to the Constitution of 1946 ...

Article 2 France is an indivisible, lay (secular), democratic and social Republic. It ensures the equality before the law of all citizens without distinction as to origin, race or religion. It respects all beliefs ...

Article 5 The President of the Republic ensures respect for the Constitution. He provides, by his arbitration, the regular functioning of the public authorities as well as the continuity of the State.

He is the protector of national independence, of territorial integrity, of respect for Community agreements and for treaties.

Article 6 (as amended by the Law of 6 November 1962) The President of the Republic is elected for seven years by universal direct suffrage ...

Article 8 The President of the Republic names the Prime Minister. He puts an end to his period of office on the presentation by the Prime Minister of the resignation of the Government.

He names the other members of the Government on the proposal of the Prime Minister.

Article 9 The President of the Republic presides over the Cabinet.

Article 11 On the proposal of the Government during Parliamentary sessions or on the joint proposal of the two Chambers of Parliament, published in the *Journal officiel*, the President of the Republic can submit to Referendum every Bill bearing on the organisation of the public authorities, involving approval of a Community agreement or tending to authorise the ratification of a treaty which, without being contrary to the Constitution, would have effects on the functioning of institutions.

When the Referendum has approved the adoption of the Bill, the President of the Republic promulgates it ...

Article 12 The President of the Republic can, after consulting the Prime Minister and the presidents of the two Chambers of Parliament, pronounce the dissolution of the National Assembly (lower Chamber). The general elections take place at least twenty days and not more than forty days after the dissolution.

Article 47 Parliament votes Finance Bills according to the conditions established in an organic law ...

If Parliament has reached no decision within seventy days, the provisions of the Bill may be put into force by Ordinance.

If the Finance Bill determining revenue and expenditures for the financial year has not been introduced in time to be promulgated before the beginning of the financial year, the Government asks Parliament, as a matter of urgency, for authorisation to levy the taxes and allocates by decree the credits relating to the estimates already approved ...

Article 49 The Prime Minister, after Cabinet deliberation, engages the Confidence of the Government before the National Assembly (lower Chamber), on its programme or eventually on a declaration of general policy.

The National Assembly challenges Confidence in the Government by adopting a motion of censure. A censure motion is only in order if it is signed by at least one tenth of the members of the National Assembly. The vote may not take place until forty-eight hours after its introduction. Only votes in favour of the motion of censure are counted, and it can only be adopted if it receives the votes of a majority of the members of the Assembly ...

The Prime Minister can, after deliberation of the Cabinet, engage the Confidence of the Government before the National Assembly on the vote on a text of a Bill. In this case, the text is considered as adopted unless a censure motion, introduced within the next twenty four hours, is adopted in the conditions set out in the preceding paragraph ...

Article 50 When the National Assembly passes a motion of censure or when it rejects the Government's programme or a declaration of general policy of the Government, the Prime Minister must submit the Government's resignation to the President of the Republic.

Article 54 If the Constitutional Council, when its jurisdiction has been invoked by the President of the Republic, by the Prime Minister or by the president of one or other Assembly (Chamber), has declared that an international agreement includes a clause contrary to the Constitution, the authorisation to ratify it or to approve it cannot take place except after amendment of the Constitution.

Article 56 The Constitutional Council is composed of nine members whose mandate lasts for nine years and is not renewable. The Constitutional Council's membership is renewed by thirds every three years. Three of its members are named by the President of the Republic, three by the president of the National Assembly (lower Chamber), three by the president of the Senate.

Over and above the nine members provided for above, former Presidents of the Republic are *ex officio* life members of the Constitutional Council.

The president is named by the President of the Republic. He has a casting vote in case of a tie vote.

Article 61 Organic laws before their promulgation, and the rules of procedure of the Parliamentary assemblies before their coming into force, must be submitted to the Constitutional Council which pronounces on their conformity to the Constitution.

– (As amended, 1974) For the same purposes, ordinary laws can be submitted to the Constitutional Council, before their promulgation, by the President of the Republic, the Prime Minister, the president of the National Assembly (lower Chamber), the president of the Senate or sixty deputies (members of the National Assembly) or sixty Senators.

In the cases envisaged in the two preceding paragraphs, the Constitutional Council must decide within one month. However, on the request of the Government, if it is a matter of urgency, this period is reduced to eight days ...

Article 89 The right to propose the amendment of the Constitution belongs concurrently to the President of the Republic on the proposal of the Prime Minister and to the members of Parliament.

The amending project or proposal must be voted by the two parliamentary Assemblies in identical terms. The amendment becomes effective after it has been approved by Referendum.

However, the project of amendment is not presented to the Referendum when the President of the Republic decides to submit it to Parliament meeting as a Congress; in this case the project of amendment is not approved unless it obtains a three fifths majority of the votes cast ...

The republican form of government is not open to amendment.

Germany

Constitution of the German Reich (Weimar Constitution) of 11 August 1919

Preamble The German people, at one in its roots, and inspired by its will to renew and consolidate its Reich in freedom and justice and to serve internal and external peace and to promote social progress, has given itself this Constitution.

Article 1 The German Reich is a Republic. The State authority stems from the people.

Article 4 The general, recognised rules of International Law are valid as binding components of German Reich law.

Article 25 The President of the Reich can dissolve the Reichstag (National Assembly), but only once for the same cause. The new elections take place, at the latest, sixty days after the dissolution.

Article 41 The President of the Reich is elected by all the German people ...

Article 43 The office of Reich President lasts seven years. Reelection is permitted ...

Article 48 If a Province (Land) does not fulfil the obligations placed upon it by the Constitution of the Reich or by statutes of the Reich, the Reich President can hold it to those obligations with the aid of the armed forces.

If public safety and order in the German Reich are materially disturbed or endangered, the Reich President can undertake the necessary measures for the restoration of public safety and order, if necessary intervening with the aid of the armed forces. To this end he may temporarily suspend, wholly or in part, the basic rights established in Articles 114 (personal freedom), 115 (inviolability of the home), 117 (secrecy of letters and communications), 118 (freedom of expression), 123 (freedom of assembly), 124 (freedom of association), and 153 (right to private property) of the Constitution.

The Reich President must immediately inform the Reichstag (National Assembly) of all measures adopted under (such) authority. The measures are to be revoked on the demand of the Reichstag.

Article 53 The Chancellor of the Reich and, on his proposal, the Reich Ministers are appointed and dismissed by the Reich President.

Article 54 The Reich Chancellor and the Reich Ministers require, for their continuance in office, the confidence of the Reichstag. They must resign if the Reichstag, by express resolution, withdraws its confidence.

Basic Law of the Federal Republic of Germany of 23 May 1949

Preamble
The German People
in the Laender of Baden*, Bavaria, Bremen, Hamburg, Hesse, Lower Saxony, North Rhine-Westphalia, Rhineland-Palatinate, Schleswig-Holstein, Wuerttemberg-Baden* and Wuerttemberg-Hohenzollern*,
Conscious of their responsibility before God and men,
Animated by the resolve to preserve their national and political unity and to serve the peace of the world as an equal partner in a united Europe,
Desiring to give a new order to political life for a transitional period,
Have enacted, by virtue of their constituent power, this Basic Law for the Federal Republic of Germany.
They have also acted on behalf of those Germans to whom participation was denied.
The entire German people are called upon to achieve in free self-determination the unity and freedom of Germany.
[Baden, Wuerttemberg-Baden, and Wuerttemberg-Hohenzollern were amalgamated by federal law of 4 May 1951.]

II / THE FEDERATION AND THE CONSTITUENT STATES

Article 20 (Basic principles of the Constitution – Right to resist)
1 The Federal Republic of Germany is a democratic and social federal state.
2 All state authority emanates from the people. It shall be exercised by the people by means of elections and voting and by specific legislative, executive, and judicial organs.
3 Legislation shall be subject to the constitutional order; the executive and the judiciary shall be bound by law and justice.
4* All Germans shall have the right to resist any person or persons seeking to abolish that constitutional order, should no other remedy be possible.
[inserted by federal law of 24 June 1968]

Article 21 (Political parties)
1 The political parties shall participate in the forming of the political will of the people. They may be freely established. Their internal organization must conform to democratic principles. They must publicly account for the sources of their funds.

2 Parties which, by reason of their aims or the behaviour of their adherents, seek to impair or abolish the free democratic basic order or to endanger the existence of the Federal Republic of Germany, shall be unconstitutional. The Federal Constitutional Court shall decide on the question of unconstitutionality.
3 Details shall be regulated by federal laws.

Article 25 (International law integral part of federal law)
The general rules of public international law shall be an integral part of federal law. They shall take precedence over the laws and shall directly create rights and duties for the inhabitants of the federal territory.

Article 28 (Federal guarantee of Laender constitutions)
1 The constitutional order in the Laender must conform to the principles of republican, democratic and social government based on the rule of law, within the meaning of this Basic Law. In each of the Laender, counties (Kreise), and communes (Gemeinden), the people must be represented by a body chosen in general, direct, free, equal, and secret elections. In the communes the assembly of the commune may take the place of an elected body.
2 The communes must be guaranteed the right to regulate on their own responsibility all the affairs of the local community within the limits set by law. The associations of communes (Gemeindeverbaende) shall also have the right of self-government in accordance with the law and within the limits of the functions assigned to them by law.
3 The Federation shall ensure that the constitutional order of the Laender conforms to the basic rights and to the provisions of paragraphs 1 and 2 of this Article.

Article 29* (Reorganization of the federal territory)
[as amended, 23 August 1976]
1 The federal territory may be reorganized to ensure that the Laender by their size and capacity are able effectively to fulfil the functions incumbent upon them. Due regard shall be given to regional, historical and cultural ties, economic expediency, regional policy, and the requirements of town and country planning.
2 Measures for the reorganization of the federal territory shall be introduced by federal laws which shall be subject to confirmation by referendum. The Laender thus affected shall be consulted.

3 A referendum shall be held in the Laender from whose territories or partial territories a new Land or Land with redefined boundaries is to be formed (affected Laender) ...

Article 32 (Foreign relations)
1 Relations with foreign states shall be conducted by the Federation.
2 Before the conclusion of a treaty affecting the special circumstances of a Land, that Land must be consulted in sufficient time.
3 In so far as the Laender have power to legislate, they may, with the consent of the Federal Government, conclude treaties with foreign states.

IV / THE COUNCIL OF CONSTITUENT STATES (BUNDESRAT)

Article 50 (Function)
The Laender shall participate through the Bundesrat in the legislation and administration of the Federation.

Article 51 (Composition)
1 The Bundesrat shall consist of members of the Land governments which appoint and recall them. Other members of such governments may act as substitutes.
2 Each Land shall have at least three votes; Laender with more than two million inhabitants shall have four, Laender with more than six million inhabitants five votes.
3 Each Land may delegate as many members as it has votes. The votes of each Land may be cast only as a block vote and only by members present or their substitutes.

Article 52 (President, Rules of procedure)
1 The Bundesrat shall elect its President for one year.
2 The President shall convene the Bundesrat. He must convene it if the members for at least two Laender or the Federal Government so demand.
3 The Bundesrat shall take its decisions with at least the majority of its votes. It shall draw up its rules of procedure. Its meetings shall be public. The public may be excluded.
4 Other members of, or persons commissioned by, Land governments may serve on the committees of the Bundesrat.

Article 53 (Participation of the Federal Government)
The members of the Federal Government shall have the right, and on demand the duty, to attend the meetings of the Bundesrat and of its commit-

tees. They must be heard at any time. The Bundesrat must be currently kept informed by the Federal Government of the conduct of affairs.

V / THE FEDERAL PRESIDENT

Article 54 (Election by the Federal Convention)
1 The Federal President shall be elected, without debate, by the Federal Convention (Bundesversammlung). Every German shall be eligible who is entitled to vote for Bundestag candidates and has attained the age of forty years.
2 The term of office of the Federal President shall be five years. Re-election for a consecutive term shall be permitted only once.
3 The Federal Convention shall consist of the members of the Bundestag and an equal number of members elected by the diets of the Laender according to the principles of proportional representation ...

VI / THE FEDERAL GOVERNMENT

Article 62 (Composition)
The Federal Government shall consist of the Federal Chancellor and the Federal Ministers.

Article 63 (Election of the Federal Chancellor –
Dissolution of the Bundestag)
1 The Federal Chancellor shall be elected, without debate, by the Bundestag upon the proposal of the Federal President.
2 The person obtaining the votes of the majority of the members of the Bundestag shall be elected. The person elected must be appointed by the Federal President.
3 If the person proposed is not elected, the Bundestag may elect within fourteen days of the ballot a Federal Chancellor by more than one half of its members ...

Article 64 (Appointment of Federal Ministers)
1 The Federal Ministers shall be appointed and dismissed by the Federal President upon the proposal of the Federal Chancellor ...

Article 67 (Vote of no-confidence)
1 The Bundestag can express its lack of confidence in the Federal Chancellor only by electing a successor with the majority of its members and by request-

ing the Federal President to dismiss the Federal Chancellor. The Federal President must comply with the request and appoint the person elected.

2 Forty-eight hours must elapse between the motion and the election.

Article 68 (Vote of confidence – Dissolution of the Bundestag)

1 If a motion of the Federal Chancellor for a vote of confidence is not assented to by the majority of the members of the Bundestag, the Federal President may, upon the proposal of the Federal Chancellor, dissolve the Bundestag within twenty-one days. The right to dissolve shall lapse as soon as the Bundestag with the majority of its members elects another Federal Chancellor.

2 Forty-eight hours must elapse between the motion and the vote thereon.

Article 73 (Exclusive legislation, catalogue)

The Federation shall have exclusive power to legislate in the following matters:

1* foreign affairs as well as defence including the protection of the civilian population; [as amended by federal laws of 26.3.54 and 24.6.68]
2 citizenship in the Federation;
3 freedom of movement, passport matters, immigration, emigration, and extradition;
4 currency, money and coinage, weights and measures, as well as the determination of standards of time;
5 the unity of the customs and commercial territory, treaties on commerce and on navigation, the freedom of movement of goods, and the exchanges of goods and payments with foreign countries, including customs and other frontier protection;
6 federal railroads and air transport;
7 postal and telecommunication services;
8 the legal status of persons employed by the Federation and by federal corporate bodies under public law;
9 industrial property rights, copyrights and publishers' rights;
10* co-operation of the Federation and the Laender in matters of
   a criminal police,
   b protection of the free democratic basic order, of the existence and the security of the Federation or of a Land (protection of the constitution) and
   c protection against efforts in the federal territory which, by the use of force or actions in preparations for the use of force, endanger the foreign interests of the Federal Republic of Germany,

as well as the establishment of a Federal Criminal Police Office and the international control of crime. [as amended by federal law of 28.1.72]
11 statistics for federal purposes.

Article 76 (Bills)
1 Bills shall be introduced in the Bundestag by the Federal Government or by members of the Bundestag or by the Bundesrat.
2+ Bills of the Federal Government shall be submitted first to the Bundesrat. The Bundesrat shall be entitled to state its position on such bills within six weeks. A bill exceptionally submitted to the Bundesrat as being particularly urgent by the Federal Government may be submitted by the latter to the Bundestag three weeks later, even though the Federal Government may not yet have received the statement of the Bundesrat's position; such statement shall be transmitted to the Bundestag by the Federal Government without delay upon its receipt ... [as amended by federal law of 15.11.69]

Article 80a* (State of tension) [inserted by federal law of 24 June 1968]
1 Where this Basic Law or a federal law on defence, including the protection of the civilian population, stipulates that legal provisions may only be applied in accordance with this Article, their application shall, except when a state of defence exists, be admissible only after the Bundestag has determined that a state of tension (Spannungsfall) exists or if it has specifically approved such application. In respect of the cases mentioned in the first sentence of paragraph 5 and the second sentence of paragraph 6 of Article 12a, such determination of a state of tension and such specific approval shall require a two-thirds majority of the votes cast.
2 Any measures taken by virtue of legal provisions enacted under paragraph 1 of this Article shall be revoked whenever the Bundestag so requests.
3 In derogation of paragraph 1 of this Article, the application of such legal provisions shall also be admissible by virtue of, and in accordance with, a decision taken with the consent of the Federal Government by an international organ within the framework of a treaty of alliance. Any measures taken pursuant to this paragraph shall be revoked whenever the Bundestag so requests with the majority of its members.

Article 81 (State of legislative emergency)
1 Should, in the circumstances of Article 68, the Bundestag not be dissolved, the Federal President may, at the request of the Federal Government and with the consent of the Bundesrat, declare a state of legislative emergency with respect to a bill, if the Bundestag rejects the bill although the

Federal Government has declared it to be urgent. The same shall apply if a bill has been rejected although the Federal Chancellor had combined with it the motion under Article 68.

2 If, after a state of legislative emergency has been declared, the Bundestag again rejects the bill or adopts it in a version stated to be unacceptable to the Federal Government, the bill shall be deemed to have become a law to the extent that the Bundesrat consents to it. The same shall apply if the bill is not passed by the Bundestag within four weeks of its reintroduction.

3 During the term of office of a Federal Chancellor, any other bill rejected by the Bundestag may become a law in accordance with paragraphs 1 and 2 of this Article within a period of six months after the first declaration of a state of legislative emergency. After the expiration of this period, a further declaration of a state of legislative emergency shall be inadmissible during the term of office of the same Federal Chancellor.

4 This Basic Law may not be amended nor repealed nor suspended in whole or in part by a law enacted pursuant to paragraph 2 of this Article.

Article 91* (Aversion of dangers to the existence of the Federation or of a Land) [as amended, 24 June 1968]

1 In order to avert any imminent danger to the existence or to the free democratic basic order of the Federation or a Land, a Land may request the services of the police forces of other Laender, or of the forces and facilities of other administrative authorities and of the Federal Border Guard.

2 If the Land where such danger is imminent is not itself willing or able to combat the danger, the Federal Government may place the police in that Land and the police forces of other Laender under its own instructions and commit units of the Federal Border Guard. The order for this shall be rescinded after the removal of the danger or else at any time upon the request of the Bundesrat. If the danger extends to a region larger than a Land, the Federal Government may, in so far as is necessary for effectively combating such danger, issue instructions to the Land governments; the first and second sentences of this paragraph shall not be affected by this provision.

IX / THE ADMINISTRATION OF JUSTICE

Article 92* (Court organization) [as amended, 18 June 1968]
Judicial power shall be vested in the judges; it shall be exercised by the Federal Constitutional Court, by the federal courts provided for in this Basic Law, and by the courts of the Laender.

Article 93 (Federal Constitutional Court, competency)

1 The Federal Constitutional Court shall decide:

 1 on the interpretation of this Basic Law in the event of disputes concerning the extent of the rights and duties of a highest federal organ or of other parties concerned who have been vested with rights of their own by this Basic Law or by rules of procedure of a highest federal organ;

 2 in case of differences of opinion or doubts on the formal and material compatibility of federal law or Land law with this Basic Law, or on the compatibility of Land law with other federal law, at the request of the Federal Government, of a Land government, or of one third of the Bundestag members;

 3 in case of differences of opinion on the rights and duties of the Federation and the Laender, particularly in the execution of federal law by the Laender and in the exercise of federal supervision;

 4 on other disputes involving public law, between the Federation and the Laender, between different Laender or within a Land, unless recourse to another court exists;

 4a* on complaints of unconstitutionality, which may be entered by any person who claims that one of his rights under paragraph 4 of Article 20, under Article 33, 38, 101, 103, or 104 has been violated by public authority; [inserted by federal law of 29 January 1969]

 4b* on complaints of unconstitutionality, entered by communes or associations of communes on the ground that their right to self-government under Article 28 has been violated by a law other than a Land law open to complaint to the respective Land constitutional court; [inserted by federal law of 29 January 1969]

 5 in the other cases provided for in this Basic Law.

2 The Federal Constitutional Court shall also act in such other cases as are assigned to it by federal legislation.

Article 94 (Federal Constitutional Court, composition)

1 The Federal Constitutional Court shall consist of federal judges and other members. Half of the members of the Federal Constitutional Court shall be elected by the Bundestag and half by the Bundesrat. They may not be members of the Bundestag, the Bundesrat, the Federal Government, nor of any of the corresponding organs of a Land.

2 The constitution and procedure of the Federal Constitutional Court shall be regulated by a federal law which shall specify in what cases its decisions shall have the force of law*. Such law may require that all other legal

remedies must have been exhausted before any such complaint of unconstitutionality can be entered, and may make provision for a special procedure as to admissibility. [inserted by federal law of 29 January 1969]

Article 95* (Highest courts of justice of the Federation – Joint Panel)
[as amended, 18 June 1968]

1 For the purposes of ordinary, administrative, fiscal, labour, and social jurisdiction, the Federation shall establish as highest courts of justice the Federal Court of Justice, the Federal Administrative Court, the Federal Fiscal Court, the Federal Labour Court, and the Federal Social Court.

2 The judges of each of these courts shall be selected jointly by the competent Federal Minister and a committee for the selection of judges consisting of the competent Land Ministers and an equal number of members elected by the Bundestag.

3 In order to preserve uniformity of jurisdiction, a Joint Panel (Senate) of the courts specified in paragraph 1 of this Article shall be set up. Details shall be regulated by a federal law.

Japan

Constitution of Japan
(promulgated 3 November 1946)

We, the Japanese people, acting through our duly elected representatives in the National Diet, determined that we shall secure for ourselves and our posterity the fruits of peaceful cooperation with all nations and the blessings of liberty throughout this land, and resolved that never again shall we be visited with the horrors of war through the action of government, do proclaim that sovereign power resides with the people and do firmly establish this Constitution. Government is a sacred trust of the people, the authority for which is derived from the people, the powers of which are exercised by the representatives of the people, and the benefits of which are enjoyed by the people. This is a universal principle of mankind upon which this Constitution is founded. We reject and revoke all constitutions, laws, ordinances, and rescripts in conflict herewith.

We, the Japanese people, desire peace for all time and are deeply conscious of the high ideals controlling human relationship, and we have determined to preserve our security and existence, trusting in the justice and faith of the peace-loving peoples of the world. We desire to occupy an honored place in an international society striving for the preservation of peace, and the banishment of tyranny and slavery, oppression and intolerance for all time from the earth. We recognize that all peoples of the world have the right to live in peace, free from fear and want.

We believe that no nation is responsible to itself alone, but that laws of political morality are universal; and that obedience to such laws is incumbent upon all nations who would sustain their own sovereignty and justify their sovereign relationship with other nations.

We, the Japanese people, pledge our national honor to accomplish these high ideals and purposes with all our resources.

CHAPTER I / THE EMPEROR

Article 1 The Emperor shall be the symbol of the State and of the unity of the people, deriving his position from the will of the people with whom resides sovereign power.

Article 2 The Imperial Throne shall be dynastic and succeeded to in accordance with the Imperial House Law passed by the Diet.

Article 3 The advice and approval of the Cabinet shall be required for all acts of the Emperor in matters of state, and the Cabinet shall be responsible therefor.

Article 4 The Emperor shall perform only such acts in matters of state as are provided for in this Constitution and he shall not have powers related to government ...

CHAPTER II / RENUNCIATION OF WAR

Article 9 Aspiring sincerely to an international peace based on justice and order, the Japanese people forever renounce war as a sovereign right of the nation and the threat or use of force as a means of settling international disputes.

2 In order to accomplish the aim of the preceding paragraph, land, sea, and air forces, as well as other war potential, will never be maintained. The right of belligerency of the state will not be recognized.

CHAPTER III / RIGHTS AND DUTIES OF THE PEOPLE

Article 10 The conditions necessary for being a Japanese national shall be determined by law.

Article 11 The people shall not be prevented from enjoying any of the fundamental human rights. These fundamental human rights guaranteed to the people by this Constitution shall be conferred upon the people of this and future generations as eternal and inviolate rights.

Article 12 The freedoms and rights guaranteed to the people by this Constitution shall be maintained by the constant endeavor of the people, who shall refrain from any abuse of these freedoms and rights and shall always be responsible for utilizing them for the public welfare.

Article 13 All of the people shall be respected as individuals. Their right to life, liberty, and the pursuit of happiness shall, to the extent that it does not interfere with the public welfare, be the supreme consideration in legislation and in other governmental affairs.

Article 14 All of the people are equal under the law and there shall be no discrimination in political, economic or social relations because of race, creed, sex, social status or family origin ...

Article 19 Freedom of thought and conscience shall not be violated.

Article 20 Freedom of religion is guaranteed to all. No religious organization shall receive any privileges from the State nor exercise any political authority.

2 No person shall be compelled to take part in any religious acts, celebration, rite or practice.

3 The State and its organs shall refrain from religious education or any other religious activity.

Article 21 Freedom of assembly and association as well as speech, press and all other forms of expression are guaranteed.

2 No censorship shall be maintained, nor shall the secrecy of any means of communication be violated.

Article 22 Every person shall have freedom to choose and change his residence and to choose his occupation to the extent that it does not interfere with the public welfare.

2 Freedom of all persons to move to a foreign country and to divest themselves of their nationality shall be inviolate.

Article 23 Academic freedom is guaranteed.

Article 24 Marriage shall be based only on the mutual consent of both sexes and it shall be maintained through mutual cooperation with the equal rights of husband and wife as a basis.

2 With regard to choice of spouse, property rights, inheritance, choice of domicile, divorce and other matters pertaining to marriage and the family, laws shall be enacted from the standpoint of individual dignity and the essential equality of the sexes.

Article 25 All people shall have the right to maintain the minimum standards of wholesome and cultured living.

2 In all spheres of life, the State shall use its endeavors for the promotion and extension of social welfare and security, and of public health.

Article 26 All people shall have the right to receive an equal education correspondent to their ability, as provided by law.

2 All people shall be obligated to have all boys and girls under their protection receive ordinary educations as provided for by law. Such compulsory education shall be free.

Article 27 All people shall have the right and the obligation to work.

2 Standards for wages, hours, rest and other working conditions shall be fixed by law.

3 Children shall not be exploited.

Article 28 The right of workers to organize and to bargain and act collectively is guaranteed.

Article 29 The right to own or to hold property is inviolable.

Property rights shall be defined by law, in conformity with the public welfare.

3 Private property may be taken for public use upon just compensation therefor.

Article 30 The people shall be liable to taxations as provided by law.

Article 31 No person shall be deprived of life or liberty, nor shall any other criminal penalty be imposed, except according to procedure established by law.

CHAPTER IV / THE DIET

Article 41 The Diet shall be the highest organ of state power, and shall be the sole law-making organ of the State.

Article 42 The Diet shall consist of two Houses, namely the House of Representatives and the House of Councillors.

Article 43 Both Houses shall consist of elected members, representative of all the people.

2 The number of the members of each House shall be fixed by law.

Article 44 The qualifications of members of both Houses and their electors shall be fixed by law. However, there shall be no discrimination because of race, creed, sex, social status, family origin, education, property or income.

Article 59 A bill becomes a law on passage by both Houses, except as otherwise provided by the Constitution.

2 A bill which is passed by the House of Representatives, and upon which the House of Councillors makes a decision different from that of the House of Representatives, becomes a law when passed a second time by the House of Representatives by a majority of two-thirds or more of the members present.

3 The provision of the preceding paragraph does not preclude the House of Representatives from calling for the meeting of a joint committee of both Houses, provided for by law.

4 Failure by the House of Councillors to take final action within sixty (60) days after receipt of a bill passed by the House of Representatives, time in recess excepted, may be determined by the House of Representatives to constitute a rejection of the said bill by the House of Councillors.

Article 60 The Budget must first be submitted to the House of Representatives.

2 Upon consideration of the budget, when the House of Councillors makes a decision different from that of the House of Representatives, and when no agreement can be reached even through a joint committee of both Houses, provided for by law, or in the case of failure by the House of Councillors to take final action within thirty (30) days, the period of recess excluded, after

the receipt of the budget passed by the House of Representatives, the decision of the House of Representatives shall be the decision of the Diet.

Article 61 The second paragraph of the preceding article applies also to the Diet approval required for the conclusion of treaties.

CHAPTER V / THE CABINET

Article 65 Executive power shall be vested in the Cabinet.

Article 66 The Cabinet shall consist of the Prime Minister, who shall be its head, and other Ministers of State, as provided for by law.

2 The Prime Minister and other Ministers of State must be civilians.

3 The Cabinet, in the exercise of executive power, shall be collectively responsible to the Diet.

Article 67 The Prime Minister shall be designated from among the members of the Diet by a resolution of the Diet. This designation shall precede all other business ...

Article 68 The Prime Minister shall appoint the Ministers of State. However, a majority of their number must be chosen from among the members of the Diet.

2 The Prime Minister may remove the Ministers of State as he chooses.

Article 69 If the House of Representatives passes a nonconfidence resolution, or rejects a confidence resolution, the Cabinet shall resign en masse, unless the House of Representatives is dissolved with ten (10) days.

CHAPTER VI / JUDICIARY

Article 76 The whole judicial power is vested in a Supreme Court and in such inferior courts as are established by law.

2 No extraordinary tribunal shall be established, nor shall any organ or agency of the Executive be given final judicial power.

3 All judges shall be independent in the exercise of their conscience and shall be bound only by this Constitution and the laws.

Article 78 Judges shall not be removed except by public impeachment unless judicially declared mentally or physically incompetent to perform official duties. No disciplinary action against judges shall be administered by any executive organ or agency.

Article 79 The Supreme Court shall consist of a Chief Judge and such number of judges as may be determined by law; all such judges excepting the Chief Judge shall be appointed by the Cabinet.

2 The appointment of the judges of the Supreme Court shall be reviewed by the people at the first general election of members of the House of Representatives following their appointment, and shall be reviewed again at the first general election of members of the House of Representatives after a lapse of ten (10) years, and in the same manner thereafter.

3 In cases mentioned in the foregoing paragraph, when the majority of the voters favors the dismissal of a judge, he shall be dismissed.

4 Matters pertaining to review shall be prescribed by law.

5 The judges of the Supreme Court shall be retired upon the attainment of the age as fixed by law.

6 All such judges shall receive, at regular stated intervals, adequate compensation which shall not be decreased during their terms of office.

Article 81 The Supreme Court is the court of last resort with power to determine the constitutionality of any law, order, regulation or official act.

Article 82 Trials shall be conducted and judgment declared publicly. Where a court unanimously determines publicity to be dangerous to public order or morals, a trial may be conducted privately, but trials of political offenses, offenses involving the press or cases wherein the rights of people as guaranteed in Chapter III of this Constitution are in question shall always be conducted publicly.

CHAPTER IX / AMENDMENTS

Article 96 Amendments to this Constitution shall be initiated by the Diet, through a concurring vote of two-thirds or more of all the members of each House and shall thereupon be submitted to the people for ratification, which shall require the affirmative vote of a majority of all votes cast thereon, at a special referendum or at such election as the Diet shall specify.

2 Amendments when so ratified shall immediately be promulgated by the Emperor in the name of the people, as an integral part of this Constitution.

CHAPTER X / SUPREME LAW

Article 97 The fundamental human rights by this Constitution guaranteed to the people of Japan are fruits of the age-old struggle of man to be free; they have survived the many exacting tests for durability and are conferred upon this and future generations in trust, to be held for all time inviolate.

Article 98 This Constitution shall be the supreme law of the nation and no law, ordinance, imperial rescript or other act of government, or part thereof, contrary to the provisions hereof, shall have legal force or validity.

2 The treaties concluded by Japan and established laws of nations shall be faithfully observed.

Article 99 The Emperor or the Regent as well as Ministers of State, members of the Diet, judges, and all other public officials have the obligation to respect and uphold this Constitution.

India

Constitution of India
(adopted 26 November 1949;
entered into force 26 January 1950)

Preamble
We, the People of India, having solemnly resolved to constitute India into a Sovereign Democratic Republic and to secure to all its citizens:
  Justice, social, economic and political;
  Liberty of thought, expression, belief, faith and worship;
  Equality of status and of opportunity;
and to promote among them all
  Fraternity assuring the dignity of the individual and the unity of the Nation:
  In our Constituent Assembly this twenty-sixth day of November, 1949, do hereby Adopt, Enact and Give to ourselves this Constitution.

PART III / FUNDAMENTAL RIGHTS

GENERAL

Article 12 / Definition In this Part, unless the context otherwise requires, 'the State' includes the Government and Parliament of India and the Government and the Legislature of each of the States and all local or other authorities within the territory of India or under the control of the Government of India.
Article 13 / Laws inconsistent with or in derogation of the fundamental rights 1 All laws in force in the territory of India immediately before the commencement of this Constitution in so far as they are inconsistent with the provisions of this Part, shall, to the extent of such inconsistency, be void.
2 The State shall not make any law which takes away or abridges the rights conferred by this Part and any law made in contravention of this clause shall, to the extent of the contravention, be void ...
4 Nothing in this Article shall apply to any amendment of this Constitution made under Article 368.

RIGHT TO EQUALITY

Article 14 / Equality before law The State shall not deny to any person equality before the law or the equal protection of the laws within the territory of India.

Article 15 / Prohibition of discrimination on grounds of religion, race, caste, sex or place of birth 1 The State shall not discriminate against any citizen on grounds only of religion, caste, sex, place of birth or any of them.
2 No citizen shall on grounds only of religion, race, caste, sex, place of birth or any of them, be subject to any disability, liability, restriction with regard to –
a access to shops, public restaurants, hotels and places of public entertainment; or
b the use of wells, tanks, bathing ghats, roads and places of public resort maintained wholly or partly out of State funds or dedicated to the use of the general public.
3 Nothing in this Article shall prevent the State from making any special provision for women and children.
4 Nothing in this Article or in clause 2 of Article 29 shall prevent the State from making any special provision for the advancement of any socially and educationally backward classes of citizens or for the Scheduled Castes and the Tribes.

Article 16 / Equality of opportunity in matters of public employment 1 There shall be equality of opportunity for all citizens in matters relating to employment or appointment to any office under the State.
2 No citizen shall, on grounds only of religion, race, caste, sex, descent, place of birth, residence or any of them, be ineligible for, or discriminated against, in respect of any employment or office under the State.
3 Nothing in this Article shall prevent Parliament from making any law prescribing, in regard to a class or classes of employment or appointment to an office under the Government of, or any local or other authority within, a State or Union territory, any requirement as to residence within that State or Union territory prior to such employment or appointment.
4 Nothing in this Article shall prevent the State from making any provision for the reservation of appointments or posts in favour of any backward class of citizens which, in the opinion of the State, is not adequately represented in the services under the State.
5 Nothing in the Article shall affect the operation of any law which provides that the incumbent of an office in connection with the affairs of any religious

or denominational institution or any member of the governing body thereof shall be a person professing a particular religion or belonging to a particular denomination.

Article 17 / Abolition of Untouchability 'Untouchability' is abolished and its practice in any form is forbidden. The enforcement of any disability arising out of 'Untouchability' shall be an offence punishable in accordance with law.

Article 18 / Abolition of titles 1 No title, not being a military or academic distinction, shall be conferred by the State.

2 No citizen of India shall accept any title from any foreign State.

3 No person who is not a citizen of India shall, while he holds any office of profit or trust under the State, accept without the consent of the President any title from any foreign S'ate.

4 No person holding any office of profit or trust under the State shall, without the consent of the President, accept any present, emolument, or office of any kind from or under any foreign State.

RIGHT TO FREEDOM

Article 19 / Protection of certain rights regarding freedom of speech, etc. 1 All citizens shall have the right, –

a to freedom of speech and expression;

b to assemble peaceably and without arms;

c to form associations or unions;

d to move freely throughout the territory of India;

e to reside and settle in any part of the territory of India;

f to acquire, hold and dispose of property; and

g to practise any profession, or to carry on any occupation, trade or business.

2 Nothing in sub-clause a of clause 1 shall affect the operation of any existing law, or prevent the State from making any law, in so far as such law imposes reasonable restrictions on the exercise of the right conferred by the said sub-clause in the interests of the sovereignty and integrity of India, the security of the State, friendly relations with foreign States, public order, decency or morality, or in relation to contempt of court, defamation or incitement to an offence.

3 Nothing in sub-clause b of the said clause shall affect the operation of any existing law in so far as it imposes, or prevent the State from making any law imposing, in the interests of the sovereignty and integrity of India or public

order, reasonable restrictions on the exercise of the right conferred by the said sub-clause.

4 Nothing in sub-clause c of the said clause shall affect the operation of any existing law in so far as it imposes, or prevent the State from making any law imposing, in the interest of the sovereignty and integrity of India or public order or morality, reasonable restrictions on the exercise of the right conferred by the said sub-clause.

5 Nothing in sub-clauses d, e and f of the said clause shall affect the operation of any existing law in so far as it imposes, or prevent the State from making any law imposing, reasonable restrictions on the exercise of any of the rights conferred by the said sub-clauses either in the interests of the general public or for the protection of the interests of any Scheduled Tribe.

6 Nothing in sub-clause g of the said clause shall affect the operation of any existing law in so far as it imposes, or prevent the State from making any law imposing, in the interests of the general public, reasonable restrictions on the exercise of the right conferred by the said sub-clause, and, in particular nothing in the said sub-clause shall affect the operation of any existing law in so far as it relates to, or prevent the State from making any law relating to, –

i the professional or technical qualifications necessary for practising any profession or carrying on any occupation, trade or business; or

ii the carrying on by the State, or by a corporation owned or controlled by the State, of any trade, business, industry or service, whether to the exclusion, complete or partial, of citizens or otherwise.

Article 21 / Protection of life and personal liberty No person shall be deprived of his life or personal liberty except according to procedure established by law.

Article 22 / Protection against arrest and detention in certain cases No person who is arrested shall be detained in custody without being informed, as soon as may be, of the grounds for such arrest nor shall he be denied the right to consult, and to be defended by, a legal practitioner of his choice.

2 Every person who is arrested and detained in custody shall be produced before the nearest Magistrate within a period of twenty-four hours of such arrest excluding the time necessary for the journey from the place of arrest to the Court of the Magistrate and no such person shall be detained in custody beyond the said period without the authority of a Magistrate.

3 Nothing in clauses 1 and 2 shall apply –

a to any person who for the time being is an enemy alien; or

b to any person who is arrested or detained under any law providing for preventive detention.

4 No law providing for preventive detention shall authorise the detention of a person for a longer period than three months unless –

a an Advisory Board consisting of persons who are, or have been or are qualified to be appointed as, Judges of a High Court has reported before the expiration of the said period of three months that there is in its opinion sufficient cause for such detention:

Provided that nothing in this sub-clause shall authorise the detention of any person beyond the maximum period prescribed by any law made by Parliament under sub-clause b of clause 7; or

b such person is detained in accordance with the provisions of any law made by Parliament under sub-clauses a and b of clause 7.

5 When any person is detained in pursuance of an order made under any law providing for preventive detention, the authority making the order shall, as soon as may be, communicate to such person the grounds on which the order has been made and shall afford him the earliest opportunity of making a representation against the order.

Nothing in clause 5 shall require the authority making any such order as is referred to in that clause to disclose fact which such authority considers to be against the public interest to disclose.

7 Parliament may by law prescribe –

a the circumstances under which, and the class or classes of cases in which, a person may be detained for a period longer than three months under any law providing for preventive detention without obtaining the opinion of an Advisory Board in accordance with the provisions of sub-clause a of clause 4;

b the maximum period for which any person may in any class or classes of cases be detained under any law providing for preventive detention; and

c the procedure to be followed by an Advisory Board in an inquiry under sub-clause a of clause 4.

RIGHT AGAINST EXPLOITATION

Article 23 / Prohibition of traffic in human beings and forced labour
1 Traffic in human beings and *begar* and other similar forms of forced labour are prohibited and any contravention of this provision shall be an offence punishable in accordance with law.

2 Nothing in this Article shall prevent the State from imposing compulsory service for public purposes, and in imposing such service the State shall not make any discrimination on grounds only of religion, race, caste or class or any of them.

Article 24 / Prohibition of employment of children in factories, etc No child below the age of fourteen years shall be employed to work in any factory or mine or engaged in any other hazardous employment.

RIGHT TO FREEDOM OF RELIGION

Article 25 / Freedom of conscience and free profession, practice, and propagation of religion 1 Subject to public order, morality and health and to the other provisions of this Part, all persons are equally entitled to freedom of conscience and the right freely to profess, practise and propagate religion.

2 Nothing in this Article shall affect the operation of any existing law or prevent the State from making any law:

a regulating or restricting any economic, financial, political or other secular activity which may be associated with religious practice.

b providing for social welfare and reform or the throwing open of Hindu religious institutions of a public character to all classes and sections of Hindus.

Explanation I The wearing and carrying of *Kirpans* shall be deemed to be included in the profession of the Sikh religion.

Explanation II In sub-clause b of clause 2, the reference to Hindus shall be construed as including a reference to persons professing the Sikh, Jaina or Buddhist religion, and the reference to Hindu religious institutions shall be construed accordingly.

Article 28 / Freedom as to attendance at religious instruction or religious worship in certain educational institutions 1 No religious instruction shall be provided in any educational institution wholly maintained out of State funds ...

CULTURAL AND EDUCATIONAL RIGHTS

Article 29 / Protection of interest of minorities 1 Any section of the citizens residing in the territory of India or any part thereof having a distinct language, script or culture of its own shall have the right to conserve the same.

2 No citizen shall be denied admission into any educational institution maintained by the State or receiving aid out of State funds on grounds only of religion, race, caste, language or any of them.

Article 30 / Right of minorities to establish and administer educational institutions 1 All minorities, whether based on religion or language, shall have the right to establish and administer educational institutions of their choice.

2 The State shall not, in granting aid to educational institutions, discriminate against any educational institution on the ground that it is under the management of a minority, whether based on religion or language.

RIGHT TO PROPERTY

Article 31 / Compulsory acquisition of property No person shall be deprived of his property save by authority of law.

2 No property shall be compulsorily acquired or requisitioned save for a public purpose and save by authority of a law which provides for acquisition or requisitioning of the property for an amount which may be fixed by such law or which may be determined in accordance with such principles and given in such manner as may be specified in such law: and no such law shall be called in question in any court on the ground that the amount so fixed or determined is not adequate or that the whole or any part of such amount is to be given otherwise than in cash ...

Article 31A / Saving of laws providing for acquisition of estates etc
1 Notwithstanding anything contained in Article 13, no law providing for –

a the acquisition by the State of any estate or any rights therein or the extinguishment or modification of any such rights, or

b the taking over of the management of any property by the State for a limited period either in the public interest or in order to secure the proper management of the property, or

c the amalgamation of two or more corporations either in the public interest or in order to secure the proper management of any of the corporations ...

shall be deemed to be void on the ground that it is inconsistent with, or takes away or abridges any of the rights conferred by Article 14, Article 19 or Article 31.

Provided that where such law is a law made by the Legislature of a State, the provisions of this Article shall not apply thereto unless such law, having been reserved for the consideration of the President, has received his assent ...

PART IV / DIRECTIVE PRINCIPLES OF STATE POLICY

Article 36 / Definition In this Part, unless the context otherwise requires, 'the State' has the same meaning as in Part III.

Article 37 / Application of the principles contained in this Part The provisions contained in this Part shall not be enforceable by any court, but the principles therein laid down are nevertheless fundamental in the governance of the country and it shall be the duty of the State to apply these principles in making laws.

Article 38 / State to secure a social order for the promotion of welfare of the people The State shall strive to promote the welfare of the people by securing and protecting as effectively as it may a social order in which justice, social, economic and political, shall inform all the institutions of the national life.

Article 39 / Certain principles of policy to be followed by the State The State shall, in particular, direct its policy towards securing –

a that the citizens, men and women equally, have the right to an adequate means of livelihood;

b that the ownership and control of the material resources of the community are so distributed as best to subserve the common good;

c that operation of the economic system does not result in the concentration of wealth and means of production to the common detriment;

d that there is equal pay for equal work for both men and women;

e that the health and strength of workers, men and women, and the tender age of children are not abused and that citizens are not forced by economic necessity to enter avocations unsuited to their age or strength;

f that childhood and youth are protected against exploitation and against moral and material abandonment;

Article 40 / Organization of village panchayats The State shall take steps to organize village panchayats and endow them with such powers and authority as may be necessary to enable them to function as units of self-government.

Article 41 / Right to work, to education and to public assistance in certain cases The State shall, within the limits of its economic capacity and development, make effective provision for securing the right to work, to education and to public assistance in cases of unemployment, old age, sickness and disablement, and in other cases of undeserved want.

Article 42 / Provision for just and humane conditions of work and maternity relief The State shall make provision for securing just and humane conditions of work and for maternity relief.

Article 45 / Provision for free and compulsory education for children The State shall endeavour to provide, within a period of ten years from the commencement of this Constitution, for free and compulsory education for all children until they complete the age of fourteen years.

Article 46 / Promotion of educational and economic interests of Scheduled Castes, Scheduled Tribes and other weaker sections The State shall promote with special care the educational and economic interests of the weaker sections of the people, and, in particular, of the Scheduled Castes and the Scheduled Tribes, and shall protect them from social injustice and all forms of exploitation.

Article 47 / Duty of the State to raise the level of nutrition and the standard of living and to improve public health The State shall regard the raising of the level of nutrition and the standard of living of its people and the improvement of public health as among its primary duties and, in particular, the State shall endeavour to bring about prohibition of the consumption, except for medicinal purposes, of intoxicating drinks and of drugs which are injurious to health.

Article 51 / Promotion of international peace and security The State shall endeavour to –

a   promote international peace and security;

b   maintain just and honourable relations between nations;

c   foster respect for international law and treaty obligations in the dealings of organised peoples with one another; and

d   encourage settlement of international disputes by arbitration.

CHAPTER IV / THE UNION JUDICIARY

Article 124 / Establishment and constitution of Supreme Court 1 There shall be a Supreme Court of India consisting of a Chief Justice of India and, until Parliament by law prescribes a larger number, of not more than seven[1] other Judges. [amended by Act No 17 of 1960 to increase to thirteen judges]

2 Every Judge of the Supreme Court shall be appointed by the President by warrant under his hand and seal after consultation with such of the Judges of the Supreme Court and of the High Courts in the States as the President may deem necessary for the purpose and shall hold office until he attains the age of sixty-five years:

Provided that in the case of appointment of a Judge other than the Chief Justice, the Chief Justice of India shall always be consulted ...

Article 143 / Power of Parliament to consult Supreme Court 1 If at any time it appears to the President that a question of law or fact has arisen, or is likely to arise, which is of such a nature and of such public importance that it is expedient to obtain the opinion of the Supreme Court upon it, he may refer the question to that Court for consideration and the Court may, after such hearing as it thinks fit, report to the President its opinion thereon ...

PART XVIII / EMERGENCY PROVISIONS

Article 352 / Proclamation of Emergency 1 If the President is satisfied that a grave emergency exists whereby the security of India or of any part of the territory thereof is threatened, whether by war or external aggression or internal disturbance, he may, by Proclamation, make a declaration to that effect.
2 A Proclamation issued under clause 1 –
a may be revoked by a subsequent Proclamation;
b shall be laid before each House of Parliament;
c shall cease to operate at the expiration of two months unless before the expiration of that period it has been approved by resolutions of both Houses of Parliament ...
3 A Proclamation of Emergency declaring that the security of India or of any part of the territory thereof is threatened by war or by external aggression or by internal disturbance may be made before the actual occurrence of war or any such aggression or disturbance if the President is satisfied that there is imminent danger thereof.

Article 353 / Effect of Proclamation of Emergency While a Proclamation of Emergency is in operation, then –
a notwithstanding anything in this Constitution, the executive power of the Union shall extend to the giving of directions to any State as to the manner in which the executive power thereof is to be exercised;
b the power of Parliament to make laws with respect to any matter shall include power to make laws conferring powers and imposing duties, or authorising the conferring of powers and the imposition of duties upon the Union or officers and authorities of the Union as respects that matter, notwithstanding that it is one which is not enumerated in the Union List.

Article 355 / Duty of the Union to protect States against external aggression and internal disturbance It shall be the duty of the Union to protect every State against external aggression and internal disturbance and to ensure that the Government of every State is carried on in accordance with the provisions of this Constitution.

Article 356 / Provisions in case of failure of constitutional machinery in States 1 If the President on receipt of a report from the Governor of a State or otherwise is satisfied that a situation has arisen in which the government of the State cannot be carried on in accordance with the provisions of the Constitution, the President may by Proclamation –

a assume to himself all or any of the functions of the Government of the State and all or any of the powers vested in or exercisable by the Governor or any body or authority in the State other than the Legislature of the State;

b declare that the powers of the Legislature of the State shall be exercisable by or under the authority of Parliament;

c make such incidental and consequential provisions as appear to the President to be necessary or desirable for giving effect to the objects of the Proclamation, including provisions for suspending in whole or in part the operation of any provisions of this Constitution relating to any body or authority in the State:

Provided that nothing in this clause shall authorise the President to assume to himself any of the powers vested in or exercisable by a High Court, or to suspend in whole or in part the operation of any provision of this Constitution relating to High Courts.

2 Any such Proclamation may be revoked or varied by a subsequent Proclamation.

3 Every Proclamation under this Article shall be laid before each House of Parliament and shall, except where it is a Proclamation revoking a previous Proclamation, cease to operate at the expiration of two months unless before the expiration of that period it has been approved by resolutions of both Houses of Parliament.

Article 358 / Suspension of provisions of Article 19 during emergencies While a Proclamation of Emergency is in operation, nothing in Article 19 shall restrict the power of the State as defined in Part III to make any law or to take any executive action which the State would but for the provisions contained in that Part be competent to make or to take, but any law so made shall, to the extent of the incompetency, cease to have effect as soon as the Proclamation ceases to operate, except as respects things done or omitted to be done before the law so ceases to have effect.

Article 359 / Suspension of the enforcement of the rights conferred by Part III during emergencies 1 Where a Proclamation of Emergency is in operation, the President may by order declare that the right to move any Court for the enforcement of such of the rights conferred by Part III as may be mentioned in the order and all proceedings pending in any court for the enforcement of the rights so mentioned shall remain suspended for the period during which the Proclamation is in force or for such shorter period as may be specified in the order.

2 An order made as aforesaid may extend to the whole or any part of the territory of India.

3 Every order made under clause 1 shall, as soon as may be after it is made, be laid before each House of Parliament.

Article 360 / Provisions as to financial emergency 1 If the President is satisfied that a situation has arisen whereby the financial stability or credit of India or of any part of the territory thereof is threatened, he may by a Proclamation make a declaration to that effect.

2 The provisions of clause 2 of Article 352 shall apply in relation to a Proclamation issued under this Article as they apply in relation to a Proclamation of Emergency issued under Article 352.

3 During the period any such Proclamation as is mentioned in clause 1 is in operation, the executive authority of the Union shall extend to the giving of directions to any State to observe such canons of financial propriety as may be specified in the directions, and to the giving of such other directions as the President may deem necessary and adequate for the purpose.

4 Notwithstanding anything in this Constitution –

    a any such direction may include –

        i a provision requiring the reduction of salaries and allowances of all or any class of persons serving in connection with the affairs of a State;

        ii a provision requiring all Money Bills or other Bills to which the provisions of Article 207 apply to be reserved for the consideration of the President after they are passed by the Legislature of the State;

    b it shall be competent for the President during the period any Proclamation issued under this Article is in operation to issue directions for the reduction of salaries and allowances of all or any class of persons serving in connection with the affairs of the Union including the Judges of the Supreme Court and the High Courts.

PART XX / AMENDMENT OF THE CONSTITUTION

Article 368 / Power of Parliament to amend the Constitution and Procedure therefor 1 Notwithstanding anything in this Constitution, Parliament may in exercise of its constituent power amend by way of addition, variation or repeal any provision of this Constitution in accordance with the procedure laid down in this Article.

2 An amendment of the Constitution may be initiated only by the introduction of a Bill for the purpose in either House of Parliament, and when the Bill is passed in each House by a majority of the total membership of that House and by a majority of not less than two-thirds of the members of that House

present and voting, it shall be presented to the President who shall give his assent to the Bill and thereupon the Constitution shall stand amended in accordance with the terms of the Bill ...
3 Nothing in Article 13 shall apply to any amendment under this Article.

Soviet Union

Constitution (Basic Law) of the Union of Soviet Socialist Republics (published 8 October 1977)

[Additions to the original draft, or new wordings, are italicized; deletions from the original draft, or old wordings, are in brackets.]

The Great October Socialist Revolution, carried out by the workers and peasants of Russia under the leadership of the Communist Party headed by V.I. Lenin, overthrew the power of the capitalists and landowners, broke the fetters of oppression, *established the dictatorship of the proletariat* and created the Soviet state – a new type of state and the basic instrument for the defense of revolutionary gains and the construction of socialism and communism. *Mankind's world-historic turn from capitalism to socialism began.*

After winning victory in the Civil War and repulsing imperialist intervention, Soviet power carried out profound social and economic transformations and once and for all ended the exploitation of man by man, class antagonisms and national enmity. *The unification of the Soviet republics in the USSR multiplied the forces and possibilities of the country's peoples in the construction of socialism.* Public ownership of the means of production and genuine democracy for the masses of working people were established. For the first time in the history of mankind, a socialist society has been created.

The unfading exploit of the Soviet people and their Armed Forces in winning the historic victory in the Great Patriotic War was a brilliant manifestation of the strength of socialism. This victory strengthened the *prestige and* international position of the USSR and opened up new and favorable possibilities for the growth of the forces of socialism, national liberation, democracy and peace the world over.

Continuing their creative activity, *the working people of the Soviet Union* [Soviet people] have ensured the country's rapid and comprehensive development and the improvement of the socialist system. The alliance of the working class, the collective farm peasantry and the people's intelligentsia and the friendship of the USSR's nations and nationalities have been consolidated. Social, political *and ideological* unity has come about in Soviet society, in which the working class is the leading force. Having fulfilled the tasks of the dictatorship of the proletariat, the Soviet state has become a state of all the people. The leading role of the Communist Party – the vanguard of all the people – has grown.

A developed socialist society has been built in the USSR. At this stage, when socialism is developing on its own foundation, the creative forces of the new system and the advantages of the socialist way of life are being disclosed more and more fully, and the working people are making ever wider use of the fruits of the great revolutionary gains.

This is a society in which mighty productive forces and advanced science and culture have been created, in which the people's well-being is growing steadily and increasingly favorable conditions for the all-round development of the individual are taking shape.

This is a society of mature socialist social relations, in which a new historical community of people – the Soviet people – has come into being on the basis of the drawing together of all *classes and* social strata and the juridical and actual equality of all nations and nationalities *and their fraternal cooperation*.

This is a society in which the working people – patriots and internationalists – have a high degree of organization, ideological conviction and class consciousness.

This is a society in which the law of life is the concern of all for the *welfare* [well-being] of each and the concern of each for the *welfare* [well-being] of all.

This is a society of genuine democracy, whose political system ensures the effective administration of all public affairs, the increasingly active participation of the working people in state life and the combination of real *citizens'* [human] rights and liberties with *their duties and responsibility to society* [civic responsibility].

The developed socialist society is a logically necessary stage on the path to communism.

The supreme goal of the Soviet state is the building of a classless communist society *in which public communist self-government will receive development*. The principal tasks of the *socialist* state *of all the people* are: creating the material and technical base of communism, improving socialist social relations and transforming them into communist relations, rearing the man of communist society, raising the working people's material and cultural living standard, safeguarding the country's security and helping to strengthen peace and to develop international cooperation.

The Soviet people,

guided by the ideas of scientific communism and maintaining fidelity to their revolutionary traditions,

relying on the great social, economic and political gains of socialism,

striving for the further development of socialist democracy,

taking into account the international position of the USSR as a component part of the world socialist system, and conscious of their international responsibility,

preserving the continuity of the ideas and principles of the *first*, 1918 *Soviet* [RSFSR] Constitution, the 1924 USSR Constitution and the 1936 USSR Constitution,

formalize the principles of the USSR's social system and policy, establish the rights, liberties and duties of citizens and the principles of organization and aims of the socialist state of all the people, and proclaim them in this Constitution.

I / PRINCIPLES OF THE SOCIAL (SOCIOPOLITICAL AND ECONOMIC) SYSTEM AND POLICY OF THE USSR

CHAPTER 1 / THE POLITICAL SYSTEM

Article 1 The Union of Soviet Socialist Republics is a socialist state of all the people, expressing the will and interests of the *workers* [working class], *peasants* [the peasantry] and the intelligentsia and of *the working people of* all the country's nations and nationalities.

Article 2 All power in the USSR belongs to the people. The people exercise state power through the Soviets of People's Deputies, which constitute the political foundation of the USSR.

All other state agencies are under the control of and accountable to the Soviets *of People's Deputies.*

Article 3 The organization and activity of the Soviet state are constructed in accordance with the principle of democratic centralism: the elective nature of all bodies of state power, from top to bottom, their accountability to the people, and the binding nature of the decisions of higher bodies on lower. Democratic centralism combines single leadership with local initiative and creative activeness, with the responsibility of every state agency and official for the assigned task.

Article 4 The Soviet state and all its agencies operate on the basis of socialist legality and ensure the protection of law and order, the interests of society and the rights *and liberties* of citizens.

State [institutions] and public organizations and officials are obliged to observe the USSR Constitution and Soviet laws.

Article 5 The most important questions of state life are submitted for nationwide discussion and are also put up for a nationwide vote (referendum).

Article 6 The Communist Party of the Soviet Union is the leading and guiding force of Soviet society, the nucleus of its political system and of [all] state and public organizations. The CPSU exists for the people and serves the people.

Armed with the Marxist-Leninist teaching, the Communist Party determines general prospects for the development of society and the lines of the USSR's domestic and foreign policy, directs the great creative activity of the Soviet people, and gives their struggle for the victory of communism a planned, scientifically substantiated nature.

All Party organizations operate within the framework of the USSR Constitution.

Article 7 In accordance with their statutory tasks, trade unions, the All-Union Lenin Young Communist League and cooperative and other [mass] public organizations participate in the administration of state and public affairs and in the resolution of political, economic, social and cultural questions.

Article 9 [Article 8 in the draft] The basic direction of the development of the political system of Soviet society is the further unfolding of socialist democracy: the ever wider participation of *citizens* [the working people] in the administration of the affairs of the state and of society, the improvement of the state apparatus, an increase in the activeness of public organizations, the intensification of people's control, the strengthening of the legal foundations of state and public life, greater publicity, and constant consideration for public opinion.

CHAPTER 2 / THE ECONOMIC SYSTEM

Article 10 [Article 9] Socialist ownership of the means of production, in the form of state ownership (that of all the people) and collective farm-cooperative ownership [and ownership by trade union and other public organizations], is the foundation of the USSR's economic system.

Socialist ownership also extends to the property of trade union and other public organizations needed to carry out their statutory tasks.

The state protects socialist property and creates conditions for its multiplication.

No one has the right to use socialist property for purposes of personal gain *or for other selfish purposes.*

Article 11 [Article 10] State ownership – the common property of all the Soviet people – is the principal form of socialist ownership.

The land, its mineral wealth, the waters and the forests are the exclusive property of the state. The principal means of production in industry, construction and agriculture, means of transport and communication, banks, *the property of* trade, *municipal-service and other* [social and consumer-service] enterprises *organized by the state* and the bulk of the urban housing stock, *as well as other property necessary to carry out the state's tasks*, belong to the state.

Article 12 [Article 11] The property of collective farms and other cooperative organizations and of their associations is the means of production and other property *necessary for* [that serves] the implementation of their statutory tasks.

The land occupied by collective farms is assigned to them for free use for an unlimited time.

The state assists the development of collective farm-cooperative ownership and its approximation to state ownership.

The collective farms, like other land users, are obliged to use land effectively, take a solicitous attitude toward it and increase its fertility.

Article 13 [Article 12] *Earned income constitutes the foundation of the personal property of USSR citizens. Personal property may include* [USSR citizens may have in their personal possession] household articles, articles of personal consumption and convenience, *articles needed for auxiliary household farming operations*, a house and earned [income and] savings [and an auxiliary farming operation]. The personal property of citizens and their right to its inheritance are protected by *the state* [law].

Citizens may have the use of plots of land made available [by the state or by collective farms], under a procedure established by law, for auxiliary farming operations (including the keeping of livestock and poultry), the growing of fruit and vegetables, and also for individual housing construction. *Citizens are obliged to make rational use of the plots of land made available to them. The state and the collective farms provide assistance to citizens in auxiliary farming operations.*

Property in the personal possession or use of citizens may not serve for the derivation of unearned income or be used to harm *the interests of* society.

Article 14 [Article 13] The [free] labor of Soviet people, *free from exploitation*, is the source of the growth of social wealth and of the well-being of the people and of every Soviet person.

The state exercises control over the measure of labor and consumption in accordance with the principle *of socialism*: 'From each according to his ability, to each according to his work.' It determines the size of the income tax *on taxable income* [and establishes the level of wages exempted from the payment of taxes].

Socially useful labor and its results determine the status of a person in society. By combining material and moral incentives *and encouraging innovation and a creative attitude toward work*, the state helps turn labor into a prime necessity in the life of every Soviet person.

Article 15 [Article 14] The highest goal of social production under socialism is the fullest possible satisfaction of people's growing material and spiritual requirements.

Relying on the creative activeness of the working people, socialist competition and the achievements of scientific and technical progress *and improving the forms and methods of economic management*, the state ensures the growth of labor productivity, increases in production efficiency and the quality of work, and the dynamic, *planned* and proportional development of the national economy.

Article 16 [Article 15] The economy of the USSR is a single national-economic complex embracing all elements of social production, distribution and exchange on the country's territory.

Management of the economy is carried out on the basis of state plans *of economic and social development* [for the development of the national economy and social and cultural construction], taking branch and territorial principles into account, and combining centralized management with the economic independence and initiative of enterprises, associations and other organizations. In this process, active use is made of economic accountability, profit, unit cost *and other economic levers and incentives*.

Article 17 Individual labor activity in the sphere of handicrafts, agriculture and consumer services for the population, as well as other types of activity based exclusively on the personal labor of citizens and members of their families, is permitted in the USSR in accordance with the law. *The state regulates individual labor activity, seeing to it that it is used in the interests of society.*

Article 18 In the interests of present and future generations, the necessary steps are being taken in the USSR to protect and make scientifically substantiated and rational use of the land and its mineral wealth, *water resources* and flora and fauna, to preserve the purity of the air and water, to ensure the reproduction of natural resources, and to improve man's environment.

CHAPTER 4 / FOREIGN POLICY

Article 28 The USSR [Soviet state] *steadfastly* [consistently] pursues a Leninist policy of peace, and it stands for the consolidation of the security of peoples and broad international cooperation.

The USSR's foreign policy is aimed at ensuring favorable international conditions for building communism in the USSR, *protecting the Soviet Union's state interests*, strengthening the positions of world socialism, supporting the peoples' struggle for national liberation and social progress, preventing wars of aggression, *achieving general and complete disarmament* and consistently implementing the principle of the peaceful coexistence of states with different social systems.

In the USSR, war propaganda is forbidden [by law].

Article 29 The USSR's relations with other states are constructed on the basis of observance of the principles of sovereign equality; mutual renunciation of the use of force or the threat of force; the inviolability of borders; the territorial integrity of states; the peaceful settlement of disputes; noninterference in internal affairs; respect for human rights and basic liberties; equality and the right of peoples to decide their own fate; cooperation between states; and the conscientious fulfillment of commitments stemming from generally recognized principles and norms of international law and from international treaties concluded by the USSR.

Article 30 The USSR [Soviet Union], as a component part of the world socialist system and the socialist commonwealth, develops and strengthens friendship, cooperation and comradely mutual assistance with other socialist countries on the basis of *the principle of* socialist internationalism and actively participates in economic integration and in the international socialist division of labor.

II / THE STATE AND THE INDIVIDUAL

CHAPTER 6 / USSR CITIZENSHIP, THE EQUALITY OF CITIZENS

Article 33 Uniform Union citizenship is established in the USSR. Every citizen of a Union republic is a USSR citizen.

The grounds and procedure for acquiring and losing Soviet citizenship are *defined* [established] by *the Law on USSR Citizenship* [USSR law].

USSR citizens abroad enjoy the protection of the Soviet state.

Article 34 USSR citizens are equal before the law, regardless of origin, social or property status, race or nationality, sex, education, language, attitude to religion, nature or type of employment, place of residence or other circumstances.

Equal rights for USSR citizens are ensured in all fields of economic, political, social and cultural life.

Article 35 Women and men have equal rights in the USSR.

The exercise of these rights is ensured by providing women with opportunities equal *to those of men* in receiving an education and vocational training, in labor, remuneration and promotion and in social, political and cultural activity, as well as by special measures to protect women's labor and health; *by the creation of conditions enabling women to combine labor and motherhood*; by legal protection and material and moral support for mother and child, including the granting of paid leave and other benefits to pregnant women and mothers; and by *the gradual reduction of working time for women with small children* [state aid to single mothers.]

Article 36 USSR [Soviet] citizens of different races and nationalities have equal rights.

The exercise of these rights is ensured by the policy of the all-round development and drawing together of all the USSR's nations and nationalities, the fostering in citizens of a spirit of Soviet patriotism and socialist internationalism, and the opportunity to use the mother tongue and languages of other peoples of the USSR.

Any kind of direct or indirect restriction of the rights of citizens or the establishment of any direct or indirect advantages for citizens on a racial or national basis, as well as any preaching of racial or national exclusiveness, hostility or contempt, is punishable by law.

CHAPTER 7 / THE BASIC RIGHTS,
LIBERTIES AND DUTIES OF USSR CITIZENS

Article 39 USSR citizens possess the whole range of social, economic, political and personal rights and liberties proclaimed in and guaranteed by the USSR Constitution and Soviet laws. The socialist system ensures the expansion of rights and liberties and the continuous improvement of the living conditions of citizens in step with the fulfillment of programs of social, economic and cultural development.

The exercise of rights and liberties by citizens must not injure the interests of society and the state or the rights of other citizens.

Article 40 USSR citizens have the right to labor – that is, to receive guaranteed work and remuneration for labor in accordance with its quantity and quality *and not below the minimum amount established by the state* – including the right to choice of occupation, type of employment and work in accordance with one's primary vocation, capabilities, vocational training and education and with consideration for social requirements.

This right is ensured by the socialist economic system, the steady growth of productive forces [of society], free vocational instruction, the improvement of labor skills and training in new specialties, *and the development of the systems of vocational guidance and job placement.*

Article 41 USSR citizens have the right to rest.

This right is ensured by the *establishment of a* [41-hour] workweek *not exceeding 41 hours* for workers and office employees, a shortened working day for a number of occupations and production sectors, and shorter working hours at night; the provision of annual paid vacations and weekly days off, and also by the expansion of the network of cultural-enlightenment and health-improvement institutions and the large-scale development of sports, physical culture and tourism; and the creation of favorable opportunities for rest at one's place of residence and other conditions for the rational use of free time.

The length of working time and of rest for collective farmers is regulated by the collective *farms* [farm charters].

Article 42 USSR citizens have the right to health care.

This right is ensured by free and qualified medical assistance, provided by state public health institutions; by the expansion of the network of institutions for providing citizens with medical treatment and health-improvement services; by the development and improvement of safety measures and industrial sanitation; by conducting wide-scale preventive-medicine measures; by measures to improve the environment; by special concern for the health of the growing generation, including the prohibition of child labor *not involving training and labor upbringing;* and by the development of scientific research aimed at preventing disease, reducing its incidence and ensuring long and active lives for citizens.

Article 43 USSR citizens have the right to material security in old age, in case of illness, and in the event of complete or partial disability or loss of breadwinner.

This right is guaranteed by social insurance for workers, office employees and collective farmers and by temporary disability allowances; by *the payment by the state and by collective farms of* old-age and disability pensions and pensions for loss of breadwinner; by the job placement of citizens with partial disability; by care for [single] elderly citizens and for invalids; *and by other forms of social insurance.*

Article 44 USSR citizens have the right to housing.

This right is ensured by the development and protection of the state and public housing stock, by assistance to cooperative and individual housing construction, by the fair distribution, under public control, of housing space allotted in accordance with the implementation of the program for the construction of *well-appointed* housing, and also by low apartment rents *and charges for municipal services. USSR citizens must take good care of the housing allocated to them.*

Article 45 USSR citizens have the right to education.

This right is ensured by the free nature of all types of education, the implementation of the universal compulsory secondary education of young people and the broad development of vocational-technical, specialized secondary and higher education based on the linkage of instruction with life and production; by the development of correspondence and evening education; by the provision of state stipends and other benefits for pupils and students; by the free issuance of school textbooks; by the opportunity for school instruction in one's native tongue; and by the [development of the vocational guidance system and the] creation of conditions for [the working people's] self-education.

Article 46 USSR citizens have the right to use cultural achievements.

This right is ensured by general access to the values of Soviet and world culture in state and public collections; by the development and balanced distribution of cultural-enlightenment institutions in the country; *by the development of television, radio, book publishing, the periodical press and the network of free libraries*; and by the expansion of cultural exchanges with foreign states.

Article 47 USSR citizens, in accordance with the goals of communist construction, are guaranteed freedom of scientific, technical and artistic creation. This freedom is ensured by the extensive development of scientific research, invention and rationalization activity and by the development of *literature and the arts*. The state creates the necessary material conditions for this, gives support to voluntary societies and unions of creative artists, *and organizes the introduction of inventions and rationalization proposals in the national economy and other spheres of life.*

The rights of authors, inventors and rationalizers are protected by *the state* [law].

Article 48 USSR citizens have the right to participate in the administration of state and public affairs *and in the discussion and adoption of laws and decisions of nationwide and local importance.*

This right is ensured by the opportunity to elect and be elected to Soviets of People's Deputies and other elective state agencies, to take part in nationwide discussions and votes in people's control, in the work of state agencies, public organizations and public-initiative agencies, and in meetings of labor collectives and meetings at places of residence.

Article 49 Every USSR citizen has the right to submit to state agencies and public organizations proposals on improving their activity and to criticize shortcomings in work.

Officials are obliged, within the established [by law] time periods, to examine proposals and statements by citizens, to reply to them and to take the necessary steps.

Persecution for criticism is prohibited. *Persons who persecute others for criticism will be called to account.*

Article 50 In accordance with the [working] people's interests and for the purpose of strengthening *and developing* the socialist system, USSR citizens are guaranteed freedom of speech, of the press, of assembly, of mass meetings and of street processions and demonstrations.

The exercise of these political freedoms is ensured by putting public buildings, streets and squares at the disposal of the working people and their organizations, by the broad dissemination of information, and by the opportunity to use the press, television and radio.

Article 51 In accordance with the goals of communist construction, USSR citizens have the right to unite in public organizations that facilitate the development of political activeness and initiative and the satisfaction of their diverse interests.

Public organizations are guaranteed conditions for the successful performance of their statutory tasks.

Article 52 *USSR citizens are guaranteed* freedom of conscience [is recognized for USSR citizens], that is, the right to profess any religion or to profess none, to perform religious worship or to conduct atheistic propaganda. The incitement of hostility and hatred in connection with religious beliefs is prohibited.

In the USSR the church is separate from the state, and the school is separate from the church.

Article 53 The family is under the protection of the state.

Marriage is *based on* [entered into with] the voluntary agreement of the bride and groom; the spouses are completely equal in family relations.

The state *shows concern for* [aids] the family by creating and developing an extensive network of children's institutions, by organizing and improving consumer services and public catering, by paying childbirth allowances, by providing allowances and benefits for large families, *and by other types of allowances and family assistance.*

Article 54 USSR citizens are guaranteed inviolability of the person. No one can be arrested except *on the basis of a court decision* [by court order] or with the sanction of a prosecutor.

Article 55 USSR citizens are guaranteed inviolability of the home. No one has the right, without lawful grounds, to enter a home against the will of the persons living therein.

Article 56 The private lives of citizens and the confidentiality of correspondence, telephone conversations and telegraph messages are protected by law.

Article 57 Respect for the individual and the protection of the rights and liberties of *citizens* [Soviet persons] are the obligation of all state agencies, public organizations and officials.

USSR citizens have the right to legal protection against attempts on their honor and dignity, their lives and health, and their personal freedom and property.

Article 58 USSR citizens have the right to file complaints against the actions of officials and state *and public* agencies [and public organizations]. These complaints are to be examined according to the procedure and within the time periods established by law.

Actions of officials, performed in violation of the law and exceeding their authority, that infringe on the rights of citizens may be protested to a court according to the procedure established by law.

USSR citizens have the right to compensation for damages caused by illegal actions of state [institutions] and public organizations, and also of officials during the performance of their duties [according to the procedure and within the limits established by law].

Article 59 The exercise of rights and liberties is inseparable from the performance by citizens of their duties.

USSR citizens are obliged to observe the USSR Constitution and Soviet laws, to respect the rules of the Socialist community, and to bear with dignity the lofty title of USSR citizen.

Article 60 Conscientious labor in one's chosen field of socially useful activity and the [strict] observance of labor discipline are the duty of, and a matter of honor for, every able-bodied USSR citizen. *The evasion of socially useful labor is incompatible with the principles of a socialist society.*

Article 61 The USSR citizen is obliged to protect and enhance socialist property. It is the duty of the USSR citizen to combat the theft and waste of state and public property *and to take good care of the people's property.*

Persons encroaching on socialist property are punishable by law.

Article 65 The USSR citizen is obliged to respect the rights and legitimate interests of other persons, to be intolerant of antisocial acts, and to assist in every way in the safeguarding of public order.

III / THE NATIONAL-STATE STRUCTURE OF THE USSR

CHAPTER 8 / THE USSR IS A FEDERAL STATE

Article 70 [Article 69] The Union of Soviet Socialist Republics is a unitary, federal and multinational state, formed *on the basis of the principle of socialist federalism and* as a result of the free self-determination of nations and the voluntary union of equal Soviet Socialist Republics.

The USSR embodies the state unity of the Soviet people and unites all nations and nationalities for the purpose of the joint construction of communism.

Article 72 [Article 71] Each Union republic retains the right freely to secede from the USSR.

V / THE SUPREME BODIES OF STATE POWER
AND ADMINISTRATION IN THE USSR

CHAPTER 15 / THE USSR SUPREME SOVIET

Article 108 [Article 106] The USSR Supreme Soviet is the supreme body of state power in the USSR.

The USSR Supreme Soviet is empowered to resolve all questions placed within the jurisdiction of the USSR by this Constitution.

The adoption of the USSR Constitution and its amendment; the admission of new republics to the USSR and the ratification of the formation of new autonomous republics and autonomous provinces; the ratification of state plans for the *economic and social development of* [development of the national economy and for social and cultural construction in] the USSR, the USSR State Budget and reports on their fulfillment; and the formation of USSR agencies accountable to the USSR Supreme Soviet are exercised exclusively by that body.

USSR laws are adopted [solely] by the USSR Supreme Soviet *or by a nationwide vote (referendum), conducted by decision of the USSR Supreme Soviet.*

Article 109 [Article 107] The USSR Supreme Soviet consists of two chambers: the Council of the Union and the Council of Nationalities.

The chambers of the USSR Supreme Soviet have equal rights.

Article 110 [Article 108] The Council of the Union and the Council of Nationalities have an equal number of Deputies.

The Council of the Union is elected on the basis of election districts with equal populations.

The Council of Nationalities is elected according to the following norms: 32 Deputies from each Union republic, 11 Deputies from each autonomous republic, 5 Deputies from each autonomous province and 1 Deputy from each autonomous region ...

CHAPTER 16 / THE USSR COUNCIL OF MINISTERS

Article 128 [Article 127] The USSR Council of Ministers – the USSR government – is the supreme executive and administrative body of state power in the USSR.

Article 129 [Article 128] The USSR Council of Ministers is formed by the USSR Supreme Soviet at a joint meeting of the Council of the Union and the Council of Nationalities and consists of the Chairman of the USSR Council of Ministers, the First Vice-Chairmen and Vice-Chairmen [of the USSR Council of Ministers], the USSR ministers and the chairmen of USSR state committees.

The Chairmen of the Union-republic Councils of Ministers are ex-officio members of the USSR Council of Ministers.

On a representation by the Chairman of the USSR Council of Ministers, the USSR Supreme Soviet may include the heads of other USSR agencies and organizations in the USSR government.

VII / JUSTICE, ARBITRATION AND PROSECUTOR'S SUPERVISION

CHAPTER 20 / THE COURTS AND ARBITRATION

Article 151 [Article 150] In the USSR, justice is administered solely by the courts.

In the USSR there are the USSR Supreme Court, the Union-republic Supreme Courts, the autonomous-republic Supreme Courts, territory, province and city courts, autonomous-province courts, autonomous-region courts, district (city) people's courts, and the military tribunals in the Armed Forces.

Article 152 [Article 151] All courts in the USSR are formed on the principle that the posts of judges and people's assessors are elective ...

Article 153 [Article 152] The USSR Supreme Court is the supreme judicial body of the USSR and exercises supervision over the judicial activity of USSR courts, as well as of Union-republic courts, within the limits established by law.

The USSR Supreme Court is elected by the USSR Supreme Soviet [for a term of five years] and is composed of a chairman, vice-chairmen, members and people's assessors. The chairmen of the Union-republic Supreme Courts are ex-officio members of the USSR Supreme Court.

CHAPTER 21 / THE PROSECUTOR'S OFFICE

Article 164 [Article 163] Supreme supervision over the precise and uniform execution of laws by all ministries, state committees and departments, enterprises, institutions and organizations, executive and administrative agencies of local Soviets of People's Deputies, collective farms, cooperative and other public organizations, officials and citizens is vested in the USSR Prosecutor General and in prosecutors subordinate to him.

Article 165 [Article 164] The USSR Prosecutor General is appointed by the USSR Supreme Soviet, is responsible and accountable to it and, in intervals between sessions of the Supreme Soviet, to the Presidium of the USSR Supreme Soviet.

Article 166 [Article 165] The prosecutors of Union republics, autonomous republics, territories, provinces and autonomous provinces are appointed by the USSR Prosecutor General. The prosecutors of autonomous regions and district and city prosecutors are appointed by the Union-republic prosecutors and approved by the USSR Prosecutor General.

Article 167 [Article 166] The term of office of the USSR Prosecutor General and of all lower-ranking prosecutors is five years ...

IX / THE LEGAL EFFECT OF THE USSR CONSTITUTION AND THE PROCEDURE FOR AMENDING IT

Article 173 [Article 172] The USSR Constitution has supreme legal force. All laws and other acts of state agencies are issued on the basis of and in conformity with the USSR Constitution. [The USSR Constitution goes into effect at the time it is adopted.]

Article 174 [Article 173] The USSR Constitution is changed by a decision of the USSR Supreme Soviet, adopted by a majority of at least two-thirds of the total number of Deputies in each of its chambers.

China

Constitution of the People's Republic of China (adopted 5 March 1978)

Preamble

After more than a century of heroic struggle the Chinese people, led by the Communist Party of China headed by our great leader and teacher Chairman Mao Tsetung, finally overthrew the reactionary rule of imperialism, feudalism and bureaucrat-capitalism by means of people's revolutionary war, winning complete victory in the new-democratic revolution, and in 1949 founded the People's Republic of China.

The founding of the People's Republic of China marked the beginning of the historical period of socialism in our country. Since then, under the leadership of Chairman Mao and the Chinese Communist Party, the people of all our nationalities have carried out Chairman Mao's proletarian revolutionary line in the political, economic, cultural and military fields and in foreign affairs and have won great victories in socialist revolution and socialist construction through repeated struggles against enemies both at home and abroad and through the Great Proletarian Cultural Revolution. The dictatorship of the proletariat in our country has been consolidated and strengthened, and China has become a socialist country with the beginnings of prosperity.

Chairman Mao Tsetung was the founder of the People's Republic of China. All our victories in revolution and construction have been won under the guidance of Marxism-Leninism-Mao Tsetung Thought. The fundamental guarantee that the people of all our nationalities will struggle in unity and carry the proletarian revolution through to the end is always to hold high and staunchly to defend the great banner of Chairman Mao.

The triumphant conclusion of the first Great Proletarian Cultural Revolution has ushered in a new period of development in China's socialist revolution and socialist construction. In accordance with the basic line of the Chinese Communist Party for the entire historical period of socialism, the general task for the people of the whole country in this new period is: To persevere in continuing the revolution under the dictatorship of the proletariat, carry forward the three great revolutionary movements of class struggle, the struggle for production and scientific experiment, and make China a great and powerful socialist country with modern agriculture, industry, national defence and science and technology by the end of the century.

We must persevere in the struggle of the proletariat against the bourgeoisie and in the struggle for the socialist road against the capitalist road. We must oppose revisionism and prevent the restoration of capitalism. We must be prepared to deal with subversion and aggression against our country by social-imperialism and imperialism.

We should consolidate and expand the revolutionary united front which is led by the working class and based on the worker-peasant alliance, and which unites the large numbers of intellectuals and other working people, patriotic democratic parties, patriotic personages, our compatriots in Taiwan, Hongkong and Macao, and our countrymen residing abroad. We should enhance the great unity of all the nationalities in our country. We should correctly distinguish and handle the contradictions among the people and those between ourselves and the enemy. We should endeavour to create among the people of the whole country a political situation in which there are both centralism and democracy, both discipline and freedom, both unity of will and personal ease of mind and liveliness, so as to help bring all positive factors into play, overcome all difficulties, better consolidate the proletarian dictatorship and build up our country more rapidly.

Taiwan is China's sacred territory. We are determined to liberate Taiwan and accomplish the great cause of unifying our motherland.

In international affairs, we should establish and develop relations with other countries on the basis of the Five Principles of mutual respect for sovereignty and territorial integrity, mutual non-aggression, non-interference in each other's internal affairs, equality and mutual benefit, and peaceful coexistence. Our country will never seek hegemony, or strive to be a superpower. We should uphold proletarian internationalism. In accordance with the theory of the three worlds, we should strengthen our unity with the proletariat and the oppressed people and nations throughout the world, the socialist countries, and the third world countries, and we should unite with all countries subjected to aggression, subversion, interference, control and bullying by the social-imperialist and imperialist superpowers to form the broadest possible international united front against the hegemonism of the superpowers and against a new world war, and strive for the progress and emancipation of humanity.

CHAPTER ONE / GENERAL PRINCIPLES

Article 1 The People's Republic of China is a socialist state of the dictatorship of the proletariat led by the working class and based on the alliance of workers and peasants.

Article 2 The Communist Party of China is the core of leadership of the whole Chinese people. The working class exercises leadership over the state through its vanguard, the Communist Party of China.

The guiding ideology of the People's Republic of China is Marxism-Leninism-Mao Tsetung Thought.

Article 3 All power in the People's Republic of China belongs to the people. The organs through which the people exercise state power are the National People's Congress and the local people's congresses at various levels.

The National People's Congress, the local people's congresses at various levels and all other organs of state practise democratic centralism.

Article 4 The People's Republic of China is a unitary multinational state.

All the nationalities are equal. There should be unity and fraternal love among the nationalities and they should help and learn from each other. Discrimination against, or oppression of, any nationality, and acts which undermine the unity of the nationalities are prohibited. Big-nationality chauvinism and local-nationality chauvinism must be opposed.

All the nationalities have the freedom to use and develop their own spoken and written languages, and to preserve or reform their own customs and ways.

Regional autonomy applies in an area where a minority nationality lives in a compact community. All the national autonomous areas are inalienable parts of the People's Republic of China.

Article 5 There are mainly two kinds of ownership of the means of production in the People's Republic of China at the present stage: socialist ownership by the whole people and socialist collective ownership by the working people.

The state allows non-agricultural individual labourers to engage in individual labour involving no exploitation of others, within the limits permitted by law and under unified arrangement and management by organizations at the basic level in cities and towns or in rural areas. At the same time, it guides these individual labourers step by step onto the road of socialist collectivization.

Article 6 The state sector of the economy, that is, the socialist sector owned by the whole people, is the leading force in the national economy.

Mineral resources, waters and those forests, undeveloped lands and other marine and land resources owned by the state are the property of the whole people.

The state may requisition by purchase, take over for use, or nationalize land under conditions prescribed by law.

Article 9 The state protects the right of citizens to own lawfully earned income, savings, houses and other means of livelihood.

Article 10 The state applies the socialist principles: 'He who does not work, neither shall he eat' and 'from each according to his ability, to each according to his work.'

Work is an honourable duty for every citizen able to work. The state promotes socialist labour emulation, and, putting proletarian politics in command, it applies the policy of combining moral encouragement with material reward, with the stress on the former, in order to heighten the citizens' socialist enthusiasm and creativeness in work.

Article 11 The state adheres to the general line of going all out, aiming high and achieving greater, faster, better and more economical results in building socialism, it undertakes the planned, proportionate and high-speed development of the national economy, and it continuously develops the productive forces, so as to consolidate the country's independence and security and improve the people's material and cultural life step by step.

In developing the national economy, the state adheres to the principle of building our country independently, with the initiative in our own hands and through self-reliance, hard struggle, diligence and thrift, it adheres to the principle of taking agriculture as the foundation and industry as the leading factor, and it adheres to the principle of bringing the initiative of both the central and local authorities into full play under the unified leadership of the central authorities.

The state protects the environment and national resources and prevents and eliminates pollution and other hazards to the public.

Article 12 The state devotes major efforts to developing science, expands scientific research, promotes technical innovation and technical revolution and adopts advanced techniques wherever possible in all departments of the national economy. In scientific and technological work we must follow the practice of combining professional contingents with the masses, and combining learning from others with our own creative efforts.

Article 13 The state devotes major efforts to developing education in order to raise the cultural and scientific level of the whole nation. Education must serve proletarian politics and be combined with productive labour and must enable everyone who receives an education to develop morally, intellectually and physically and become a worker with both socialist consciousness and culture.

Article 14 The state upholds the leading position of Marxism-Leninism-Mao Tsetung Thought in all spheres of ideology and culture. All cultural undertakings must serve the workers, peasants and soldiers and serve socialism.

The state applies the policy of 'letting a hundred flowers blossom and a hundred schools of thought contend' so as to promote the development of the arts and sciences and bring about a flourishing socialist culture.

Article 18 The state safeguards the socialist system, suppresses all treasonable and counter-revolutionary activities, punishes all traitors and counter-revolutionaries, and punishes new-born bourgeois elements and other bad elements.

The state deprives of political rights, as prescribed by law, those landlords, rich peasants and reactionary capitalists who have not yet been reformed, and at the same time it provides them with the opportunity to earn a living so that they may be reformed through labour and become law-abiding citizens supporting themselves by their own labour.

SECTION V / THE PEOPLE'S COURTS
AND THE PEOPLE'S PROCURATORATES

Article 42 The Supreme People's Court is the highest judicial organ.

The Supreme People's Court supervises the administration of justice by local people's courts at various levels and by special people's courts; people's courts at the higher levels supervise the administration of justice by people's courts at the lower levels.

The Supreme People's Court is responsible and accountable to the National People's Congress and its Standing Committee. Local people's courts at various levels are responsible and accountable to local people's congresses at the corresponding levels.

Article 43 The Supreme People's Procuratorate exercises procuratorial authority to ensure observance of the Constitution and the law by all the departments under the State Council, the local organs of state at various levels, the personnel of organs of state and the citizens. Local people's procuratorates and special people's procuratorates exercise procuratorial authority within the limits prescribed by law. The people's procuratorates are formed as prescribed by law.

The Supreme People's Procuratorate supervises the work of local people's procuratorates at various levels and of special people's procuratorates; people's procuratorates at the higher levels supervise the work of those at the lower levels.

The Supreme People's Procuratorate is responsible and accountable to the National People's Congress and its Standing Committee. Local people's procuratorates at various levels are responsible and accountable to people's congresses at the corresponding levels.

CHAPTER THREE / THE FUNDAMENTAL RIGHTS
AND DUTIES OF CITIZENS

Article 44 All citizens who have reached the age of eighteen have the right to vote and to stand for election, with the exception of persons deprived of these rights by law.

Article 45 Citizens enjoy freedom of speech, correspondence, the press, assembly, association, procession, demonstration and the freedom to strike, and have the right to 'speak out freely, air their views fully, hold great debates and write big-character posters.'

Article 46 Citizens enjoy freedom to believe in religion and freedom not to believe in religion and to propagate atheism.

Article 47 The citizens' freedom of person and their homes are inviolable.

No citizen may be arrested except by decision of a people's court or with the sanction of a people's procuratorate, and the arrest must be made by a public security organ.

Article 48 Citizens have the right to work. To ensure that citizens enjoy this right, the state provides employment in accordance with the principle of overall consideration, and, on the basis of increased production, the state gradually increases payment for labour, improves working conditions, strengthens labour protection and expands collective welfare.

Article 49 Working people have the right to rest. To ensure that working people enjoy this right, the state prescribes working hours and systems of vacations and gradually expands material facilities for the working people to rest and recuperate.

Article 50 Working people have the right to material assistance in old age, and in case of illness or disability. To ensure that working people enjoy this right, the state gradually expands social insurance, social assistance, public health services, co-operative medical services, and other services.

The state cares for and ensures the livelihood of disabled revolutionary armymen and the families of revolutionary martyrs.

Article 51 Citizens have the right to education. To ensure that citizens enjoy this right, the state gradually increases the number of schools of various types and of other cultural and educational institutions and popularizes education.

The state pays special attention to the healthy development of young people and children.

Article 52 Citizens have the freedom to engage in scientific research, literary and artistic creation and other cultural activities. The state encourages and assists the creative endeavours of citizens engaged in science, education, literature, art, journalism, publishing, public health, sports and other cultural work.

Article 53 Women enjoy equal rights with men in all spheres of political, economic, cultural, social and family life. Men and women enjoy equal pay for equal work.

Men and women shall marry of their own free will. The state protects marriage, the family, and the mother and child.

The state advocates and encourages family planning.

Article 54 The state protects the just rights and interests of overseas Chinese and their relatives.

Article 55 Citizens have the right to lodge complaints with organs of state at any level against any person working in an organ of state, enterprise or institution for transgression of law or neglect of duty. Citizens have the right to appeal to organs of state at any level against any infringement of their rights. No one shall suppress such complaints and appeals or retaliate against persons making them.

Article 56 Citizens must support the leadership of the Communist Party of China, support the socialist system, safeguard the unification of the motherland and the unity of all nationalities in our country and abide by the Constitution and the law.

Article 57 Citizens must take care of and protect public property, observe labour discipline, observe public order, respect social ethics and safeguard state secrets.

Article 58 It is the lofty duty of every citizen to defend the motherland and resist aggression.

It is the honourable obligation of citizens to perform military service and to join the militia according to the law.

Article 59 The People's Republic of China grants the right of residence to any foreign national persecuted for supporting a just cause, for taking part in revolutionary movements or for engaging in scientific work.

European Communities

Treaty instituting the European Economic Community (Treaty of Rome, signed 25 March 1957; entered into force 1 January 1958)

HIS MAJESTY THE KING OF THE BELGIANS, THE PRESIDENT OF THE FEDERAL REPUBLIC OF GERMANY, THE PRESIDENT OF THE FRENCH REPUBLIC, THE PRESIDENT OF THE ITALIAN REPUBLIC, HER ROYAL HIGHNESS THE GRAND DUCHESS OF LUXEMBOURG, HER MAJESTY THE QUEEN OF THE NETHERLANDS,

DETERMINED to lay the foundations of an ever closer union among the peoples of Europe,

RESOLVED to ensure the economic and social progress of their countries by common action to eliminate the barriers which divide Europe,

AFFIRMING as the essential objective of their efforts the constant improvement of the living and working conditions of their peoples,

RECOGNISING that the removal of existing obstacles calls for concerted action in order to guarantee steady expansion, balanced trade and fair competition,

ANXIOUS to strengthen the unity of their economies and to ensure their harmonious development by reducing the differences existing between the various regions and the backwardness of the less favoured regions,

DESIRING to contribute, by means of a common commercial policy, to the progressive abolition of restrictions on international trade,

INTENDING to confirm the solidarity which binds Europe and the overseas countries and desiring to ensure the development of their prosperity, in accordance with the principles of the Charter of the United Nations,

RESOLVED by thus pooling their resources to preserve and strengthen peace and liberty, and calling upon the other peoples of Europe who share their ideal to join in their efforts,

HAVE DECIDED to create a European Economic Community ...

Article 1

By this Treaty, the High Contracting Parties establish among themselves a EUROPEAN ECONOMIC COMMUNITY.

Article 2

The Community shall have as its task, by establishing a common market and progressively approximating the economic policies of Member States, to promote throughout the Community a harmonious development of economic activities, a continuous and balanced expansion, an increase in stability, an accelerated raising of the standard of living and closer relations between the States belonging to it.

Article 3

For the purposes set out in Article 2, the activities of the Community shall include, as provided in this Treaty and in accordance with the timetable set out therein

a / the elimination, as between Member States, of customs duties and of quantitative restrictions on the import and export of goods, and of all other measures having equivalent effect;

b / the establishment of a common customs tariff and of a common commercial policy towards third countries;

c / the abolition, as between Member States, of obstacles to freedom of movement for persons, services and capital;

d / the adoption of a common policy in the sphere of agriculture;

e / the adoption of a common policy in the sphere of transport;

f / the institution of a system ensuring that competition in the common market is not distorted;

g / the application of procedures by which the economic policies of Member States can be coordinated and disequilibria in their balances of payments remedied;

h / the approximation of the laws of Member States to the extent required for the proper functioning of the common market;

i / the creation of a European Social Fund in order to improve employment opportunities for workers and to contribute to the raising of their standard of living;

j / the establishment of a European Investment Bank to facilitate the economic expansion of the Community by opening up fresh resources;

k / the association of the overseas countries and territories in order to increase trade and to promote jointly economic and social development.

Article 4

1 The tasks entrusted to the Community shall be carried out by the following institutions:

an ASSEMBLY,
a COUNCIL,
a COMMISSION,
a COURT OF JUSTICE.

Each institution shall act within the limits of the powers conferred upon it by this Treaty.

2 The Council and the Commission shall be assisted by an Economic and Social Committee acting in an advisory capacity.

Article 5

Member States shall take all appropriate measures, whether general or particular, to ensure fulfilment of the obligations arising out of this Treaty or resulting from action taken by the institutions of the Community. They shall facilitate the achievement of the Community's tasks.

They shall abstain from any measure which could jeopardise the attainment of the objectives of this Treaty.

Article 6

1 Member States shall, in close cooperation with the institutions of the Community, coordinate their respective economic policies to the extent necessary to attain the objectives of this Treaty.

2 The institutions of the Community shall take care not to prejudice the internal and external financial stability of the Member States.

Article 7

Within the scope of application of this Treaty, and without prejudice to any special provisions contained therein, any discrimination on grounds of nationality shall be prohibited.

The Council may, on a proposal from the Commission and after consulting the Assembly, adopt, by a qualified majority, rules designed to prohibit such discrimination.

Article 8

1 The common market shall be progressively established during a transitional period of twelve years.

This transitional period shall be divided into three stages of four years each; the length of each stage may be altered in accordance with the provisions set out below.

2 To each stage there shall be assigned a set of actions to be initiated and carried through concurrently.

3 Transition from the first to the second stage shall be conditional upon a finding that the objectives specifically laid down in this Treaty for the first stage have in fact been attained in substance and that, subject to the exceptions and procedures provided for in this Treaty, the obligations have been fulfilled ...

5 The second and third stages may not be extended or curtailed except by a decision of the Council, acting unanimously on a proposal from the Commission.

6 Nothing in the preceding paragraphs shall cause the transitional period to last more than fifteen years after the entry into force of this Treaty.

7 Save for the exceptions or derogations provided for in this Treaty, the expiry of the transitional period shall constitute the latest date by which all the rules laid down must enter into force and all the measures required for establishing the common market must be implemented.

Article 232

1 The provisions of this Treaty shall not affect the provisions of the Treaty establishing the European Coal and Steel Community, in particular as regards the rights and obligations of Member States, the powers of the institutions of that Community and the rules laid down by that Treaty for the Functioning of the common market in coal and steel.

2 The provisions of this Treaty shall not derogate from those of the Treaty establishing the European Atomic Energy Community.

Article 233

The provisions of this Treaty shall not preclude the existence or completion of regional unions between Belgium and Luxembourg, or between Belgium, Luxembourg and the Netherlands, to the extent that the objectives of these regional unions are not attained by application of this Treaty.

Article 234

The rights and obligations arising from agreements concluded before the entry into force of this Treaty between one or more Member States on the one hand, and one or more third countries on the other, shall not be affected by the provisions of this Treaty.

To the extent that such agreements are not compatible with this Treaty, the Member State or States concerned shall take all appropriate steps to eliminate the incompatibilities established. Member States shall, where necessary, assist each other to this end and shall, where appropriate, adopt a common attitude.

In applying the agreements referred to in the first paragraph, Member States shall take into account the fact that the advantages accorded under this

Treaty by each Member State form an integral part of the establishment of the Community and are thereby inseparably linked with the creation of common institutions, the conferring of powers upon them and the granting of the same advantages by all the other Member States.

Article 236

The Government of any Member State or the Commission may submit to the Council proposals for the amendment of this Treaty.

If the Council, after consulting the Assembly and, where appropriate, the Commission, delivers an opinion in favour of calling a conference of representatives of the Governments of the Member States, the conference shall be convened by the President of the Council for the purpose of determining by common accord the amendments to be made to this Treaty.

The amendments shall enter into force after being ratified by all the Member States in accordance with their respective constitutional requirements.

Article 237

Any European State may apply to become a member of the Community. It shall address its application to the Council, which shall act unanimously after obtaining the opinion of the Commission.

The conditions of admission and the adjustments to this Treaty necessitated thereby shall be the subject of an agreement between the Member States and the applicant State. This agreement shall be submitted for ratification by all the Contracting States in accordance with their respective constitutional requirements.

Article 238

The Community may conclude with a third State, a union of States or an international organisation agreements establishing an association involving reciprocal rights and obligations, common action and special procedures.

These agreements shall be concluded by the Council, acting unanimously after consulting the Assembly.

Where such agreements call for amendments to this Treaty, these amendments shall first be adopted in accordance with the procedure laid down in Article 236.

Article 239

The Protocols annexed to this Treaty by common accord of the Member States shall form an integral part thereof.

Article 240

This Treaty is concluded for an unlimited period.

Bibliography

Alexandrowicz, C.H. *Constitutional Developments in India* (1957)

Apelt, W. *Geschichte der Weimarer Verfassung* (2nd ed, 1964)

Banerjee, D.N. *Our Fundamental Rights. Their nature and extent (as judicially determined)* (1960)

Baring, A. 'Gründungsstufen, Gründungsväter,' in *Nach Dreissig Jahren*, Walter Scheel ed, at p 19 (1979)

Basu, D.D. *Shorter Constitution of India* (5th ed, 1967)

Bayer, H.-W. *Die Bundestreue* (1961)

Beard, Charles A. *An Economic Interpretation of the Constitution of the United States* (1913)

– *Economic Origins of Jeffersonian Democracy* (1915)

Berlia, G. 'La dissolution et le régime des pouvoirs publics,' in *Recueil publié en hommage à la mémoire de Georges Berlia*, Georges Vedel and J. Robert eds, at p 107 (1980)

– 'L'évolution constitutionnelle française depuis 1944' ibid, at p 55

– 'Le Président de la République dans la Constitution de 1958' ibid, at p 133

– 'Le problème de la constitutionnalité du referendum du 28 octobre 1962' ibid, at p 189

Bebr, G. *Judicial Control of the European Communities* (1962)

Berber, Friedrich *Das Staatsideal im Wandel der Weltgeschichte* (1973)

Berkhouwer, C. (ed) *European Integration and the Future of Parliaments in Europe* (1975)

Biscaretti di Ruffia, P. *La Constitution comme loi fondamentale dans les Etats de l'Europe occidentale et dans les Etats socialistes*, with Stefan Rozmaryn (1966)

– *La Repubblica Popolare Cinese. Un 'modello' nuovo di ordinamento statale socialista* (Costituzione del 17 gennaio 1975) (1977)

Black, Charles L. Jr *Impeachment. A Handbook* (1974)

Blondel, J. *Comparative Legislatures* (1973)

Bracher, K.D. *Die Auflösung der Weimarer Republik* (1955)

- 'Der parlamentarische Parteienstaat zwischen Bewährung und Anfechtung' in *Nach Dreissig Jahren*, Walter Scheel ed, at p 28 (1979)

Bridel, M. *Précis de droit constitutionnel et public suisse* (1959)

Burdeau, G. *Droit constitutionnel et institutions politiques* (16th ed, 1974)

Callard, K. *Pakistan. A Political Study* (1957)

Cappelletti, Mauro *Judicial Review in the Contemporary World* (1971)

Chafee, Zechariah Jr *Free Speech in the United States* (1954)

Chapsal, J. *La Vie politique en France depuis 1940* (3rd ed, 1972)

Cole, R. Taylor 'The West German Federal Constitutional Court: An Evaluation after Six Years,' 20 *Journal of Politics* 278 (1958)

Commager, Henry Steele *The American Mind: An interpretation of American thought and character since the 1880s* (1950)

Commission des Communautés Européennes. Rapport du groupe *ad hoc* pour l'examen du problème de l'accroissement des compétences du Parlement européen ('Rapport Vedel') (1972)

Corwin, Edward S. *The Constitution and What It Means Today* (1948)

- *The 'Higher Law' Background of American Constitutional Law* (1955)

- *The President, Office and Powers 1787–1957* (1957)

de Meyer, J. 'Communautés et régions en Belgique,' 27 *Jahrbuch des öffentlichen Rechts der Gegenwart* (1978)

de Smith, S.A. *The New Commonwealth and Its Constitutions* (1964)

Deuerlein, Ernst *Der Reichstag* (1978)

Dicey, A.V. *Introduction to the Study of the Law of the Constitution* (9th ed, by E.C.S. Wade, 1939)

- *Lectures on the Relation between Law and Public Opinion in England* (2nd ed, 1914)

Doehring, Karl *Das Staatsrecht der Bundesrepublik Deutschland* (1976)

Dogos-Docovitch, G. (ed) *Le Parlement européen* (1978)

Djordjevic, J. *La Yougoslavie: Démocratie socialiste* (1959)

Dominice, C. *Fédéralisme coopératif* (1969)

Donaldson, A.G. *Some Comparative Aspects of Irish Law* (1957)

Duverger, M. *Institutions politiques et Droit constitutionnel* (12th rev ed, 1971)

- *La Monarchie républicaine* (1974)

- *L'Influence des systèmes électoraux sur la vie politique*, with François Goguel, et al (1950)

Ehrlich, Eugen *Grundlegung der Soziologie des Rechts* (1912)

Einaudi, Mario *Christian Democracy in Italy and France*, with François Goguel (1952)

Eisenmann, Charles *Bonn: Weimar. Deux constitutions de l'Allemagne* (1950)
Elias, T.O. *Government and Politics in Africa* (2nd ed, 1963)
Etzioni, A. *Political Unification: A comparative study of leaders and forces* (1965)
Favoreu, L. *Le Conseil constitutionnel*, with L. Philip (1978)
- *Les Grandes Décisions du Conseil constitutionnel*, with L. Philip (1975)
Feldman, H. *A Constitution for Pakistan* (1956)
Finer, Herman *The Future of Government* (2nd ed, 1946)
- *Theory and Practice of Modern Government* (rev ed, 1949)
Forsthoff, E. *Deutsche Verfassungsgeschichte der Neuzeit* (4th ed, 1972)
- *Rechtsstaat im Wandel, Verfassungsrechtliche Abhandlungen 1954–1973* (2nd ed, 1976)
Freudenheim, Y. *Government in Israel* (1967)
Freund, Paul A. *On Law and Justice* (1968)
- *On Understanding the Supreme Court* (1951)
Friedrich, Carl J. *Constitutional Government and Democracy* (rev ed, 1950)
- *Constitutional Reason of State: The survival of the constitutional order* (1957)
- *Limited Government. A comparison* (1974)
- *Man and His Government. An empirical theory of politics* (1963)
- (ed) *Studies in Federalism*, with Robert R. Bowie (1954)
- *The Impact of American Constitutionalism Abroad* (1967)
- *The Philosophy of Law in Historical Perspective* (1958)
- *Trends of Federalism in Theory and Practice* (1968)
Gabriel, R.H. *The Course of American Democratic Thought* (1940)
Gajendragadkar, P.B. *Indian Parliament and the Fundamental Rights* (1972)
Gledhill, A. *Fundamental Rights in India* (1955)
- *Pakistan. The development of its laws and constitution* (1957)
Goguel, François *Géographie des Elections Françaises de 1870 à 1951* (1951)
- *Sociologie électorale*, with Georges Dupeux and A. Bomier-Landowski (1951)
Grund, Henning *'Preussenschlag' und Staatsgerichtshof im Jahre 1932* (1976)
Grzybowski, K. *Soviet Legal Institutions. Doctrines and social functions* (1962)
Hazard, John N. *Law and Social Change in the U.S.S.R.* (1953)
- *Le Droit soviétique*, with René David (1954)
- (ed) *Le Fédéralisme et le Développement des Ordres juridiques* (1971)
- *The Soviet Legal System* (rev ed, with I. Shapiro and P.B. Maggs, 1969)
- *The Soviet System of Government* (1957)
- *Settling Disputes in Soviet Society* (1960)
Heidenheimer, A.J. *The Governments of Germany* (4th ed, with Donald P. Kommers, 1975)
Henderson, D.F. *The Constitution of Japan. Its first twenty years 1947–67* (1968)

Hennis, W. 'Alternativen ohne Spielraum – Möglichkeiten und Unmöglich-
keiten des politischen Systems,' in *Nach Dreissig Jahren*, Walter Scheel ed, at
p 58 (1979)

Héraud, Guy *L'Europe des Ethnies* (1963)

Hesse, K. *Grundzüge des Verfassungsrechts der Bundesrepublik Deutschland*
(11th ed, 1978)

Heuser, Robert 'Die chinesische Verfassungsrevision vom 5 März 1978 als
Hinwendung zu einem sozialistischen Rechtssystem in China' 39 *Zeitschrift für
ausl. öff. Recht u. Völkerrecht* 301 (1979)

Hildebrandt, H. *Die deutschen Verfassungen des 19 und 20 Jahrhunderts* (1977)

Holmes, Oliver Wendell *Collected Legal Papers* (1920)

Hondius, F.W. *The Yugoslav Community of Nations* (1968)

Itoh, H. (ed) *The Constitutional Law of Japan: Selected Supreme Court decisions,
1961–70*, with L.W. Beer (1978)

Jackson, Robert H. *The Supreme Court in the American System of Government*
(1955)

Jain, M.P. *Indian Constitutional Law* (1962)

– *Outlines of Indian Legal History* (2nd ed, 1966)

Japan, Commission on the Constitution *Comments and Observations by Foreign
Scholars on Problems Concerning the Constitution of Japan 1946* (1964)

Jennings, W. Ivor *Cabinet Government* (1936)

– *Constitutional Problems in Pakistan* (1957)

– *Parliament* (1938)

– *Problems of the New Commonwealth* (1958)

– *The Approach to Self-Government* (1956)

– *The Commonwealth in Asia* (1951)

– *The Law and the Constitution* (3rd rev ed, 1943)

– *The Queen's Government* (1954)

Kennedy, W.P.M. *The Law and Custom of the South African Constitution*, with
H.J. Schlosberg (1935)

Kisker, G. *Kooperation in Bundesstaat* (1971)

Kohn, L. *The Constitution of the Irish Free State* (1932)

Koopmans, T. (ed) *Constitutional Protection of Equality* (1975)

Kovacs, I. *New Elements in the Evolution of Socialist Constitution* (1968)

– (ed) *Socialist Concept of Human Rights* (1966)

Krishnaswami Aiyar, A. *The Constitution and Fundamental Rights* (1955)

Lapenna, Ivo *State and Law: Soviet and Yugoslav theory* (1964)

Laski, Harold J. *Parliamentary Government in England* (1947)

– *Reflections on the Constitution* (1951)

Lasswell, Harold D. *Politics: Who gets what, when, how* (1936)

- *Power and Society. A framework for political inquiry* (1950)
- *The Analysis of Political Behaviour. An empirical approach* (1948)

Latham, R.T.E. 'The Law and the Commonwealth,' in *Survey of British Commonwealth Affairs*, W.K. Hancock ed, vol 1, at p 533 (1937)

Laufer, Heinz *Verfassungsgerichtsbarkeit und politischer Prozess* (1968)

Lavroff, D.-M. *Les Libertés publiques en Union soviétique* (1963)

Lehmann, H. *Die Weimarer Republik* (1960)

Leibholz, Gerhard *Politics and Law* (1965)
- *Die Gleichheit vor dem Gesetz* (1959)
- *Grundgesetz für die Bundesrepublik Deutschland. Kommentar* (4th rev ed, with H.J. Rinck, 1971)
- *Strukturprobleme der Modernen Demokratie* (1958)
- *Verfassungsstaat – Verfassungsrecht* (1973)

Litchfield, E.H. (ed) *Governing Postwar Germany* (1953)

Loewenstein, Karl *Political Power and the Governmental Process* (1957)
- *Political Reconstruction* (1946)

Löwenthal, Richard 'Bonn und Weimar: Zwei deutsche Demokratien,' in *Nach Dreissig Jahren*, Walter Scheel ed, at p 69 (1979)

Macmahon, Arthur W. (ed) *Federalism: Mature and emergent* (1954)
- *Delegation and Autonomy* (1961)

McBain, H.L. *The Living Constitution* (1934)

McIlwain, Charles Howard *Constitutionalism: Ancient and modern* (rev ed, 1947)

McWhinney, Edward *Comparative Federalism. States' rights and national power* (2nd ed, 1965)
- *Constitutionalism in Germany and the Federal Constitutional Court* (1962)
- *Federal Constitution-Making for a Multi-national World* (1966)
- *Föderalismus und Bundesverfassungsrecht* (1962)
- *Judicial Review in the English-Speaking World* (4th ed, 1969)
- *Quebec and the Constitution 1960–1978* (1979)
- (ed) *Federalism and Supreme Courts and the Integration of Legal Systems*, with P. Pescatore (1973)

Maki, John M. (ed) *Court and Constitution in Japan: Selected Supreme Court decisions, 1948–60* (1964)
- *Government and Politics in Japan. The road to democracy* (1962)

Mansergh, N. *The Government of Northern Ireland* (1936)

May, H.J. *The South African Constitution* (1949)

Menzies, Sir Robert *Central Power in the Australian Commonwealth* (1967)

Minear, R.H. *Japanese Tradition and Western Law. Emperor, state and law in the thought of Hozumi Yatsuka* (1970)

Mirkine-Guetzévitch, B. *Les Constitutions européennes* (1951)

Mosler, H. (ed) *Verfassungsgerichtsbarkeit in der Gegenwart* (1961)

Murphy, W.F. *Comparative Constitutional Law. Cases and commentaries*, with J.F. Tanenhaus (1977)

Northrop, F.S.C. *European Union and United States Foreign Policy* (1954)

Pescatore, P. *Le Droit de l'intégration* (1972)

– (ed) *Federalism and Supreme Courts and the Integration of Legal Systems*, with Edward McWhinney (1973)

Popper, K.R. *The Open Society and Its Enemies* (1945)

Prélot, Marcel *Institutions politiques et Droit constitutionnel* (1969)

Rackman, E. *Israel's Emerging Constitution 1948–51* (1955)

Radruch, Gustav *Rechtsphilosophie* (4th ed, 1950)

Ray, S.N. *Judicial Review and Fundamental Rights* (1974)

Roberts, Owen J. *The Court and the Constitution* (1951)

Robertson, A.H. *European Institutions* (1959)

– *Legal Problems of European Integration* (1957)

– *The Law of International Institutions in Europe* (1961)

Rozmaryn, Stefan *La Constitution comme loi fondamentale dans les États de l'Europe occidentale et dans les États socialistes*, with P. Biscaretti di Ruffia (1966)

– *Le Concept de la Légalité dans les Pays socialistes* (1961)

Säcker, Horst *Das Bundesverfassungsgericht* (1975)

Sathe, S.P. *Fundamental Rights and the Amendment of the Indian Constitution* (1968)

Sauser-Hall, G. *Guide Politique Suisse* (1956)

Sawer, G. *Australian Federalism in the Courts* (1967)

Schlesinger, Arthur M. Jr *The Imperial Presidency* (1973)

Schmitt, Hans A. *The Path to European Unity. From the Marshall Plan to the Common Market* (1962)

Schultz, L. 'Die Neue Verfassung der Sowjetunion und die Entwicklung des Verfassungsrecht in den volksdemokratischen Ländern' 5 *Recht in Ost und West* 207 (1978)

Schweisfurth, Th. 'Verfassunggebung und Verfassung in einem Staat des "realen Sozialismus." Anmerkungen zur Verfassung der Ud SSR vom 7 Oktober 1977,' 39 *Zeitschrift für ausl. öff. Recht u. Völkerrecht* 740 (1979)

Sharlet, R. *The New Soviet Constitution of 1977: Analysis and text* (1978)

Shoup, Paul *Communism and the Yugoslav National Question* (1968)

Siegfried, André *Tableau des Partis en France* (1930)

Stone, Julius *The Province and Function of Law* (1946)

Stoyanovich, K. *Le régime socialiste yougoslave* (1961)

Swisher, Carl Brent *American Constitutional Development* (2nd ed, 1954)

Tope, T.K. *The Constitution of India* (1960)

Topornin, B.N. *Aktualnie teoreticheskie problemi razvitia gosudarstvennogo prava i sovetskogo stroitelstva* (1976)

Tournoix, Raymond *Le feu et la cendre* (1978)

Tripathi, P.K. 'Mr. Justice Gajendragadkar and Constitutional Interpretation,' 8 *Journal of the Indian Law Institute* 479 (1966)

– 'Perspectives on the American Constitutional Influence on the Constitution of India,' in *Constitutionalism in Asia. Asian views of the American influence*, L.W. Beer ed, at p 59 (1979)

Vedel, Georges *Droit constitutionnel* (1949)

Vermeil, Edmond *La Constitution de Weimar et le principe de la démocratie allemande* (1923)

Vyshinsky, A.Y. *The Law of the Soviet State* (transl, 1954)

Wahlen, F.T. *Vortragszyklus über die Anbahnung einer Totalrevision der Bundesverfassung*, with M. Imboden et al (1969)

Weber, Max *Wirtschaft und Gesellschaft* (1922)

Wedel, H. von *Das Verfahren der demokratischen Verfassungsgeben. Dargestellt am Beispiel Deutschlands 1848/49, 1919, 1948/49* (1976)

Weggel, H. von 'Die chinesische Verfassung vom 5 März 1978,' 27 *Jahrbuch des öffentlichen Rechts der Gegenwart* (1978)

Wheare, K.C. *Federal Government* (1946)

– *Modern Constitutions* (1951)

Wigny, P. *La troisième Revision de la Constitution* (1972)

Wildhaber, L. 'Das Projekt einer Totalrevision der schweizerischen Bundesverfassung,' 26 *Jahrbuch des öffentlichen Rechts der Gegenwart* 239 (1977)

Zurcher, Arnold J. (ed) *Constitutions and Constitutional Trends since World War II* (1951)

Index